ST. PAUL AND
THE MYSTERY-RELIGIONS

ST. PAUL AND THE
MYSTERY-RELIGIONS

BY

H. A. A. KENNEDY, D.D., D.Sc.
PROFESSOR OF NEW TESTAMENT LANGUAGE, LITERATURE AND THEOLOGY
NEW COLLEGE, EDINBURGH

WIPF & STOCK · Eugene, Oregon

Wipf and Stock Publishers
199 W 8th Ave, Suite 3
Eugene, OR 97401

St. Paul and the Mystery-Religions
By Kennedy, H. A. A.
ISBN 13: 978-1-5326-1882-6
Publication date 3/10/2017
Previously published by Hodder and Stoughton, 1913

TO MY WIFE

PREFACE

IT is scarcely necessary to apologise for a discussion of St. Paul's relation to the Mystery-Religions of his Hellenistic environment. One of the most noteworthy features in the trend of contemporary scholarship is the interest manifested by philological experts in the phenomena of that extraordinary religious syncretism which prevailed in the Græco-Roman world between 300 B.C. and 300 A.D. Their learned and instructive investigations touch nascent Christianity at numerous points, and raise many fascinating questions. Obscure places in early Christian literature are being illuminated, and the New Testament itself has much to gain from the historical reconstruction of the habits of thought and beliefs in the midst of which it came into being. The natural tendency, however, of explorers in remote fields is to over-estimate the significance of their discoveries. This temptation, I believe, has not been escaped by the pioneer workers in the province of Hellenistic religion. And their readiness to look in that direction for the source of various important Christian conceptions has been encouraged by the ardour of those theologians who find in the comparison of religions the main clue to the interpretation of Christianity.

As a matter of fact, the chief defect in the process is the failure to be sufficiently rigorous in the application of the historical method. The more immediate background of the Christian faith is apt to be strangely neglected. It will appear again and again in the course of the present investigation that the Old Testament supplies a perfectly adequate explanation of ideas and usages in the Epistles of Paul which it is the fashion to associate with Hellenistic influence. Perhaps Deissmann may be charged with over-statement when he declares that "if we are to understand the complete Paul from the view-point of the history of religion, we must grasp the spirit of the Septuagint" (*Paulus*, p. 70). But one has no doubt whatever that this assertion sets in bold relief an aspect of the situation which is too frequently ignored.

To dismiss the view that the Christianity of Paul is a syncretistic religion is not, however, to close one's eyes to the light which may be shed from many quarters on the conditions in which he accomplished his work as a missionary. And if we are to do full justice to his own famous statement, "I have become all things to all men that at all events I might save some," we must recognise his willingness to put himself *en rapport* with the men and women whom he sought to win for Christ. Hence it is of real value to understand something of the religious atmosphere in which his converts had lived as Pagans, if we are to grasp the more delicate implications both of his thought and language in those Letters which answered their questions and dealt with their spiritual dangers.

I have not hesitated to fill in somewhat elaborately the religious background of those communities to which Paul proclaimed the Gospel of Jesus Christ. Otherwise, the full significance of the Mystery-Religions could scarcely be appreciated. And I felt that unless the character and influence of these cults themselves were clearly outlined so far as the data permitted, it would be useless to discuss the Apostle's relation to them. Perhaps at first sight the sketch of Jewish mystical phenomena in Chapter II. may appear superfluous. But it seemed necessary to indicate forces in the religious history of Judaism sufficient to account for elements in Paul's experience which could not easily be referred to the crisis in his spiritual life and required no explanation from his Hellenistic environment. I have not attempted to discuss the question which Prof. K. Lake has emphasised in his *Earlier Epistles of St. Paul*: To what extent did Paul's converts from Paganism retain their earlier beliefs, and how far did this influence affect their conception of Christianity? The problem is one of real moment in the light of subsequent ecclesiastical developments, but it is not of necessity involved in the subject of this investigation.

The larger part of the material here incorporated appeared in a series of studies published in the *Expositor* during 1912 and the earlier part of the present year. My cordial thanks are due to the Editor and the publishers of that journal for their kind permission to use it. All of it has been carefully revised, many portions re-written, and many expanded as the result of further research. The frequent references throughout the volume to the literature on Hellenistic religion are evidence of my indebtedness to many scholars. If I have constantly been obliged to differ from one of the most distinguished of them, Prof. R. Reitzenstein, there is none from whom I have received so much real stimulus. E. Norden's elaborate monograph, *Agnostos Theos*, I could only use while my book was passing through the press, and the proofs had been finally corrected before the appearance of Clemen's *Der Einfluss der Mysterienreligionen auf älteste Christentum*.

I am under deep obligations to my friend and colleague, Prof. H. R. Mackintosh, D.D., for helping me to revise the proofs and giving me the benefit of many valuable suggestions.

H. A. A. KENNEDY.

New College, Edinburgh,
 July 5th, 1913.

CONTENTS

CHAPTER I

PROLEGOMENA

	PAGE
Mystery-theory of Pauline Christianity	1
Hellenistic Atmosphere of Paul's Missionary Labours	3
Stoicism as a Religious Force	4
Posidonius and Astral Mysticism	6
The Orphic Movement	10
Its Relation to the Dionysus-cult	13
Oriental Elements in Orphism	16
Influence of Oriental Cults in Hellenistic Period	18
Incipient Gnosticism	24

CHAPTER II

JEWISH AFFINITIES WITH THE MYSTERY-RELIGIONS

Paul's Mysticism	31
Mystic Phenomena in Israel	33

CONTENTS

	PAGE
The Spirit of Jahweh	34
"Knowledge" of God	36
Ecstatic Conditions in Ezekiel	38
Pneumatic Experiences in Judaism:—	
(a) Apocalyptic Literature	39
(b) Rabbinic Tradition	44
Rabbinic Mysticism and Allegorical Exegesis	51
The Hidden Name	54
Ethnic Influence on Judaism	57
Philo	64

CHAPTER III

THE CHARACTER AND INFLUENCE OF THE MYSTERY-RELIGIONS

Meagre Data regarding Mystery-Religions	68
Evidence of Inscriptions	72
Character and Diffusion of Religious Associations	77
Examination of Typical Mystery-Religions:—	
(a) Mysteries of Eleusis	81
(b) Mystery-cult of Cybele-Attis	88
(c) Mysteries of Isis-Serapis	95
(d) Hermetic Mystery-Literature	103

CHAPTER IV

ST. PAUL'S RELATION TO THE TERMINOLOGY OF THE MYSTERY-RELIGIONS

	PAGE
Contact of Paul with Influence of Mystery-Religions	115
Technical Mystery-terms in the Epistles	117
Does Use of Terms involve Adoption of Underlying Ideas?	119
μυστήριον	123
τέλειος	130
πνευματικός and ψυχικός	135
πνεῦμα in Mystery-Documents	141
πνευματικός and ψυχικός in Mystery-Literature	142
Reitzenstein on Two-fold Personality in Mystery-Religions	145
νοῦς as equivalent to πνεῦμα	149
Summary of Positions Established	151
Paul's Usage in the Light of the O.T.	154
Pneumatic Experiences in Paul's Environment	159
γνῶσις and ἀγνωσία in Hermetic Literature	162
γνῶσις in Paul	167
ἀποκάλυψις	172
"Transformation" in Mystery-Religions	177

	PAGE
"Transformation" in Paul	180
The "Spiritual Organism"	184
εἰκών and δόξα	189
φωτίζειν	197

CHAPTER V

St. Paul and the Central Conceptions of the Mystery-Religions

Deification by Communion with Deity as Aim of Mystery-Religions	199
Various Views of Communion :—	
Partaking of the Deity	200
ἐνθουσιασμός	201
Ecstasy	202
Contemplation and Revelation	203
Element-Mysticism	204
Marriage-Symbolism	205
Dying to Live	206
Alleged Parallels between Paul's Conception of Christ and Mystery-Deities	211
Salvation (Deification) in Mystery-Religions and in Paul	215

CONTENTS

	PAGE
Paul's Conception of Regeneration and Communion with Christ	220
Depends on Faith and the Spirit	223
Death and Resurrection with Christ wholly different from Mystery-Conceptions	225

CHAPTER VI

BAPTISMAL RITES

Rites of Purification in all Ancient Religions . .	229
Meagre Knowledge of these in Mystery-cults . .	229
Connection of Baptism with Death in Egyptian Papyrus	230
Paul's Conception of Baptism alleged to be Magical .	232
Paul's Detachment from Ritual	234
No Contrary Evidence in 1 Cor. x. 1 ff. . . .	235
Secondary Place of Sacraments in Paul . . .	237
Fundamental Importance of the Spirit . . .	238
Faith as Basis of the New Life	241
Connection in Paul between Baptism and Death to Sin	244
Significance of Baptism for Paul	246
Baptism for the Dead	253
Conclusions	254

CONTENTS

CHAPTER VII

SACRAMENTAL MEALS

	PAGE
Scanty Evidence for Sacramental Meals in Mystery-cults	256
Significance of such Meals	259
Theories of Paul's Conception of the Lord's Supper	261
The Pauline Material	263
1 Cor. x. 1-5	265
1 Cor. x. 14-21	268
1 Cor. xi. 23 ff.	274

CHAPTER VIII

CONCLUSIONS

The Mystery-Religions as Part of Paul's Environment	280
Paul and the Mystery-Ritual	282
The "Mysticism" of Paul	284
Supreme Place of Faith in it	288
Limits of Paul's Mystical Feeling	291
Criticism of Schweitzer's Eschatological Construction of Pauline Mysticism	294
Conclusion	299
INDEX	301

CHAPTER I

PROLEGOMENA

OURS is an age of new things. In no province is this more apparent than in that of New Testament interpretation. And no section of the New Testament continues to stimulate more revolutionary theories than the Pauline Epistles. It is true that discussions of authenticity have lost the importance assigned to them by scholars of the earlier time, like Baur, or by later critical investigators, like Van Manen. The emphasis has been shifted. The primary question at issue is the essential nature of St. Paul's view of the Christian faith.

The answers given to the question are extraordinarily divergent. Scholars of the calibre of Holtzmann and Deissmann are still convinced that the clue to Pauline Christianity is to be found in the apostle's experience of conversion. A. Schweitzer, in his recently published *Geschichte der Paulinischen Forschung* (Tübingen, 1911), believes that Paul's doctrine is "simply and exclusively eschatological" (p. 190). For Loisy, Paul has been the chief factor in transforming the original Gospel of Jesus into "a religion of mystery". Professor K. Lake holds that "Christianity . . . was always, at least in Europe, a mystery-religion" (*Earlier Epistles of St. Paul*, p. 215), and his statement that "Baptism is, for St. Paul and his readers, universally and unquestionably accepted as a 'mystery,' a sacrament which works *ex opere operato*" (p. 385), along with others of the same drift, suggests that the Apostle of the Gentiles played a prominent part in creating such a type of Christianity.

It is obvious that if this mystery-theory of Pauline Christianity can be established, many of our fundamental ideas regarding the Apostle's religious outlook will need to be transformed. We must courageously face such a transformation if the facts demand it. In the following chapters we propose to examine some of the available evidence and to ascertain how far it leads.

It is impossible, however, to appreciate the influences to which St. Paul and his converts were exposed, without attempting briefly to sketch, in the light of recent research, certain aspects of the

PROLEGOMENA 3

religious atmosphere of the Hellenistic world, at the time when the new faith began to be propagated throughout the Roman Empire. It is needless to say that here we are supremely indebted to the investigations of Cumont, P. Wendland, Reitzenstein, Bousset, and Dieterich. We shall discuss in turn the religious revival associated with Stoicism, more especially those elements in it which may be largely attributed to the famous Stoic-Peripatetic, Posidonius; the Orphic strain so widely diffused over the Hellenistic area; certain influential tendencies prominently at work in those Oriental cults which began to press westwards; and, finally, various significant features of current (popular) religion which, for convenience' sake, may be grouped under the designation of Earlier Gnosticism. It will often be difficult to draw sharp lines of division between those divergent but related phases of religious thought and aspiration.

It has long since been recognised that Stoicism [1]

---

[1] By "Stoicism" we mean that phase of development in the Stoic school which had become highly eclectic, adopting to a large extent Platonic conceptions, more particularly in its idea of God. See Wendland, *Die urchristlichen Literaturformen*, p. 397, note 2.

contributed many of the elements best fitted to satisfy popular cravings at the time when the national faiths of the Græco-Roman world were falling to pieces. The general drift towards a more or less vague monotheism was accelerated by a process, mediated at least in great measure by prominent Stoic teachers. This was the transformation of earlier deities, with the help of the allegorical method, into a hierarchy of hypostases of the supreme Divinity. Many of the Hellenistic speculations dealing with νοῦς, λόγος, σοφία, etc., have their origin in this circle of thought, and the bizarre outcome is apparent in the more fully developed Gnostic systems. This type of theologising had a special attractiveness from the Stoic point of view. On the one hand, the trained intellect regarded the abstractions referred to as attributes of the highest Deity, or as beings having a quasi-independent existence beside Deity.[1] In this aspect they did not contradict the fundamental pantheism of Stoic thought. On the other hand, they were sure to be interpreted by the popular mind as separate divinities, belonging to a purer mythology than that which it had discarded. But, in effect,

[1] See Bousset, *Hauptprobleme der Gnosis*, pp. 234, 235.

they ministered to a far higher religious ideal than the earlier, just because their function was to lead men's minds beyond themselves to the Divine Source from which they had emanated, and apart from which they had no real existence.

This effort of Stoicism, however, was not merely an artifice. It was not merely a compromise between truth and error, intended to preserve what was useful in the beliefs of the masses, while paving the way for a higher type of religion. Through the instrumentality, mainly, of Oriental teachers, the doctrine came to be associated with a Mysticism which had far-reaching influence. An important feature of the transformation-process which we have described was the metamorphosis of the elements of the kosmos into Divine forces. Of course we are here reminded of an original element-worship, *e.g.*, in Babylonia and Persia. In that quarter of Asia, also, from the most primitive times, the worship of the starry heavens had not only been an all-powerful feature in practical religion, but had gradually been developed by a learned priesthood on theoretical lines. The development seems to have been conditioned by the advancing knowledge of astronomy, so that gradually there emerged a notable combination between science and faith. But the ancient Chaldaean worship passed into a new phase under the influence of Hellenised Orientals, and, pre-eminently, of Posidonius, the renowned Stoic of Apamea in Syria.

The acute investigations of scholars like Cumont and Wendland have succeeded in demonstrating that Posidonius was perhaps the most remarkable figure of the transition period between the old era and the new. Cumont describes him [1] as a scholar of encyclopædic knowledge, a rhetorician of a rich and harmonious style, the builder of "a vast system whose summit was the adoration of that God who penetrates the universal organism and manifests Himself with clearest purity and radiance in the brightness of the stars". Posidonius was probably supreme among those Platonising Stoic teachers who liberated the abstruse and formal astral worship from the domain of the purely intellectual, and wedded it to the highest emotions. For him a reverent con-

[1] *Le Mysticisme astral*, Bulletin de la Classe des Lettres, Acad. Royale de Belgique, 1909, 5, p. 259; *Astrology and Religion*, p. 83 ff.

templation of the heavens culminated in a mystic ecstasy.[1] The soul which is stirred to its depths by the vision of the starry sky is itself akin to that upon which it gazes. For it was a Stoic doctrine that the soul is a fragment detached from the cosmic fires. Like is drawn to like. The rapture of contemplation becomes real communion. The gazer is possessed by a divine love. He cannot rest until he participates in the divinity of those living, sparkling beings above. And the experience is intimately associated with ethical purity. Thus, the astrological writer, Vettius Valens, page 242, 15 (ed. Kroll) : " I desired to obtain a divine and adoring contemplation of the heavens and to purify my ways from wickedness and all defilement ". In an impressive passage Cumont contrasts the calm ecstasy of this sidereal mysticism with the delirious transports of Dionysiac worship.[2]

Its influence on Hellenistic religious thought was very notable. It seems practically certain [3]

[1] Cumont, *Astrology and Religion*, pp. 140-5.

[2] *Le Mysticisme astral*, pp. 268, 269.

[3] Apelt, *De rationibus quibusdam quae Philoni Alexandrino cum Posidonio intercedunt*.

that Philo was largely indebted to Posidonius in some of his finest mystical ideas,[1] and numerous echoes of his doctrine are found, *e.g.*, in Cicero and Seneca. One of the most convincing proofs of the religious domination of Posidonius appears in the pseudo-Aristotelian treatise περὶ κόσμου, which has been carefully investigated by W. Capelle.[2] The book is a document of the current popular philosophy, probably dating from the beginning of the second century A.D. The author begins with a survey of the realm of nature, dealing with various sciences, such as meteorology and geography. But the treatise reaches its climax in what is a truly religious meditation upon the harmony of the kosmos in God, *from* whom and *through* whom all has its being.[3] We may note in passing the tendency of the semi-philosophical literature of the period to define in this way the relationship of the constituents of man or the universe to God. So Plutarch, *Quaestiones Platonicae*, ii., 2: " Now the soul [of the universe] has come into being not by

---

[1] See an instructive conspectus of passages in the appendix to Cumont, *op. cit.*, pp. 281, 282.

[2] *Neue Jahrb. f. klass. Altert.*, 1905, pp. 529-568.

[3] See especially *op. cit.*, pp. 556, 563.

PROLEGOMENA

Him (ὑπ' αὐτοῦ) but actually from Him (ἀπ' αὐτοῦ) and out of Him (ἐξ αὐτοῦ)". The facts suggest that Paul is using current phrases in various passages such as 1 Cor. viii. 6 : " One God the Father, from whom (ἐξ οὗ) are all things and we unto Him, and one Lord Jesus Christ, through whom are all things and we through Him ".[1] Here, therefore, there is presented a religious view of the world, based on a virtual monotheism, which can be traced back to Posidonius' reshaping of the ancient astral worship of Babylon by means of Stoic-Platonic conceptions.

We have emphasised this remarkable strain of thought in St. Paul's Hellenistic environment because, while in certain situations it would inevitably be bound up with the ritual of a cult,[2] it bears witness to the existence of a yearning for communion with God, which could be felt and expressed without the aid of sensuous ceremonies which are so often scarcely distinguishable from magic.

But the development of religious ideas, highly important in their bearing on the appeal of the Christian mission, had been proceeding in another direction. This was distinctly ritual in

[1] See especially the rich collection of material in Norden's *Agnostos Theos*, pp. 240-250.

[2] We know, *e.g.*, that Posidonius believed in divination.

its origin, and probably continued all along to be associated with mystic rites. Plato,[1] in one of his most remarkable speculations on the destiny of the soul (*Phædo*, 69 C), speaks of "those who established our mysteries" as affirming in parables "that whosoever comes to Hades uninitiated and profane will lie in the mire: while he that has been purified and initiated shall dwell with the gods. For 'the thyrsus-bearers (ναρθη-κοφόροι) are many,' as they say in the mysteries, 'but the inspired (βάκχοι) few'." This reference is assigned by early commentators to that cycle of thought known as Orphism. Probably such passages as *Phædo*, 70 C, and *Phædrus*, 350 C, have a similar bearing. Indeed Prof. Taylor suggests that wherever we meet ἔρως in Plato we are face to face with Orphic influence. The origins of Orphism are shrouded in obscurity. Miss J. E. Harrison, in her fascinating exposition of the Orphic movement,[2] collects and emphasises the ancient evidence for the historicity of Orpheus, "a real man, a mighty singer, a prophet and a teacher, bringing with him a new religion,

---

[1] Prof. Burnet would say Socrates. See the introduction to his recently published edition of the *Phædo*.

[2] *Prolegomena to the Study of Greek Religion*, pp. 455-659.

PROLEGOMENA 11

seeking to reform an old one" (*op. cit.*, p. 470). While her arguments on the point are not convincing, it is plain that from the sixth century B.C.[1] there had been a remarkable re-moulding of certain central elements in the older Dionysus-worship which was to have far-reaching influence in the Hellenistic world. This refining of grosser ideas is found embodied in mystic doctrines imparted to the initiated.

The writers on Greek religion often speak of Orphic sects or communities. These were bound together by their theological beliefs.[2] Behind their theology seems to have lain the famous myth of the rending of Zagreus (a Chthonian designation of Dionysus), son of Zeus and Persephone, by the Titans, in the form of a bull. They devour the various parts, but the heart is rescued by Athene, and given to Zeus who swallows it. From him springs the new Dionysus, the son of Semele, and Zagreus comes to life again in him. Zeus blasts the Titans by a lightning-flash. From their ashes there arises the race of men who thus possess a good element, handed down from Dionysus-Zagreus, and

[1] *Cf.* Rohde, *Psyche*,[3] ii., p. 105 ff.
[2] See Rohde, *op. cit.*, ii., p. 111 ff.

an evil from the Titans. The myth symbolises the dividing up of the Divine unity by evil forces into the Manifold of this world's forms. That unity is restored in the new Dionysus-Zagreus. The task of man is " to shake himself free from the evil (Titanic) element of his nature and to return in purity to the God to whom he owes a vital part of his being ".[1] This will mean above all else deliverance of the soul from the prison-house of the body. That can only be a gradual process. For the soul is subject to re-incarnations. Finally, through mystic ritual and a life of ascetic purity, he will be enabled to escape from the wheel of births. The Orphic tablets found in Southern Italy [2] bear out the references in Greek authors to a connection between Orphic doctrine and Pythagoreanism. This connection has been suggestively dealt with by Mr. F. M. Cornford in his recent study, *From Religion to Philosophy* (see especially pp. 180, 198-200). He believes that " as Orphism was a reformation of Dionysian religion, so Pythagoreanism may be regarded as a further reformation of Orphism". Orphic

[1] See Rohde, *op. cit.*, ii., p. 121.

[2] See Prof. Gilbert Murray's appendix to Miss Harrison's *Prolegomena*.

theology had been specially concerned with the salvation, by rites of purification, of the individual soul. As this individualism became more pronounced, "the Orphic could no longer find a complete satisfaction in the immediate union with his God in orgiastic ecstasy : his Way of Righteousness was a long and painful round of ritual forms, which easily degenerated into external observances". Pythagoras rekindled the mystic faith inherent in Orphism by transforming the cult into a way of life. He substituted for ritual cleansing a purification by means of the "pursuit of wisdom" (φιλοσοφία), while still retaining certain elements of the Orphic ἄσκησις. Much that is hypothetical must enter into any reconstruction of this kind. But its general truth is at various points corroborated by the Pythagorean elements which appear in the *Symposium*, the *Phædo*, the *Republic*, and the *Phædrus* of Plato.[1]

For our purpose the relation of Orphism to the Dionysus-cult is of primary importance. Both had apparently come to Greece by way of the north. Fundamental for the Dionysiac religion was the delirious frenzy, common to all orgiastic

[1] See especially Prof. A. E. Taylor's brilliant essay on "The Impiety of Socrates," *Varia Socratica*, i., pp. 1-39.

ritual, in which the votary believed himself to be possessed by his deity. See Euripides, *Bacchœ* (ed. Wecklein), 300 f. :—

ὅταν γὰρ ὁ θεὸς εἰς τὸ σῶμ' ἔλθῃ πολύς,
λέγειν τὸ μέλλον τοὺς μεμηνότας ποιεῖ.

The union was felt to be so complete that the person possessed came to be called by the name of the god. To attain this condition was virtually to share in the immortal life of the divinity. And no doubt, even in the crudest form of their ἐνθουσιασμός, in which the worshippers identified the bull which they slew and devoured raw with the god himself, there were dim hints of a craving for a life which should defy the restrictions of mortality. The Orphic sects seem to have adhered more or less closely to the Dionysiac ritual, but they liberated it from savage excesses, elevating its central conception of union with the god, and, as a preparation for this highest religious attainment, inculcating a life of austere purity. We cannot share in Miss Harrison's certainty as to a personal Orpheus, but there is probably abundant truth in her statement (which will apply to the action of a community as well as to that of an individual) : "The great step that Orpheus took was that, while he kept the old Bacchic faith that man might become a god, he altered the conception of what a god was, and he sought to obtain that godhead by wholly different means. The grace he sought was not physical intoxication, but spiritual ecstasy; the means he adopted not drunkenness, but abstinence and rites of purification."[1]

It is possible that Orphism had cultivated an ascetic life before its association with the religion of Dionysus. But from this time onwards the significance of its cathartic ritual and practice has a new emphasis. Purity, as we have seen, is needful in order to be set free from the "cycle of generation" (κύκλος τῆς γενέσεως). It takes the form especially of ὁσιότης, consecration. The man who is fully initiated in the Orphic rites is ὁσιωθείς. What that involves is suggested by the mystic formulae of the Compagno tablet. In answer to the confession of the mystic : "Out of the pure I come. . . . For I also avow me that I am of your blessed race. . . . I have flown out of the sorrowful weary wheel . . . I have passed with eager feet from the circle desired," the assurance is given : "Happy and blessed one, thou shalt be

[1] *Op. cit.*, p. 477.

god instead of mortal ".[1] That these cathartic rites were often degraded there is evidence in many Greek writers, *e.g.*, Plato, *Republ.*, 364 E : " They [*i.e.*, those whom in 364 B he names ' mendicant prophets '] produce a host of books written by Musaeus and Orpheus, according to which they perform their ritual, and persuade not only individuals, but whole cities, that expiations and atonements for sin may be made by sacrifices and amusements which fill a vacant hour, and are equally at the service of the living and the dead ". Apparently the purifying priest was able to carry on a lucrative business among the credulous, and his ritual was mixed up with all manner of superstition and trickery. But that is a feature involved in the history of all religious movements. The new emphasis on purity was destined to make an ever-widening appeal, and to rank as one of the most impressive factors in the evolution of Hellenic religion.

It is possible that from the beginning the Orphic Theogonies, of which fragments have survived, contained Oriental elements (Babylonian ?). Eisler argues for the direct influence of Persian religion which came into touch with Ionian colonies

[1] J. E. Harrison, *op. cit.*, p. 586.

in Asia Minor in the sixth century B.C.[1] In the course of their diffusion these Theogonies were confronted with the various types of Oriental speculation. So that by the opening centuries of our era Orphism had been swept into that many-sided syncretistic movement which must be regarded as the source of the main currents and systems of belief usually designated by the safely indefinite title of Gnosticism. There is enough evidence to indicate that from the sixth century B.C. onwards the Orphic strain of religion had never died out. The collection of hymns which is extant,[2] and whose redaction in its present form is assigned by Dieterich[3] to the second century A.D., contains elements of high antiquity. But in the Hellenistic period Orphism received new life through its touch with Eastern cults. It enriched them and was enriched by them in turn.[4]

[1] See his *Weltenmantel und Himmelszelt*, vol. ii., *passim*.

[2] *Orphica*, ed. Abel.

[3] *Abraxas*, p. 31. But Eisler and others would date the "Theogony" at least as far back as the Persian wars or even earlier.

[4] On its contact with Phrygian cults, see Eisele, *Neue Jahrb. f. klass. Altert.*, 1909, p. 630.

In this movement, which struck its roots in a typically Hellenic soil, it is evident that genuinely religious aspirations emerged, intimately associated with purifying rites and mystic initiation. In the various combinations which it would form it must have been pervasively present in St. Paul's spheres of operation. But we must now turn to certain features of primary importance in those Oriental cults, with which Orphism had many affinities, features contributed by them to the environment of the Pauline mission. In a later chapter we shall sketch more in detail the main characteristics of the Mystery-Religions of Hellenism, with which terms and ideas in the Epistles of Paul have been brought into definite relation.

In view of the fragmentary nature of our sources it is often easier to point to a distinctively Oriental phase of religious faith or practice than to analyse its component parts, and assign their origin. The task, moreover, is endlessly complicated by the dominant syncretism of the Hellenistic period. No more crucial example could be found than that of Egypt. Apart altogether from the influence of primitive Egyptian doctrines, which has certainly been exaggerated by

Reitzenstein[1] in his investigations of the Hermetic literature, but which must surely be reckoned with, there appear the phenomena of Babylonian theology, such as the conception of the seven spheres and the sway of the planets,[2] along with the related belief in εἱμαρμένη, that fatalism which has mysticism as its counterpart.[3] Here also are found the curious dogma of the Heavenly Man, whose origin is lost in the mists of antiquity, the typically syncretistic cult of Osiris-Serapis and Isis, and the elaborate practice of magic, with its quaint apparatus of efficacious "names". In this whirlpool of ideas, too, may be discerned the elements of confusing Gnostic systems.

The fact, however, of Oriental influence on the Hellenistic civilisation which grew up from the time of Alexander's conquests, is perhaps the most vital which confronts us in attempting to understand its religious developments. Various aspects of the situation claim attention. It need not surprise us that forces of mighty potency in religion,

[1] See especially W. Otto's *Priester u. Tempel im Hellenistischen Aegypten*, ii., pp. 218-224 (with the notes), and Kroll's art. "Hermes Trismegistos" in Pauly-Wissowa, *R.E.* (*Neue Bearb.*, ed. Kroll), viii. 1, *sp.* 792 ff.

[2] For the connection of the planetary spirits with demons, see Bousset, *op. cit.*, p. 54 f.

[3] See Reitzenstein, *Poimandres*, pp. 70 f., 77 f., 79.

as in all other spheres of human thought or achievement,[1] pressed in from the East. For in Egypt, Syria, and Asia Minor, an intellectual life was pulsing to which there was no parallel in the Western world at the beginning of the Roman Empire. Science, literature, industry, were in this era the province of Orientals, not of Greeks or Romans.[2] And, moreover, as Cumont has impressively put it, "if the triumph of Oriental cults appears at times like a revival of savagery, as a matter of fact, in the evolution of religious forms, these cults represent a more advanced type than the ancient national devotions".[3]

There were many features of Oriental belief and worship which possessed a fascination for the Græco-Roman world. A halo of reverence surrounded the mystic lore emanating from the East. Thus, *e.g.*, the Egyptian priesthood was supposed to have preserved in greater purity the earliest rites of Divine worship. Chaldaeans and Brahmins stood closer to the origins of things than Greeks or Romans.[4] And the Gospel which

[1] Except, perhaps, the military and legal, see Eisele, *op. cit.*, p. 633.
[2] See Cumont, *Les Religions Orientales*,[2] pp. 8-14.
[3] *Op. cit.*, p. 40.
[4] See Anrich, *Das antike Mysterienwesen*, p. 36.

Paul preached could count on this predilection in its favour. But such a conviction would not have sufficed to extend the sway of exotic faiths. As Reitzenstein has cogently shown, the influence of Oriental cults throughout the Roman Empire became intensely personal. Perhaps this was partly the result of a zealous propaganda.[1] But it was involved in the very method of the propaganda. This was carried on by priests who travelled hither and thither, bearing a message of hope, which was often delivered in ecstatic utterances.[2] These would impress audiences accustomed to a cold and formal ceremonial. Moreover, when they won the interest of yearning souls, they played upon them by the weird rites of mystic initiation. Every means was used to excite the feelings. Overpowering spectacles amidst the darkness of night, seductive music, delirious dances, the impartation of mysterious formulæ— these made a unique appeal to men and women who had prepared for the solemn experience by

[1] *Die hellenistischen Mysterienreligionen*, p. 6.

[2] *Cf.* in this whole connection Dill's fascinating chapters on the "philosophic director" and the "philosophic missionary," *Roman Society from Nero to Marcus Aurelius*, pp. 289-383.

long courses of rigid abstinence. But even more potent was the profounder side of the appeal: that which directly touched consciences unsatisfied by their ancestral rites. What Cumont has said of the Oriental priests in Italy gives the clue to the whole situation which we are trying to review. They brought with them " two new things, mysterious means of purification by which they proposed to cleanse away the defilements of the soul, and the assurance that an immortality of bliss would be the reward of piety ".[1] The full significance of these truths will appear in a later chapter, when we examine the fundamental doctrines of the Mysteries in their relation to Paulinism.

One effect of this individualistic appeal is very suggestive. Many devout people, not content with a single initiation, embraced every fresh opportunity that came to them of using this means of communion with deity. They felt they could not have too intense a consciousness of the deifying of their own individuality. And, doubtless, behind it all lay the thought, now dimmer, now

[1] *Op. cit.*, p. 61. It is of importance to note, as Cumont points out, that Oriental cults had a more *restricted* influence in Greece because there analogous doctrines were familiar from the Hellenic mysteries. See *op. cit.*, p. 324, note 23.

clearer, expressed in *Diogenes Laertius*, vii., 135 : ἕν τε εἶναι θεὸν καὶ νοῦν καὶ εἱμαρμένην καὶ Δία πολλαῖς τε ἑτέραις ὀνομασίαις προσονομάζεσθαι : "God and Reason and Fate and Zeus are identical, and they have many other designations besides". The assurance as to the supernatural, confirmed by so many solemn sanctions, opened a new vista to their spiritual vision. The truth which they would fain grasp was presented to them in the guise of Divine revelations, esoteric doctrines to be carefully concealed from the gaze of the profane, doctrines which placed in their hands a powerful apparatus for gaining deliverance from the assaults of malicious demonic influences, and above all, for overcoming the relentless tyranny of Fate. It is not difficult to see how various aspects of Paul's message might be superficially interpreted on parallel lines. The word of the Cross might readily appear as a mysterious talisman with superhuman potencies.[1]

Here we touch a crucial feature in the religious life of the Hellenistic period. Anz, in his important study, *Zur Frage nach dem Ursprung des*

[1] *Cf.* the mystery associated with the term σταυρός by the Valentinian Gnostics, as in Barth, *Die Interpretation d. N.T. in der Valent. Gnosis*, pp. 84-87.

Gnosticismus, is disposed to find in the doctrine of escape from the rule of εἱμαρμένη the pivotal conception of Gnosticism. This is scarcely probable. Gnosticism is too chameleon-like in its hues to allow of a single unifying idea. But there can be no question that conceptions like that of the seven Archons, who, from their planetary realm, determine the destinies of mortals, were almost universally influential. Dieterich has briefly sketched the range of diffusion of such doctrines.[1] Originating in Babylon, they have penetrated into the religions of Persia and Egypt. They appear in Jewish Apocalyptic, in Orphic fragments, in Hermetic documents, in Greek astrological texts, in every variety of Gnostic system. They can be discerned in the background of the Pauline Epistles, in those hierarchies of evil forces ruled by the θεὸς τοῦ αἰῶνος τούτου, the ἄρχων τῆς ἐξουσίας τοῦ ἀέρος.

Perhaps this was the most crushing weight which oppressed human souls in the period with which we are dealing. It is scarcely possible to doubt that the ἀσθενῆ καὶ πτωχὰ στοιχεῖα, against whose bondage Paul warns in Galatians iv. 9, are the elemental spirits whose iron yoke was so

[1] *Abraxas*, p. 43 ff.

grievously felt throughout the Hellenistic world. Indeed, his words in verse 8 remove all uncertainty : τότε μὲν οὐκ εἰδότες θεὸν ἐδουλεύσατε τοῖς φύσει μὴ οὖσιν θεοῖς. Redemption from this servitude, which embittered daily existence, was probably the object of intensest craving in the higher life of pagan society. It was realised by fellowship with higher powers too strong for these lower. In the present life it could be attained through mystic ecstasy. After death it would be consummated by the ascent of the soul to heaven. The actual apparatus of ritual and magic by which communion with higher divinities was reached is vividly exemplified in the prayers and incantations of the so-called Liturgy of Mithra.[1] The possession of means for escaping the thraldom of the Archons came at an early stage to be regarded and described as Gnosis *par excellence*. However intellectual might be the original basis of the idea involved, it now indicated the highest practical attainment of the religious life. Gnosis was pre-eminently δύναμις. It made possible mystic communion with deity. It was a religious rather than a speculative con-

[1] Edited and elucidated by A. Dieterich. The second edition, considerably enlarged, was brought out after Dieterich's death by R. Wünsch, Leipzig, Teubner, 1910.

ception. But when we pass from the term to the communities or sects within which it found its chief realisation, we enter a field bristling with problems. Gnosticism is one of the most flexible designations in the vocabulary of the history of religion. It is used to cover phenomena which, while more or less closely allied to each other, are far from being identical. Some writers restrict the name to those fantastic developments of speculation within the life of the early Church, on which the Fathers pour their scorn. Others include under the title a variety of tendencies in the Hellenistic period, of which some took shape inside the Church, some remained completely pagan, while some belonged to a debateable borderland, hard to define. But the complexity of the term is still further aggravated. Harnack, *e.g.*, using the designation in its narrower sense, would lay the emphasis on its affinities with Greek philosophy. "Almost everything," he says, "which was matter of controversy between Gnosticism and the Church would have also been in dispute between the Church, on the one hand, and Plato, Aristotle, Stoicism, etc., on the other."[1] Wendland, while acknowledging that Gnosticism knew how to provide cultivated minds with specu-

[1] *Theol. L.Z.*, 1908, 1, *sp.* 11.

PROLEGOMENA 27

lations, finds the clue to its origin and pervasive influence in Oriental-Hellenistic syncretism.[1] It is not our purpose to discuss these more or less conflicting views. We are not concerned here with Gnostic phenomena inside the Church. What we wish to indicate in a sentence or two is that drift of tendencies in the Hellenistic period which makes itself felt in the environment of Paul's mission, and which, for convenience' sake, may be described as incipient Gnosticism. This must directly affect our investigation of the main problem to be dealt with, the relation of Paul to the Mystery-Religions.

For incipient Gnosticism and the Mystery-Religions are phenomena which overlap. There is an instructive passage in Hippolytus, v., 20 (ed. Duncker and Schneidewin), in which, describing the Gnostic sect of the Sethians, he derives their peculiar doctrine from " the ancient theologians, Musaeus and Linus and Orpheus, who, above all others, introduced the rites of initiation and the mysteries," and asserts of a particular teaching that " it is found in this very form in the Bacchic rites of Orpheus ". Whether the explanation

[1] See also the very suggestive remarks of Norden, *Agnostos Theos*, p. 95 f., which must, however, be accepted with caution.

given by Hippolytus has any foundation or not, it suggests a feature of undoubted significance in the movement we are concerned with. In fully-fledged Gnostic systems like the Valentinian, for all its curious mythological formations, we are confronted by philosophical constructions, which seem far removed from a traffic in magical formulæ. But there is a " vulgar " Gnosis, of which traces appear even in those sects which exhibit metaphysical developments. It is found, *e.g.*, to a marked degree, in the Hermetic literature of Egypt, as Zielinski has shown,[1] side by side with elaborate cosmological speculations, and makes abundant use of alchemy and magic. It reveals the influence of all manner of ancient beliefs and superstitions which, in a time of religious disintegration, have forced themselves up from various levels of popular fancy and tradition. These are associated with ritual (or magical) actions and mystic sacraments, some of which have their origin in early Greek Chthonian worship, and others in the multifarious Oriental rites which were being carried westwards in an unceasing stream. Behind most phases of this earlier

[1] *Archiv f. Religionswiss.*, 1906, p. 27 f. But Kroll, *op. cit.*, *sp.* 819, denies the appearance of magical rites in the Hermetic literature strictly so called.

PROLEGOMENA

"Gnosticism," as later at the basis of its more philosophical expressions, there seems to lie an essentially dualistic view of the universe. Bousset would associate the phenomenon with the direct influence of the religion of Persia, while admitting that in its Hellenistic environment Persian dualism lost its more concrete mythological embodiment, and made way for a new antithesis, that between "the good spiritual and the evil corporeal world".[1] His view is highly probable. In any case, the ground-tone of the movement is a thorough-going pessimism, which often issues, on the one hand, in a rigid asceticism, in unbridled immorality on the other. These are features which Paul has definitely to deal with side by side in the Epistle to the Colossians, *e.g.*, ii. 20 ff. : " If you died with Christ from the elements of the world, why, as though living in the world, do you subject yourselves to ordinances. Handle not, nor taste, nor touch . . . which things have indeed a show of wisdom in self-imposed worship and humility and severity to the body, but are not of any value against the indulgence of the flesh." The truth is that this chaotic outgrowth of Hellenistic religion is our most faithful mirror of the prevailing syncretism of the period. Large addi-

[1] *Op. cit.*, p. 118.

tions to the knowledge of its essential character have been made in recent years by the magical papyri unearthed in Egypt. These have preserved fragments of hymns and spells and mystic names of Babylonian, Egyptian, Hellenic, and even Jewish origin. With ritual and liturgical texts are blended, in a bewildering medley, curious theogonies and cosmologies, which find their affinities in documents so far removed from each other as the poems of Hesiod and the Apocalypses of Judaism, and have undoubted associations with Stoic allegorisings. The process of which this is the product must have had a long and chequered history. Corresponding to the extended period of its development would be the width of area over which it was diffused. The graphic delineation of the burning of the books at Ephesus (Acts xix. 18, 19) gives us a casual glimpse of the forces which were potent in the common life of the cities of the Empire. This was a movement which in vague forms must continually have confronted the Apostle Paul as he moved from one great centre to another. Its atmosphere would surround him like the air which he breathed. Was he influenced by it consciously or unconsciously? Is the Christianity of Paul, as Gunkel asserts, "a syncretistic religion"?

CHAPTER II

JEWISH AFFINITIES WITH THE MYSTERY-RELIGIONS

It is a custom almost universal among writers on the religion of the New Testament to speak of the "Mysticism" or "Faith-Mysticism" of St. Paul. Now "Mysticism" is one of the most elastic terms in the vocabulary of religion. Hence, when it is used to designate an important element in the complex of Paul's religious experience, its precise significance in this connection must be as clearly defined as possible. It is not our purpose at the present stage to attempt such a definition. It is enough to indicate the features in the Apostle's experience which are commonly grouped under this name. Prominent among them are those which he himself describes as "crucified with Christ," "baptised into His death," "risen with Christ," "joined to the Lord," "putting on Christ," being "in Christ," having "Christ living in" him. To a somewhat different side of the same general category belong the "visions" and "revelations" which he occasionally claims to have had: the pneumatic endowments of a unique kind which he shares with other spirit-possessed Christians: and the remarkable ecstatic experience which he recalls in 2 Corinthians xii. 1 ff. Some recent investigators have been disposed to associate these spiritual phenomena with the influence of the Mystery-Religions, and at a later point we must, in the light of their researches, make a careful comparison of the terminology of these religions with the religious vocabulary of Paul. On a surface view of the facts, however, it seems relevant, meanwhile, to suggest that in the Pauline phrases quoted above, we have examples of a spiritual experience which comes to light wherever religion exercises an intense and sovereign control over the personality. The soul for which God is all in all craves for and continually attains a relationship to the Divine which can only be expressed in terms of absorbing personal intimacy, and in such terms symbolic elements must always have a place. For Paul access to God is only and altogether through Christ. Hence, speaking generally, the language he employs is true to his whole Christian standpoint. On the other hand, the peculiar experience described in 2 Corinthians xii. 1 ff., the visions and revelations, and perhaps the unique spiritual endowments, while traceable over a very wide area of religious history both in ancient and modern times, are nevertheless more temperamental in character, and belong more essentially to a definite environment. If we are to do justice to that environment in Paul's case, we must attempt to examine those elements in Judaism, his ancestral faith, which may broadly be grouped under the comprehensive term "Mysticism". For there certainly may be a germ of truth in Reitzenstein's statement : " Paul was a mystic before his conversion : this is attested by his allegorical exegesis of Scripture ".[1]

We should expect to find phenomena of the kind called " mystic " in experiences which reveal religious feeling at its highest pitch of intensity. These, in the history of Israel, are associated with the *prophetic* function.

The earliest descriptions of the *Nebî'îm* (*e.g.*, 1 Sam. x. 5, 6, 10 ; xix. 20, 24) are extraordinarily significant. The prophets appear in bands, swayed by a common religious excitement, accompanied by stirring music. Their frenzy is con-

[1] *Die hellenistischen Mysterienreligionen*, p. 199.

tagious. Saul is swept away by it, strips himself of his clothing, and falls exhausted to the ground. Even at a later date, according to 2 Kings iii. 15, Elisha calls for music, and while the minstrel plays the prophetic inspiration comes upon him and he declares the word of the Lord. In the Samuel-passages these phenomena are attributed to the *Ruach Elohim*. The Ruach-conception, in the most primitive phases of the popular religion, had probably stood for anything "demonic" that had to be accounted for, but in the oldest documents of the Old Testament has already been incorporated with the person of Jahweh.[1] In the case of Elisha, the phrase used is "the hand of Jahweh". This phrase occurs again and again in the book of Ezekiel, where it is apparently connected with trance or ecstatic conditions. It is almost needless to recall the parallels to these primitive ideas both in Semitic and Hellenic religions. The ecstatic influence of Apollo over the Pythia is typical.[2] It is worth noting that in Egypt certain classes of priests who are re-

[1] See Volz, *Der Geist Gottes im A.T.*, p. 62, *et al.*

[2] See Rohde, *Psyche*,³ ii., pp. 60, 61. A conspectus of most striking passages from Greek authors in De Jong, *Das antike Mysterienwesen*, pp. 163-165.

THE MYSTERY-RELIGIONS 35

garded as being in immediate contact with the supernatural world are designated προφῆται.

The development of Hebrew religion has nowhere left more impressive traces than in the sphere of the prophetic activity. A characteristic feature of the great pre-exilic prophets is their lack of emphasis on the conception of the *Ruach Jahweh* in connection with their own prophetic equipment. Perhaps this is due to the fact, as Volz suggests,[1] that they still felt in it something of the primitive idea, which, as not necessarily ethical, was alien to them. But their usage is no indication that they were less conscious of the Divine Presence. It is the very reverse. They feel themselves to be in direct touch with Jahweh. "The Lord God hath spoken," says Amos (iii. 8) "who can but prophesy?" "Thou shalt be as my mouth," says the Lord to Jeremiah (Jer. xv 19). And Isaiah's solemn vision represents the same type of experience. At certain crises they were peculiarly sensitive to the Divine compulsion. Isaiah, *e.g.*, tells how the Lord spake to him "with strong pressure of the hand" (viii. 11) Jeremiah in an appeal to God exclaims: "I sat alone because of thy hand" (xv. 17).

[1] *Op. cit.*, p. 67 f.

While visions are rare in the experience of the greatest prophets, their conception of intimate fellowship with Jahweh is central for their religion. It is often described as "knowing God," or the "knowledge" of Him. This is something more profound than any activity of the intellect. It is essentially experimental. Very significant for its meaning are the words of Hosea : " I will even betroth thee unto me in faithfulness, and thou shalt know the Lord " (ii. 20). The "knowledge" is a revelation of God in the inner being. "The word is very nigh unto thee in thy mouth, and in thy heart, that thou mayest do it " (Deut. xxx. 14).[1] God gives Himself to men in experience. And the experience is essentially moral. This point of view is peculiarly characteristic of Jeremiah. For him all ethical activity has as its foundation a personal communion with the living God.[2] Perhaps the climax of this aspect of Old Testament religion appears in some of the later Psalms : *e.g.*, Psalm li. 11 : " Cast me not away from thy presence : and take not thy holy spirit from me ". In Psalm lxxiii. 23-26, the "mysti-

---

[1] *Cf.* Kohler, *Grundriss einer systematischen Theologie des Judentums*, pp. 25, 26.

[2] *Cf.* Duhm, *Theologie der Propheten*, p. 243.

cal" element is still more prominent : " Nevertheless I am continually with thee. . . . Whom have I in heaven but thee, and there is none on earth that I desire beside thee."

It is obvious that there are intimate relations between the prophetic idea of the "knowledge of God" which we have just emphasised, and Paul's conception of γνῶσις, which must be examined at a later stage. Meanwhile, if, following the development, we inquire into the standpoint of Ezekiel, we are confronted by experiences which remind us forcibly of the earlier popular beliefs. Ezekiel, like his great predecessors, sets high moral truths in the forefront of his message. But his is plainly a nature sensitive to ecstatic conditions, and these occupy a prominent place in his own descriptions of his prophetic work. In his first overpowering vision of the glory of God he narrates how he fell upon his face, and then heard a voice which commanded him to stand up that he might receive the Divine commission. "And spirit entered into me when he spake unto me, and set me upon my feet, and I heard him that spake unto me" (ii. 2). In chapter viii. 3, he describes spirit as lifting him up between earth and heaven, and bringing him in the visions of

God to Jerusalem. This takes place after "the hand of the Lord God" has fallen upon him. No doubt the experience belongs to a trance-condition. It is futile to explain such descriptions as merely literary artifice. They belong to the very essence of his prophetic activity. The fact that he narrates them so vividly attests the importance which they had for him. Of interest in this connection is the eating of the book which was given him (ii. 9 ff.). It is quite possible that this was not a mere symbol, but rather an indication that "Ezekiel received the Divine message in an ecstatic condition, associated with intense bodily sensations".[1] It is not without importance for our subject that the later Apocalyptic, with its emphasis on esoteric lore, its delineation of mysterious events, the elaborate symbolism of its visions, and its pictures of the Divine judgment, lies in the direct descent from Ezekiel. Even in view of the phenomena already examined, Dean Inge's remark requires some modification: "The Jewish mind . . . was alien to Mysticism".[2]

Ezekiel, in contrast to the pre-exilic prophets, makes fairly frequent mention of the Spirit of Jahweh in connection with his inspired utter-

[1] Volz, *op. cit.*, p. 15.   [2] *Christian Mysticism*, p. 39.

ances. And in the post-exilic period, as a whole, the *Ruach Jahweh* comes gradually to be regarded as the special charism of the prophet. The conception has become highly ethicised, as, *e.g.*, in Deutero-Isaiah. Here we have, as Volz points out,[1] the monotheistic transformation of the Ruach which had possessed the earlier *Nebi'im*. One cannot help comparing the process with that by which Paul ethicised the ecstatic conception of the $\pi\nu\epsilon\hat{\upsilon}\mu\alpha$, current in early Christianity. The parallel has a vital bearing on the meaning of the Apostle's " mysticism ".

When we pass into the Judaistic period we are confronted by a variety of phenomena which may be called " pneumatic ". This is the era of apocalyptic literature, and the descriptions given by the seers in the Apocalypses of their visions and of the conditions and circumstances in which these were granted to them afford rich material for study. Now it is true that the writers of the Apocalypses associate the revelations embodied in their books with famous names of the past. And the experiences related are constantly embellished and elaborated in a more or less formal way. But throughout there is abundance of

[1] *Op. cit.*, p. 96.

unconscious evidence that the writers themselves had personal and intimate knowledge of ecstatic conditions. These conditions are again and again ascribed to the influence of the Spirit. A noteworthy instance occurs in 4 Ezra xiv. 38 ff. : "On the following day there cried to me a voice : Ezra, open thy mouth, and drink that which I give thee. Then I opened my mouth, and behold, a full cup was handed to me. It was filled as if with water, but the colour of the water was like fire. This I took and drank, and when I had drunk, understanding streamed from my heart, my breast swelled with wisdom, my soul preserved its memory. Then my mouth was opened, and was not again closed." In his illuminating notes (ed. Kautzsch) Gunkel points out that the flame-coloured liquid represented the Spirit; when the seer had drunk, he was inspired. An interesting feature of the description is the reference to the memory of the experience. Persons in ecstasy often lost consciousness, and after the condition had passed away, were unable to recall that which had been given them "in the Spirit". Here consciousness and memory have suffered no interruption. The whole passage is evidence that the writer was not dealing merely with phenomena external to himself. These mystical experiences are prepared for by ascetic practices, as in the Orphic ritual. For example, the command comes to Baruch (Apoc. of Baruch, ed. Charles, chap. xx. 5-6) : "Go therefore and sanctify thyself seven days, and eat no bread, nor drink water, nor speak to any one. And afterwards come to that place and I will reveal myself to thee . . . and I will give thee commandment regarding the method of the times." The same type of instruction is found in 4 Ezra ix. 23 f. Here, again, there is something more than second-hand tradition.

We do not forget that in the Judaistic epoch the opinion prevailed that the Divine Spirit was no longer operative in the nation. And this view could be justified by comparing the existing age with that of the great prophets. But, as Gunkel aptly remarks, "such phenomena are in reality not the possession of any single epoch; they occur at all times and in all places".[1] Frank recognition of this truism would save much irrelevant discussion on the subject of the "mysticism" of Paul.

[1] *Apokryphen u. Pseudepigraphen d. A.T.* (ed. Kautzsch), Bd. II, p. 341.

JEWISH AFFINITIES WITH

The visions and revelations of the Jewish Apocalypses, which are all to a greater or less degree related to eschatological happenings, are in many instances connected with the ascent of the soul to heaven. Some scholars believe that this conception must have entered Judaism from outside, and are inclined to find its origin in Hellenic-Egyptian culture.[1] This is quite possible. For, as we shall notice immediately, Judaism came into very intimate contact with the various phases of Hellenistic syncretism. And ever since the time of Plato, the notion of the ascent of the soul into the higher world seems to have formed an important element in the profounder strains of Greek religion.[2] The experience is described more than once in the Ethiopic Enoch, *e.g.*, xxxix. 3 f. (ed. Charles) : " In those days a cloud and a whirlwind carried me off from the earth, and set me down at the end of the heavens. And here I saw another vision, the mansions of the holy and the resting-places of the righteous." In the Slavonic Enoch, the seer is carried up through

---

[1] So, *e.g.*, Volz, *op. cit.*, p. 124. Bousset favours the hypothesis of Persian influence, *Archiv f. Religionswissenschaft*, 1901, p. 145 ff.

[2] See Dieterich, *Eine Mithrasliturgie*,[2] p. 199.

the various heavens until, in the seventh, he is set "before the face of the Lord" (chap. xxi. 5). There his earthly robe is taken off, and he is clothed with the raiment of the Divine glory (xxii. 8). This, no doubt, refers to the purification of the soul, if it is to look upon the face of God. It is scarcely possible to separate the conception from the Hellenistic idea of the ascent of the soul through the various spheres, a process in which it is gradually purified. It is obvious that in the Enoch-literature there is a large mass of imported material, mystic lore accumulated from manifold sources. But here again we have no doubt to reckon with an ecstatic "mysticism," current in certain circles of Judaism, and lying behind the delineations given in Apocalypses of religious heroes of the olden times.[1]

Many modern Jewish scholars are inclined to believe that the chief elements in the famous mystic system of the Cabala have descended in a continuous tradition from the apocalyptic literature of the second and first centuries B.C. Whether, as Josephus holds, these writings were carefully preserved in the circle of the Essenes, who are regarded by some (*e.g.*, Jellinek and Gaster) as

[1] *Cf.* Bousset, *Religion des Judentums*,² p. 342.

the originators of the Cabala, there is little evidence to determine. The description we have quoted from the Slavonic Enoch of the seer's ascent to heaven vividly reminds us of Paul's account of his mystic experience in 2 Corinthians xii. 1 ff. And we know that at many points the Apostle has links of connection with apocalyptic ideas. But whether these belong to the centre or the circumference of his religious outlook is a question which must be discussed at a later stage in our inquiry.[1]

It is probably an error to draw a sharp line of demarcation between Apocalyptic and Rabbinic thought. These provinces must certainly have overlapped. The Scribes admitted the apocalyptic book of Daniel into the Canon. Both in Daniel (*e.g.*, i. 8), and in the Apocalypse of Baruch (*e.g.*, xxxviii. 2 ff.), the observance of the Law receives a prominent place. But gradually the essential divergence of temperament between Scribe and Apocalyptist became manifest. A

---

[1] Gunkel (*op. cit.*, pp. 342 f., 349) indicates many parallels, *e.g.*, between 4 Ezra and Paul, which suggest that they belonged to the same circle of Judaism. But he clearly recognises that the contrasts are greater than the resemblances (p. 343).

THE MYSTERY-RELIGIONS 45

saying occurs in the Talmudic treatise, *Sanhedrin*, that "he who reads in the secret books (*i.e.*, the apocalypses) has no portion in the world to come ".[1] Hence there is no doubt truth in Schlatter's remark that the Palestinian Synagogue had no room for "pneumatics".[2] In Rabbinic piety ecstatic experiences seem to have been held in check. The problems of mystical lore had to be approached with much caution. The advice of the Son of Sirach is significant: "The things which have been commanded thee, ponder; for thou hast no need of secret things" (iii. 22). This shrinking from mystic raptures became more marked in the authoritative Rabbinic schools of the second century A.D. It was said of Simon ben Azzai that he died after he had cast a glance into the mysteries of the "garden".[3] To the famous Rabbi Akiba (†135 A.D.) is referred the warning found in the Mischna against discoursing on the creation of the world (Gen. i.) and the

[1] See Bertholet, *Biblische Theologie d. A.T.* (begun by Stade), vol. ii., p. 358.

[2] *Jochanan ben Zakkai*, p. 74, note 2.

[3] Interpreted by some as the realm of theosophical speculations, by others as Paradise. See Bacher, *Die Agada der Tannaiten,*[2] i., p. 408.

first chapter of Ezekiel, which became the basis of mystical speculations as to the Divine essence and the heavenly sphere of being, except before carefully selected individuals.[1] Nevertheless the existence in Rabbinic circles of "pneumatic" phenomena, parallel to those with which we have been dealing, is fully made out.

It is interesting to note that the "wise" man is regarded as possessing a special Divine endowment. "Who hath known thy counsel except thou hast given him wisdom and sent thy holy spirit from on high?" (Wisd. of Sol. ix. 17). With this may be compared a passage from the celebrated description of Wisdom: "From generation to generation passing into holy souls, she (*i.e.*, Wisdom) maketh them friends of God and prophets" (*ib.*, vii. 27). Probably under the same category may be placed the remarkable experience of Eliphaz narrated in Job iv. 13 ff.: "In thoughts from the visions of the night when deep sleep falleth on men, fear came upon me, and trembling, which made all my bones to shake. Then a spirit passed before my face; the hair of my flesh stood up: it stood still, but I could not discern the form thereof: an image was before

[1] Bacher, *op. cit.*, p. 334.

THE MYSTERY-RELIGIONS 47

mine eyes, I heard a still voice." Notable Rabbis like Hillel were looked upon as inspired by the Holy Spirit.[1] Indeed saintliness (*Chasiduth*), which is virtually imitation of God, finds its climax in communion with the Holy Spirit. Schechter, commenting on this conception, quotes from a Midrash: " Holiness means nothing else than prophecy ".[2] But on the whole, no doubt, the catastrophic aspect of the Spirit has fallen into the background. Characteristic of this situation is the idea of the Spirit as especially manifested in the Holy Scriptures, which has become a widespread belief in Rabbinic theology.[3]

But much and varied evidence can be adduced for a markedly mystical strain in Rabbinic literature. This is well exemplified by the all-important conception of the *Shechinah* which occurs far more frequently than the allied notion of the Holy Spirit, from which at times it can scarcely be discriminated. In an early phase of Rabbinic thought, the *Shechinah* is clothed in material forms, such as light, fire, etc. And this usage reappears later, but as pure symbolism. More

---

[1] See Volz, *op. cit.*, pp. 115, 165.
[2] *Some Aspects of Rabbinic Theology*, p. 217.
[3] See Volz, *op. cit.*, pp. 167, 168.

notably, the *Shechinah* is often regarded as a kind of emanation of God, embodying the Divine Presence, and occasionally it is directly personified. Indeed the variety of usages, which merge into one another, is strikingly parallel to the New Testament conceptions of the Holy Spirit.[1]

There is another group of phenomena which are closely linked to those ecstatic experiences which we discussed in the field of apocalyptic literature. As in the case of the Apocalyptists, they are associated with esoteric lore, arising out of theosophical and cosmogonic speculations. Judaism had been in touch with Babylonian-Persian ideas, as Blau points out,[2] for at least 500 years before the Christian era. The conception of Gnosis had permeated many phases of its thought. So we need not be surprised to find in it remarkable affinities with the doctrines which we meet both in Hellenistic and in Christian Gnosticism. One name stands out prominently in Rabbinic tradition as identified with such mys-

---

[1] See an interesting discussion in Abelson's *The Immanence of God in Rabbinic Literature*, pp. 367-375. His chapter on "The Rabbinic God" (especially pp. 278-295) emphasises the element we are considering.

[2] Art. "Gnosticism," in *Jewish Encyclopædia*, v., p. 681.

THE MYSTERY-RELIGIONS 49

tical speculations, that of Jochanan ben Zakkai (fl. c. 70 A.D.). Our knowledge of his Haggadic explanations of Scripture, which was the form given to esoteric doctrines of this kind, is so meagre that much caution has to be used in estimating his position.[1] But we know that the material which supplied a basis for them came from the first chapter of Genesis and the opening section of Ezekiel. The one passage was the starting-point for mystic speculations on the creation (*Ma'aseh Bereschith*), the other for esoteric theories as to the being and abode of God (*Ma'aseh Merkabah*),—Merkabah, chariot, being a concise description of Ezekiel's mysterious vision. The latter doctrine must have been elaborately developed. Traces of it, in various phases, are found throughout the Rabbinic tradition. Later, the term "Merkabah-travellers" came to be used of those who ventured on this mystic quest. Some interesting traditions survive as to Rabbis who were absorbed in such theosophical exercises. An interview is recorded between R. Joshua b. Chananja and Ben Zoma. In answer to a greeting by Joshua, Ben Zoma gave forth a mystic utterance, and Joshua said to the scholars who

[1] See Bacher, *op. cit.*, p. 39 f.

accompanied him, "Ben Zoma is gone". Bacher thinks that the saying is to be explained in the light of a tradition that Ben Zoma became mentally affected in consequence of mystical speculations.[1] But Blau's explanation, illustrated by parallel passages, which finds in the words a reference to ecstasy, seems more relevant to the whole context.[2] Ben Zoma is one of a group of Rabbis who, according to a famous tradition, had, during their lifetime, "entered Paradise". Of these Ben Azzai had his vision and died (*vide supra*). Ben Zoma saw and lost his reason. Acher became a heretic. Akiba alone suffered no harm.[3] Bousset is probably justified in connecting this tradition with visionary experiences of the Rabbis in question, reached in conditions of ecstasy. But such experiences are never conceived in the realistic fashion current, for example, in the contemporary Mystery-Religions. We are not confronted in Judaistic thought with the notion of absorption in the Deity. Nor does there ever, apparently, occur the conception of the deifi-

[1] *Op. cit.*, p. 424. [2] *Op. cit.*, p. 684.
[3] *Chagiga*, 14b-15b. *Cf.* Bousset, *Archiv f. Religionswissenschaft*, iv., p. 145 ff., a most comprehensive treatment of the conception of the ascent of the soul.

THE MYSTERY-RELIGIONS 51

cation of mortals through mystic communion with God. These facts will be found of high significance when we come to investigate the mystical ideas of Paul.

As we have already seen, the mystic phenomena of the Apocalypses are usually associated with the feverish strain of eschatological expectation which prevailed in the Judaistic period. Of course, in such books as Ethiopic Enoch, Slavonic Enoch, and 4 Ezra, much of the esoteric tradition may well fall under the category of Gnosis. But the clue to the standpoint of the writers is eschatology. On the other hand, the mysticism of Rabbinic Judaism seems to have an intimate connection with allegorical exegesis of the Old Testament. Examples have been mentioned in the case of Jochanan ben Zakkai. Significant for the whole trend of thought we are considering is the statement of Akiba: "The whole world is not worth so much as the day on which the Song of Songs was given to Israel".[1] The full import of the saying becomes plain when we remember that for Akiba the book was an allegory of the unique relationship between God and Israel. An interpretation starting with this pre-

[1] Bacher, *op. cit.*, pp. 310, 311.

supposition involved mystical conceptions at every turn. Thus, the *Rabba* on the Song of Songs (iii. 8) compares the Shechinah to a cave by the sea-shore: "The sea rushes in to the cave, filling it, but the sea is just as full as before. So the Shechinah pervades the Tabernacle or the Temple, but yet is quite as immanent, all-pervasive, in the world at large."[1] The Haggada of Simon ben Jochai, renowned as a mystic, is said to be noteworthy for the exuberance of its language as to the relation between God and Israel.[2]

Some light has been shed by recent research on this obscure field. We are able to discern dimly a group of ancient Haggadists, designated *Doresche Reschumoth, i.e.,* "interpreters of hints". The name, given them in Rabbinic tradition, would at once suggest allegorical exegetes. But this seems to be placed beyond doubt by the investigations of Lauterbach.[3] He shows that their characteristic was the estimating of Old Testament passages as symbols, whose figurative sense was far more important than the literal.

---

[1] See Abelson, *The Immanence of God in Rabbinical Literature*, p. 110.

[2] Bacher, *op. cit.*, ii., p. 79.

[3] *Jewish Quarterly Review*, Jan., 1911, esp. p. 301.

THE MYSTERY-RELIGIONS 53

While in many respects they reveal marked resemblances to Philo and the Alexandrian type of Judaism, they were apparently Palestinian theologians, independent, so far as the evidence goes, of external influences.[1] Indeed Lauterbach believes that Philo was to some extent influenced by them. It is important to observe that the chief interest of these interpreters was practical. "If thou desirest to know Him by whose word the universe came into being, study the Haggada, for from it shalt thou know the Holy One, praised be He, and cleave to His ways."[2] Klein points out that in the essentials of their piety they stand in the direct succession of the prophets.[3] Their outlook, apparently, was far wider than that of ordinary Rabbinism. And some of their utterances suggest a more or less direct affinity with the Essenes and the Therapeutæ.[4] Their mystical tendencies seem to have brought them under suspicion. For their interpretations have left very few traces in Rabbinic literature. They were felt to imperil the sacred Torah. And it is quite possible that a saying of Abtaljon's

[1] Lauterbach, *op. cit.*, pp. 305, 328.
[2] Qu. by Klein, *Der älteste christliche Katechismus*, p. 40.
[3] *Op. cit.*, p. 43.   [4] Klein, *op. cit.*, p. 41.

(*Pirque Aboth*, i., 12) is a direct polemic against them.[1] Klein believes that a chief aim of their procedure was to win the heathen for ethical monotheism. If this be so, it is all the more significant to find that Paul appears to follow their method closely in such passages as 1 Corinthians x. 1 f.[2]: "Our fathers were all under the cloud, and all passed through the sea; and were all baptized into Moses in the cloud and in the sea; and did all eat the same spiritual food; and did all drink the same spiritual drink: for they drank of a spiritual rock that followed them: and the rock was Christ".

The tragic history of R. Chanina b. Teradjon was connected in a later tradition with the fact that he had pronounced the Divine Name as it was written. "This probably implied that he had busied himself with mystic doctrine."[3] The history of the hidden Divine Name (*Schem hammephorasch*) is a complicated subject, on which we must simply touch as belonging to the essence of Rabbinic mysticism. In Ethiopic Enoch (lxix.

---

[1] Klein, *op. cit.*, p. 43, note 2.
[2] See Lauterbach, *loc. cit.*, p. 330, note 33.
[3] Bacher, *op. cit.*, i.,[2] p. 397.

THE MYSTERY-RELIGIONS 55

14), one of the evil angels asks Michael "to show him the hidden name". Various explanations have been given. Klein has collected a number of passages from Rabbinic tradition in favour of his position that the mystical name of God is *Ani we-hu,* "I and he," a combination signifying the most intimate relation conceivable between God and His people. This is an attractive hypothesis, which must not, however, be regarded as anything more. Even apart from its validity, it is quite possible that the hidden name " conceals the profoundest mystery of religion, the *unio mystica,* the demand for unity with God ". It is in any case noteworthy that direct parallels are found in Hellenistic literature. Thus, in a prayer to Hermes (in a Papyrus of the British Museum) the words occur : σὺ γὰρ ἐγὼ καὶ ἐγὼ σύ. The same formula is found in a Leiden Papyrus.[2] And in the well-known treatise of Egyptian Gnosticism, the *Pistis Sophia,* Jesus is represented as saying: "not only will you reign with Me, but all men who shall receive the mystery of the Ineffable will be kings with Me

[1] Klein, *op. cit.,* p. 48.
[2] See Dieterich, *Eine Mithrasliturgie,*[2] p. 97.

in My kingdom, and I am they and they are Me".[1] But these phenomena may also suggest traces of Hellenistic influence in Judaism. In the magical Papyri of Egypt mystic Divine names are used as incantations, and many of these are derived from the vocabulary of Judaism. The same usage is, of course, to be found in Jewish magic, which here, as at so many points, reveals Babylonian and Egyptian influence. But we have no clear data for tracing the connection which may exist between the mystic doctrine of the hidden Divine Name and those phenomena of Hellenistic religion to which reference has been made. How widely the significance of the "name" has been diffused is apparent from Ephesians i. 21 : "far above all authority and rule, and power and lordship, and every name which is named not only in this age but also in the coming one".

Philo, in a remarkable passage,[2] declares as the aim of Moses in all his legislation the establishing of "harmony, fellowship, unity of mind, blending of manners, by means of which houses and cities, nations and countries, and the whole

---

[1] Schmidt, *Koptisch-gnostische Schriften*, i., p. 148.
[2] *De Humanitate*, 119 (ed. Cohn-Wendland).

THE MYSTERY-RELIGIONS 57

human race should advance to the highest wellbeing ". This ideal is to some extent the reflection of actually existing tendencies. We have already alluded to phenomena in Judaism which suggest foreign influence. We must examine this contact more closely. The problem is of importance for our discussion, as we have to contemplate the possibility that Hellenistic (including Oriental) conceptions influenced Paul through this medium.[1]

Perhaps the most impressive example of the assimilation of Judaism and Paganism is to be found in those mixed religious communities, chiefly in Asia Minor, which recent research has been drawing out of their obscurity. Sir W. M. Ramsay has most suggestively contrasted the attitude of the Jews to Greeks and Phrygians respectively. In the first case there was an inherent racial antipathy. In the other the Jews were brought into touch with a people of fundamentally Oriental type.[2] It is evident from the narratives in Acts that before Paul's first missionary journey through Asia Minor, Judaism had appealed to the natives of Phrygia. Indeed the markedly Asiatic char-

[1] See Wendland, *Die hellenistisch-römische Kultur*,[1] p. 178.
[2] *Historical Commentary on Galatians*, pp. 193-196.

acter of the inhabitants of the Anatolian plateau was strikingly akin to the Semitic. Even in modern times, as Ramsay points out, the Jew has stood in a much more friendly relation towards the Turkish peasantry than towards the Greeks. This affinity had remarkable consequences. Antiochus the Great had founded Jewish colonies in Asia Minor about 200 B.C. It seems to have been due to their influence that the worship of the Phrygian deity, the κύριος Σαβάζιος, was blended with that of the Old Testament Jahweh, often designated in the LXX as κύριος Σαβαώθ.[1] This cult possessed mysteries closely akin to those of Attis.

But the influence of ethnic ideas upon Judaism is discernible over a wide area. Gruppe emphasises the contact of Jewish thought with Oriental mysticism at an early date in Samaria, where Chaldaean astrology seems to have been practised.[2]

---

[1] See Cumont, *Les Religions Orientales*,² pp. 97, 98; Eisele, *Neue Jahrb. f. klass. Alt.*, 1909, p. 631. There is abundant evidence also for votaries of θεὸς ὕψιστος, the typical title of the God of Israel in Asia Minor, who had not been Jews, and yet were organised in associations apparently only semi-pagan. See Schürer, *Sitzungsb. d. Berl. Akad.*, 1897, pp. 200-225.

[2] *Griechische Mythologie*, ii., p. 1608 f.

THE MYSTERY-RELIGIONS 59

This is highly probable. But we cannot by any means limit the spheres in which Judaism came into touch with Oriental syncretism. If we had any clear data regarding religious life in the regions immediately east of Palestine in the Hellenistic period, we might be able to trace the origin of that elusive sect, the Essenes, in which, alongside typically Jewish features, appear marked traces of alien beliefs and practices, as, *e.g.*, their daily prayer to the sun. But their beginnings are wrapped in obscurity. And the same may be said of the Therapeutæ, whose existence and characteristics are known to us only from Philo's treatise περὶ βίου θεωρητικοῦ.[1] His description reveals many indications of syncretism. But except for the resemblance to be found between them and ethnic associations or guilds, it is impossible to form definite conclusions. Hence it seems hazardous to regard the Essene "colonies" as the main channels through which Persian, Greek, and Egyptian ideas had penetrated Judaism.[2]

[1] Conybeare, in his masterly edition (Oxford, 1896), has adduced very convincing arguments in favour of its genuineness; see especially his excursus, pp. 258-358.

[2] So, *e.g.*, Kohler, *Jewish Quarterly Review*, April, 1893, p. 406.

Essenism may have been an important link of connection. But there are gaps in the evidence.

Unassailable testimony to the pressure of Babylonian and Persian thought upon Judaism is presented by the Apocalyptic literature. In this instance, of course, the Exile supplies the starting-point. The cosmological speculations which abound in such documents as the Ethiopic and the Slavonic Enoch are plainly traceable to the astronomical theology of Babylon, which extended its sway in all directions. It is here in all likelihood that we must look for the ultimate origin of that worship of the elements or elemental spirits ($\sigma\tau o\iota\chi\epsilon\hat{\iota}a$) which had crept into Judaism. As in the case of similar Oriental influences, the religion of Persia may have been the direct medium, for in it the elements play an exceedingly important part.[1] But since it is difficult, in this phase of religion, to make sharp distinctions between the spirits of the elements and those of the planets, Babylonian theology seems to lie in the background. Abundant evidence as to these elemental spirits occurs, *e.g.*, in Ethiopic Enoch lx. 11-23; Jubilees ii.; Ascension of Isaiah iv. 18; and the Christian Apocalypse xiv. 18, xvi.

[1] See Bousset, *Hauptprobleme d. Gnosis*, p. 223 f.

THE MYSTERY-RELIGIONS 61

5. Particularly important for our discussion is Paul's use of στοιχεῖα in Galatians iv. 3, 9, already quoted, and Colossians ii. 8, 20 : "Take heed lest there shall be any one that makes spoil of you through his philosophy and vain deceit, after the tradition of men, after the στοιχεῖα of the world, and not after Christ. . . . If you died with Christ from the στοιχεῖα of the world, why, as though living in the world, do you subject yourselves to ordinances?" And the whole subject is illumined by a passage in the second-century, Κήρυγμα Πετροῦ (Preuschen, *Antilegomena*, p. 52) : μηδὲ κατὰ Ἰουδαίους σέβεσθε · καὶ γὰρ ἐκεῖνοι μόνοι οἰόμενοι τὸν θεὸν γινώσκειν οὐκ ἐπίστανται λατρεύοντες ἀγγέλοις καὶ ἀρχαγγέλοις, Μηνὶ καὶ Σελήνῃ :[1] "Worship not after the Jewish fashion. For the Jews, supposing that they alone know God, do not know Him, rendering worship to angels and archangels, to Mên and Selênê." Both of these were lunar deities. The manifold possibilities of contact between Judaism and Babylonian doctrine are thrown into relief by such facts as the penetration of Babylonian ideas

[1] See Reitzenstein, *Poimandres*, p. 73 f., who finds an intimate relation between this Jewish mysticism and Hermetic doctrine.

into Syria, and the presence in Palmyra, where Babylonian astrology was popular, of a large Jewish colony which seems to have compromised with Paganism.[1] The influence of Persian beliefs on the Jews has at times been exaggerated.[2] Yet it would be futile to deny it in such spheres as angelology and demonology, and possibly in such apocalyptic conceptions as that of the end of the world. And there is at least some affinity between Persian dualism and the corresponding strain in Jewish Apocalyptic.[3]

We have already suggested that the Jewish idea of the all-powerful "Name" must have links of connection with Pagan magical ideas. As a matter of fact, Jacob has brought forward strong arguments for the Egyptian origin of this belief,[4] but kindred notions are universal in primitive society. It is needless to say that our knowledge of Egyptian magic has been largely augmented by the magical papyri which have recently come to light. They reveal a fundamentally Egyptian

[1] See Cumont, *op. cit.*, pp. 182 f., 367, 368.
[2] *E.g.*, in our judgment, by Bousset, *Religion des Judentums*,[2] p. 582 f., *et al.*
[3] See Bousset, *op. cit.*, p. 585 f.
[4] *Im Namen Gottes*, Berlin, 1903.

THE MYSTERY-RELIGIONS 63

ground-work. This might be expected, as from ancient times magic formed an all-important feature in Egyptian religion.[1] But these texts have incorporated many Jewish elements, more especially forms of the Divine Name, such as Ἰάω, Ἀβριάω, Ἀδωνάϊ, and famous Jewish names like Abraham, Jacob, Moses, etc. Typical examples will be found in the Μονὰς ἡ Ὀγδόη Μωϋσέως, edited by Dieterich.[2] The translation of the Old Testament into Greek has, as Hubert observes, contributed a new magical mythology to Egyptian religion.[3] But the notable fact is the action and reaction between Egyptian and Jewish ideas. For there seem to be here and there distinctly Jewish insertions in the texts, which are, no doubt, modelled on Egyptian tradition. We have here basal elements of that Jewish magical literature which reached its zenith in the Middle Ages.[4] This interchange is highly characteristic of Hel-

[1] See, *e.g.*, Erman, *Die ägyptische Religion*,[2] p. 167 ff.

[2] In *Abraxas*, see especially p. 201 ff.

[3] See his exhaustive article, "Magia," in Daremberg et Saglio, *Dictionnaire des Antiquités*, Tome iii., partie 2, pp. 1494-1521, and especially p. 1505.

[4] *Cf.* Reitzenstein, *Poimandres*, pp. 14, note 1, 186, 189, note 1.

lenistic syncretism. It leaves open the possibility of Jewish and even Christian influence in the case of conceptions which are often treated as wholly independent in their origin, and supposed to have had a share in moulding, *e.g.*, the thought of St. Paul. Gnostic communities must as frequently have been the channels for diffusing Christian ideas as for the propagation of Hellenic or Oriental doctrines. An interesting example of such a possibility is found in the remarkable resemblance between the theological ideas of the Hermetic document *Poimandres* and the letter of Ptolemæus to Flora, a product of Valentinian Gnosticism. And the terminology of various magical papyri strongly suggests Christian influence.[1]

When we speak of the accessibility of Judaism to contemporary religious syncretism, the remarkable figure of Philo inevitably stands out before us. For, in the light of our present discussion, it is scarcely legitimate to regard him, with some scholars,[2] as an isolated phenomenon. It is true

[1] See some very suggestive paragraphs in Krebs, *Der Logos als Heiland*, pp. 71 f., 147, 163. Kroll denies this possibility for Hermetic literature, but without offering any arguments, *op. cit.*, sp. 821.

[2] *E.g.*, Bousset, *op. cit.*, p. 501, as against Harnack, Schwartz, and Lebreton, *Les Théories du Logos*, who gives

THE MYSTERY-RELIGIONS 65

that Alexandrian Judaism had no transforming effect on the Jews of the Diaspora. But Philo is a crucial example of a Jewish religious thinker in whom diverse strains of thought and feeling, both inherited and acquired, are curiously amalgamated. The most common estimate of him is that of an extravagant allegoriser of the Old Testament, concerned above all else to make the Divine revelation given through Moses square completely with Greek philosophy. But the atmosphere of his allegorical activity is often ignored. Allegory he describes as dear to ὁρατικοῖς ἀνδράσιν, " men of vision ".[1] Reitzenstein gives good reasons for believing that the term ὁρατικοί in Philo is virtually equivalent to πνευματικοί or γνωστικοί, those who attain to the real vision of God.[2] And here we come at once into the circle of mysticism. Indeed Philo addresses those who reach the highest kind of knowledge as μύσται κεκαθαρμένοι τὰ ὦτα, and he beseeches them to receive it as ἱερὰ μυστήρια.[3] That these are not

a conspectus of the passages in which Philo refers to " men of deep research " who preceded him.

[1] *De Plantatione*, 36 (ed. C. W.).
[2] *Die hellenistischen Mysterienreligionen*, pp. 144-146.
[3] *De Cherubim*, 48 (ed. C. W.).

merely artificial terms taken over from the language of the mysteries is evident from his appeal to the soul. "If a yearning come upon thee to have share in Divine blessedness . . . escape from thyself and go out of thyself (ἔκστηθι σεαυτῆς) in a Bacchic frenzy and divinely inspired like those who are possessed and filled with Corybantic delirium."[1] Here is genuine ἔκστασις. And there can be no doubt that Philo speaks from personal experience. "At times, coming to my work empty, I have suddenly become full, ideas being sown upon me in showers from above, so that by Divine possession I am in a condition of frenzy (κορυβαντιᾶν) and ignorant of everything, the place, the company, myself, what was spoken, what was written. For I received a flow of interpretation [so Markland], an enjoyment of light, a vision of piercing clearness."[2] Unques-

[1] *Quis Rer. Div. Heres*, 69 (ed. C. W.). See Bousset, *op. cit.*, p. 517, note 2, for an interesting list of terms in Philo associated with ecstatic experiences.

[2] *De Migratione Abrahami*, 35 (ed. C. W.). Additional striking references in Bréhier, *Les Idées Philosophiques et Religieuses de Philon*, who gives a luminous account of Philo's conception of ecstasy and prophetic inspiration, pp. 188-200, but lays stress far too exclusively on the Platonic character of his mysticism.

tionably Platonic and Stoic influences are discernible in Philo's ecstatic mysticism. But there are elements closely akin to the prophetic ecstasy of the Old Testament. And side by side with these strains may be traced the influence of mystery-religions.

We have restricted this brief discussion of Philo to the single feature of his mystic ecstasy, partly because it suggests a parallelism with certain phenomena in the religion of Paul, and partly because it discloses as its core and kernel a genuine personal experience, which may of course be expressed in terms belonging to the religious syncretism of his age, but cannot be completely explained either from the Platonic-Stoic influence of Posidonius or from the mystery-doctrines of Hellenised Egyptian theology.[1]

[1] Kroll would virtually identify these mystery-doctrines with the tendency which appears in Posidonius. He refuses to believe in any marked Egyptian tradition in the Hermetic literature, *op. cit.*, spp. 815, 816.

CHAPTER III

THE CHARACTER AND INFLUENCE OF THE MYSTERY-RELIGIONS

WE know far less about the actual rites and doctrines of the Mystery-Religions in the Græco-Roman world than we do of their wide diffusion and potent influence. This is not surprising, for on the one hand their votaries were strictly enjoined to keep silent on their most sacred experiences,[1] and, on the other, stern critics of Paganism like the early Christian Fathers must inevitably have been biassed in their casual representations of the facts. The literary remains of these communities are very scanty. Some mystic formulæ, a few hymns and prayers, some narratives of initiations and allied ceremonial practically exhaust the list. To supplement them, there are vague illusions and isolated fragments of information which may be pieced to-

[1] *Cf.* the utterances of the Emperor Julian as to secrecy regarding his initiation into the rites of Attis (Hepding, *Attis*, p. 180).

gether from Hellenistic and early Christian writers. Further, the extant material has to be used with caution. For it is often impossible to fix dates with any certainty. Thus, *e.g.*, the *Corpus* of Hermetic writings contains elements from widely separated periods. Of the character of the so-called Liturgy of Mithra, so competent an authority as R. Wünsch can only say : " Before we are in a position to judge with certainty, we must have a much clearer view of the history of syncretism in Egypt ".[1] Some chronological landmarks, however, can be discerned. The famous description of the initiation of Lucius into the Mysteries of Isis at Cenchreæ (Apul. *Metam.* xi., 18-25) dates from the middle of the second century A.D., but the elaborate ritual and the remarkable prayers plainly presuppose a long history lying behind. The same thing is true of the mystic formulæ. They bear the stamp of antiquity, and in some instances their actual relations with primitive ideas can be demonstrated. Moreover, there are special strains of religious thought and feeling more or less common to all the Mystery-Religions, such as that of regeneration (in some sense) and union or

[1] *Eine Mithrasliturgie*, ed. 2, p. 228.

communion with deity. These appear and re-appear in documents far removed from each other, and belonging to different spheres of culture. No doubt there must have been much mutual interchange between the various types of mystic religion. But such phenomena demand time. And the time required will probably have to be measured by half-centuries rather than decades. It is perhaps true, as Schweitzer asserts, that Paul cannot have known the Mystery-Religions as we know them, because they did not yet exist in this elaborated form.[1] But the "elaborated form," which we can trace in the second and third centuries A.D., postulates a lengthy development, and it is hazardous to dogmatise as to what was or was not possible, say, in the period from 30 to 100 A.D., or even earlier. Without discussing at present the extent to which Oriental mystic cults may have been influenced by the Greek Mysteries in the Hellenistic area, a fact which is scarcely open to question,[2] it appears to us more than probable that their extraordinary sway in the opening years of

[1] *Geschichte der Paulin. Forschung*, p. 150.

[2] See, *e.g.*, Otto, *Priester u. Tempel im Hellenist. Ägypten*, i., 132; ii., 222, note 4.

the Imperial epoch was due to something deeper than their external pomp or the magical arts at their disposal.

The meagre available data we are bound to interpret in the light of parallel religious phenomena, present in every age. There is good reason to believe, *e.g.*, in the case of the State-Mysteries of Eleusis, that the effect produced on the initiated was not merely that of an imposing ritual. In a former chapter we referred to the highly complex Orphic movement. Here, too, there is a danger of confining attention to the more obvious features. There is genuine truth in Monceaux' statement that Orphism "gathered an *élite* from among the worshippers of Dionysus".[1] But it is precarious, in view of the sporadic traces of Orphic beliefs and practices found throughout the Hellenistic world from the sixth century downwards, to restrict its *bona fide* influence to philosophers and poets, as he does, and to class all other alleged adherents with the notorious Ὀρφεοτελεσταί who traded on popular credulity.[2] Indeed, the analogy of all

[1] Art. "Orphici" in Daremberg et Saglio's *Dictionnaire*, Tome iv., partie 1, p. 247.

[2] Prof. A. E. Taylor seems inclined to make the same sharp twofold division (*Varia Socratica*, i., pp. 26, 27).

similar "conventicles" in the history of religion admonishes us to leave room within them for varying shades of faith and earnestness.

A most important source of evidence for the diffusion and influence of the Mystery-Religions is to be found in the numerous inscriptions which give us glimpses into the life of religious *associations*. From the days of the Attic ὀργεῶνες, those private corporations of the worshippers of some local god or hero which we can trace as far back as the fourth century B.C., this phase of religious life becomes more and more prominent in the Hellenic world. As Kaerst has admirably shown, the religion of the Hellenistic period finds its characteristic type in the cult-brotherhood, the θίασος.[1] The old faith of the Greek πόλις had broken down. The new era inaugurated by the policy of Alexander the Great by its very expansiveness favoured individualism. Once the sanctions of the city-state had lost their validity, the individual saw the world lying open before him. In theory he became cosmopolitan, but in practice he was confronted by masses of new facts which disintegrated his traditional beliefs and threw him back upon himself. The successors of

[1] *Geschichte d. hellenistischen Zeitalters*, II., i., p. 280.

Alexander, more especially the Ptolemies and the Seleucidæ, attempted to replace the state-religion by worship of the ruler. The attempt succeeded as a political symbol. But the pressure of religious need banded men together in larger and smaller groups, dedicated to the worship and service of a deity or group of deities.

It is interesting to note that the earliest inscriptions in Attica which record these associations of θιασῶται reveal a largely preponderating element of foreigners among their members.[1] And they are found predominantly at busy seaports like the Piræus. On the coasts of Asia Minor and in the islands of the Ægæan, θίασοι can be traced in considerable numbers before the Christian era. Poland thinks that the term still points to a connection with Dionysiac worship. In the Imperial period associations of μύσται, initiates, emerge in the same regions as those in which the θίασοι flourished, especially in Asia Minor. Smyrna and Ephesus appear to have been important centres

[1] See Fr. Poland, *Geschichte d. griechischen Vereinswesens*, 1909, p. 20. Few modern scholars would support Foucart's hypothesis that *all* the Attic cult-associations were of foreign origin.

of these mystic brotherhoods.¹ It is significant that in the Imperial era Dionysus is constantly associated with cult-guilds, either as chief deity or in combination with others. His designation of βάκχος seems to have a special relation to mystery-associations. The area of his influence is extraordinarily wide. Beginning with the Διονυσιασταί of the Piræus about 180 B.C., we find similar guilds prominently represented in important centres like Rhodes and Thera.² In Thracian territory, the original home of Dionysus, a considerable number of mystic associations flourished, *e.g.*, at Philippi and in its neighbourhood (μύσται Διονύσου, *Bulletin de Corresp. Hellénique*, xxiv., p. 304 f.). Asia Minor supplies abundant material. There is little doubt that the cult of Dionysus had intimate affinities in these religious unions with those of the Phrygian deities, the Great Mother and Sabazius, although we do not possess sufficient data to elucidate the question. Here we are confronted by foreign cult-associa-

---

¹ See Poland, *op. cit.*, p. 38, and the references to Inscrr., pp. 568, 569. The dates extend over a wide period.

² See the numerous Inscrr. of first and second centuries B.C. in Poland, *op. cit.*, pp. 564, 565.

OF THE MYSTERY-RELIGIONS 75

tions, which are of such crucial importance for our discussion.

As early as the fourth century B.C., we have evidence in the Piræus of an association of ὀργεῶνες, worshippers of the Great Mother, whom they style "the goddess". In Asia Minor she is a favourite brotherhood-deity, and Attis is associated with her. The traces of Sabazius-unions are often mixed up with those of worshippers of θεὸς ὕψιστος. Egyptian deities occupy a peculiarly prominent place. Serapis-associations abound in the islands of the Ægæan, many of them earlier than the Christian era. They are found in Attica about 250 B.C. It is practically certain that Isis was reverenced along with her consort, but frequently she received independent recognition. Associations of Ἰσιασταί are found, *e.g.*, in Rhodes in the first century B.C. These phenomena are not merely due to the propaganda of a nation of enterprising traders like the Egyptians. The Ptolemaic dynasty stood in a special relation to the deities Serapis, Isis, and Osiris. They were conscious of the affinity between Isis and Demeter, between Osiris and Dionysus. Serapis seems to have been a syncretistic deity from the outset. In any case, owing to the shrewd policy of the reigning house, these deities became, as Kaerst says, "characteristic figures of religious syncretism, and at the same time symbols of the power and unique dignity which belonged to the Ptolemaic rulers, the most successful representatives of a syncretistic *Religions-politik*".[1] Accordingly, the area over which Egyptian cult-brotherhoods extend corresponds roughly to the sphere of influence of the Ptolemaic dynasty.[2]

A word must be said as to the deities of Samothrace. Possibly of Phœnician origin, they reveal Chthonian affinities, being closely allied with such Greek divinities as Hephæstus, Demeter, and Kore. They are worshipped in an influential mystery-cult. But their identification with a large variety of gods is proof of their syncretistic character. Their cult was peculiarly favoured by the monarchs who divided Alexander's dominions, especially by the Ptolemies,[3] and they also were honoured with the reverence of religious brotherhoods. A similar diffusion of religious associations

[1] *Op. cit.*, p. 273.
[2] See Poland's important discussion, *op. cit.*, pp. 522-524.
[3] See Kaerst, *op. cit.*, p. 279.

is discernible in the Roman world. Livy describes guilds of Bacchus-worshippers, who engaged in mystic ritual, as far back as 186 B.C. In the days of Sulla († 78 B.C.), *collegia* devoted to the worship of Egyptian deities, such as Osiris and Isis, can be vouched for in Italy (Apul. *Metam.* xi., 30). Isiac guilds were already notorious in the Rome of the first century A.D.[1]

One or two features of the religious situation just delineated deserve emphasis. The favourite deities of the associations are foreign. The Hellenic gods who appear among them have already been connected with a mystic worship, or are noted for their saving energies, as, *e.g.*, Æsculapius. The members of the guilds are predominantly foreigners, and a single association frequently contains representatives of many lands. Sometimes a number of deities share in the common worship of the " brethren ". The most eager religious life of these brotherhoods belongs to great commercial centres like Athens, Delos, and Rhodes, where foreigners might be expected to congregate. Such cosmopolitan communities

[1] See Kornemann, art. "Collegium," in Pauly-Wissowa, *R.E.*, vol. iv., sp. 386 f. ; Dill, *Roman Society from Nero to Marcus Aurelius*, p. 581.

would present unusual facilities for religious propaganda. It is needless to call attention to the effect of the brotherhoods in producing a spirit of equality among their members. But recent research has shown that Foucart[1] and others have exaggerated the position assigned in them to women and slaves, at least in the non-Latin area.[2] The ethical tone of Græco-Roman religious associations has been severely criticised, largely on the basis of statements found in the early Fathers. No doubt the moral standard was often low enough. But there is little unprejudiced evidence available. And we have hints here and there of a higher ideal, as, *e.g.*, in an Inscr. of Ephesus (c. 83 A.D.), in which purity is laid down as indispensable for guilds of initiates. It would be generally admitted that a large part of the fascination of these brotherhoods lay in the halo of mystery which surrounded them, and the esoteric ritual through which admission was gained. But there can be no doubt that under the influence of popular philosophy the various mystic cults became gradually purified. Whatever name

[1] *Les associations religieuses*, p. 5 f.
[2] See Poland, *op. cit.*, pp. 298, 328 f. In Roman *collegia* the circumstances were evidently much more favourable.

they bear, their ultimate aim was identical—to raise the soul above the transiency of perishable matter to an immortal life through actual union with the Divine.[1]

These associations of initiates formed an integral part of St. Paul's environment as he laboured in great centres of population like Antioch, Ephesus, Corinth, and Rome. There is nothing far-fetched in the hypothesis that many of the Pagans who were attracted to his preaching, many even of those who were already God-fearers ($\sigma\epsilon\beta\acute{o}\mu\epsilon\nu\omicron\iota$ $\tau\grave{o}\nu$ $\theta\epsilon\acute{o}\nu$), had belonged to mystic brotherhoods. When a new group of travelling preachers from the East proclaimed the promise of $\sigma\omega\tau\eta\rho\acute{\iota}\alpha$ and the assurance of life eternal, their message was bound to appeal to such an audience. Inevitably, therefore, the great missionary would be brought into personal touch with inquirers of this type. And as he sought to instruct them in "the mystery of God, even Christ, in whom are hid all the treasures of wisdom and knowledge" (Col. ii. 2), he must have gained a first-hand acquaintance with those religious conceptions by which they had

[1] See an admirable statement in Jacoby, *Die antiken Mysterienreligionen*, pp. 12, 13.

attempted to reach spiritual peace. Heinrici has tried to establish a detailed parallel between Pagan religious guilds and early Christian communities, *e.g.*, at Corinth. He has adduced many remarkable resemblances and shown some real points of contact. But we know too little about the organisation either of Pagan or early Christian societies to be able to accept his conclusion that the Christian community at Corinth was nothing else than a heathen religious guild transformed.[1] At the same time, the material which he has collected is very impressive as indicating the importance of these brotherhoods for the background of the Christian Church in the Apostolic age.

We must now attempt to estimate as concisely as possible the most typical Mystery-Religions of the Græco-Roman world, endeavouring most of all to bring out their main characteristics in the light of recent research. These characteristics will be found to blend more or less in a common complex of ideas, which cannot be explained from mere processes of mutual borrowing. We shall examine in turn the State-

[1] *Zeitschr. f. wiss. Theol.*, 1876, pp. 455-526, see esp. 484-490, 503-510.

Mysteries of Eleusis, the Mystery-Cults of the Great Mother (with Attis) and of Isis (with Serapis), and the typically Hellenistic religious phenomena connected with the Hermetic mystery-literature. This will provide an atmosphere for the detailed comparison of their conceptions with Pauline ideas.

Many scholars are still accustomed to draw a sharp line of cleavage between the State-regulated Mysteries of Eleusis and the more private and individualistic mystery-cults which proved to be such formidable rivals. A few crucial differences, of course, lie on the surface. In the hey-day of Athenian prosperity, the Mysteries of Eleusis were little less than a national Hellenic festival. As far back as the time of Herodotus, all Greeks were eligible for initiation. The accompaniments of the festival were on a public scale. Such an institution was peculiarly exposed to the risk of externalism and formality. And there is sufficient evidence that the risk was not avoided. To the multitudes which thronged the sacred precincts the whole ceremonial must often have appeared no more than an imposing religious demonstration. In contrast, the private θίασοι offered something more personal and intimate. There was the bond of a human fellowship in communion with the special deity. There was the call to a brotherhood which ignored distinctions of race or status. There was the demand for self-denial. There was the constraint of a life-long obligation.[1] Now, no doubt the influence of private associations must have reacted on the national mysteries in the way of deepening their religious significance. But we are almost compelled to believe, on the strength of the meagre data still extant, that the initiation at Eleusis already contained the germs of a higher religious outlook, admitting, of course, that these had often to be quickened into a more vigorous life. In a region where so much is matter of controversy, let us first briefly summarise some facts on which there is more or less general agreement.

Most modern scholars have rejected Foucart's hypothesis that the aim of the Eleusinian Mysteries was to furnish the initiated with a stock of magic formulæ for escaping the dangers which attended the soul on its journey to the world of the departed. The intention was to create an

[1] See Eisele, *Neue Jahrb. f. d. klass. Altertum*, 1909, p. 627.

OF THE MYSTERY-RELIGIONS 83

overpowering impression rather than to communicate esoteric doctrines. Synesius[1] quotes the judgment of Aristotle: οὐ μαθεῖν τι δεῖν ἀλλὰ παθεῖν. There was an elaborate ceremonial of preparation which included, as perhaps its most important element, rites of purification (καθαρμός), and a long interval had to elapse between admission to the Lesser Mysteries at Athens and the complete initiation at Eleusis. There was a sacred exhortation, possibly an explanation of the mystic actions performed (τελετῆς παράδοσις). The climax consisted in the ἐποπτεία,[2] the vision of the sacred scenes, accompanied by the handling of certain holy things.[3] The final rites must have been performed in an atmosphere of highly intensified feeling.

Extreme divergence of opinion prevails as to the full significance and effect of the ritual and its accompaniments. While it is universally admitted that with the secret ceremonies was

[1] *De Dione*, 10.

[2] See Theon Smyrnæus, *De Util. Mathem.*, p. 15.

[3] *Cf.* the mystic formula found in Clem. Alex. and Arnobius: ἐνήστευσα, ἔπιον τὸν κυκεῶνα, ἔλαβον ἐκ κίστης, ἐργασάμενος ἀπεθέμην εἰς κάλαθον καὶ ἐκ καλάθου εἰς κίστην.

associated, in some sense, the assurance of immortality, certain scholars, *e.g.*, Rohde, hold that this was no new conviction, reached through the mystic experience. It already existed as the basis of the widely-diffused soul-cult. It was the blissful content of the future life which was impressed on the initiates, probably (as the Homeric Hymn to Demeter would suggest) by a series of *tableaux* which glorified the goddesses of the Mysteries, and made their votaries conscious of the joy to be attained by passing under their sway.[1] Rohde will not hear of any mystical experience reached in the initiation, or of any sense of communion with the Divine. Hence he rules out the idea of a moral effect on the life of the worshipper.[2] But an important passage, whose obvious meaning he tries to evade (Aristoph., *Frogs*, 456 f.), seems to us decisive as against his view: "All we who have been initiated and lived in pious wise" ($εὐσεβῆ \ τε \ διήγομεν \ τρόπον$). The uninitiated, whom Dionysus beholds lying in thick slime, are those who wronged strangers, maltreated parents, swore false oaths

---

[1] See Rohde, *Psyche*,[3] i., pp. 294-298.
[2] *Op. cit.*, pp. 298-300.

OF THE MYSTERY-RELIGIONS 85

(*ibid.*, 148 f.).[1] These lines reflect the current opinion. The very fact that the secret of Eleusis was so inviolably kept testifies to the genuine influence of the Mysteries. It is possible to believe with Farnell,[2] that the drinking of the κυκεών points to the notion of a sacramental communion with the goddess-mother in her sorrow, although this can be no more than an hypothesis. But whatever may have been the precise nature of the "passion-play," we can scarcely separate the prominence of the conception of immortality from the recovery from the underworld of the lost Kore, the triumph of life over death.[3] Suggestive light is shed upon this phase of the Mysteries by the association with them of the mystic deity Iacchos. In spite of Rohde's arguments, he must be identified with Dionysus,

[1] We are glad to find that Wobbermin, in his valuable *Religionsgeschichtliche Studien*, p. 36 f., takes our view. He shows that ὅσιος, which is almost a technical term for the initiated, cannot be taken in a merely ritual sense, but has an ethico-religious basis, see *op. cit.*, p. 38.

[2] Art. "Mystery," *Encyc. Brit.*, ed. xi., vol. xix., p. 120 f.

[3] *Cf.* Isocr. *Panegyr.*, 28 : τὴν τελετήν, ἧς οἱ μετασχόντες περί τε τῆς τοῦ βίου τελευτῆς καὶ τοῦ σύμπαντος αἰῶνος ἡδίους τὰς ἐλπίδας ἔχουσιν.

whose cult at Athens was no doubt a much later growth than that of Demeter and Kore at Eleusis, but probably came to be fused with it in some sense, after the union of Eleusis and Athens.[1] There are various facts which seem to indicate that Iacchos was identified in the Mysteries with the son of Kore. This connection with Dionysus leads us into the heart of conceptions typical for mystery-religion, the conception of union with the Divine and attainment of undying life. We have no evidence as to the extent to which such ideas found expression. If Orphic religion with its intimate relation to the Dionysus-cult exercised any influence on the Eleusinian Mysteries,[2] the strain of thought and feeling which we have been discussing must have had a prominent place. On this problem any verdict must be hesitating. But we believe enough has been said to indicate that there is some justification for Sir W. M. Ramsay's position, that the Eleusinian Mysteries constituted "the one great attempt made by Hellenic genius to construct a religion that should keep pace

[1] See Sir W. M. Ramsay in *Encyc. Brit.*, ed. ix., vol. xvii., p. 128.

[2] So, *e.g.*, Sir W. M. Ramsay, Dieterich, and others.

OF THE MYSTERY-RELIGIONS 87

with the growth of thought and civilisation in Greece".[1]

The theory has been put forward that Eleusis was influenced by Egyptian cults, either directly at a very early date, or indirectly through the medium of the Orphic movement.[2] This is by no means impossible. But Thracian influence is more easily understood, and there were many affinities between the Thracian Dionysus and strictly Oriental deities like the Egyptian Osiris and the Phrygian Attis.[3] These affinities would have some effect in opening a path for Oriental cults into the Græco-Roman world. Considerable caution must be employed in attempting to define with any certainty the beliefs or ritual of these cults at special moments in their history. For that history remains exceedingly dim, especially for the period when Oriental faiths were confronted with Greek culture in Asia. Certain facts, however, stand out clearly. These religions, having no official prestige, could only be propagated by their appeal to the individual. The

[1] *Loc. cit.*, p. 126.

[2] See De Jong, *Das antike Mysterienwesen*, pp. 26-29.

[3] We have already referred to the theory of Eisler that Orphism was directly influenced by Persian religion.

appeal consisted above all in the promise of raising men above the dreary pressure of bodily existence into a Divine ecstasy, for the production of which they supplied the means. These means were often crass enough. For ignorant minds they became the channel of all manner of magical beliefs. For the cultivated they often served as far-reaching symbols of a high religious experience for which their souls were yearning.[1] In the light of such phenomena, it is clear why Oriental cults appear in the Hellenistic area as Mystery-Religions. The sway they thus attained is strikingly illustrated by the fact that gradually the only Hellenic gods who retained their influence beside their rivals were the mystery-deities *par excellence*, Dionysus and Hecate.[2]

We have already referred to a cult-association in honour of the Great Mother, Cybele, in the Piræus, as early as the fourth century B.C. At the instigation of a special embassy her worship was introduced into Rome from Pessinus in Galatia, in 204 B.C., when the war with Carthage was a deadly menace to the Republic. For long that

[1] See Jacoby, *op. cit.*, pp. 9-11 : a luminous description of the Dionysiac ecstasy in Rohde, *Psyche*,[3] ii., pp. 11-21.

[2] See Cumont, *Les Religions Orientales*,[3] p. 410, note 12.

worship remained an exotic, but by the time of Augustus Romans had been admitted to the religious associations of the goddess, and had served as her priests. In her Phrygian home, and indeed throughout Asia Minor, the cult of Cybele seems often to have been fused with that of Dionysus, to which it bore a remarkable resemblance. Each was an orgiastic worship, in which the votaries wrought themselves into a sacred frenzy, and thereby believed they were united with the deity.[1] Rohde and others identify with Dionysus the Phrygian god Sabazius, whose worship came to be blended with that of Cybele and Dionysus in the syncretism of Hellenistic religion.[2] Possibly, however, his origin was Phrygian.[3] Eisele holds that his cult was non-orgiastic, and symbolised in crude but quiet ritual the most intimate conceivable union of the initiate with the deity. A suggestive feature, found of course in other cults, was the designa-

[1] *Cf.* the remarkable expressions in Livy's savage account of the Bacchic Mysteries at Rome in 187 B.C., *e.g.*, 39, 13 : *viros, velut mente capta, cum jactatione fanatici corporis vaticinari . . . Raptos a diis homines,* etc.

[2] See Rohde, *op. cit.*, ii., pp. 7 (note 3), 14 f.

[3] So Eisele, *loc. cit.*, p. 625.

tion of the divinely-possessed worshippers by the name of the god, Sabos or Sabazius.[1] Central for the Phrygian cult of the Great Mother was the Attis-ritual. For it is probable that the two deities were never separated.[2] The myth of the beloved youth who, in penitence for his unfaithfulness to the goddess, mutilated himself beneath the pine-tree; the mourning of Cybele for her lover, and his restoration to undying life, formed the basis of the drama which was annually celebrated at the spring-festival of the goddess. In this was embodied the mystic revelation. The process of initiation remains in obscurity, but the unmistakable analogy of the celebration to other mystery-cults dispels all doubts as to its real character. That its mystic significance was of no recent growth [3] is obvious from the ancient formulæ which tradition has handed down. The ritual began with the felling

---

[1] So ὁ κατεχόμενος τῇ μητρὶ τῶν θεῶν was named Κύβηβος, after Κυβήβη (= Cybele). See Photius, s. Κύβηβος. The parallel usage in the Isis-Serapis cult is significant. See *infra*, and *cf.* G. Murray, *Four Stages of Greek Religion*, p. 38.

[2] See Hepding, *Attis*, p. 142.

[3] Schweitzer apparently regards it as a late development, *op. cit.*, p. 144.

of the sacred pine-tree. When the tree, bound like a corpse, and adorned with garlands and religious symbols, among them a statue of the god, was escorted into the sanctuary, the mourning for Attis broke forth. A time of abstinence followed ; then came the day of blood, when the tree was solemnly buried, and the participants in the ritual abandoned themselves to delirious dances. In a state of semi-unconsciousness they gashed themselves with knives and sprinkled the altar with their blood. On the succeeding night they met in the temple to celebrate the restoration of Attis to life. The grave was opened : a light was brought in : and the priest, as he anointed the lips of the worshippers with holy oil, uttered the consoling words : θαρρεῖτε μύσται τοῦ θεοῦ σεσωσμένου, ἔσται γὰρ ὑμῖν τῶν πόνων σωτηρία: " Be of good cheer, initiates, the god has been saved : thus for you also shall there be salvation from your troubles".[1] The joy of the *mystæ* now found expression in a kind of carnival. Masqueraders paraded the streets in disguise. There was an orgy of universal licence. Various ritual actions were per-

[1] Firmicus Maternus, *De Errore Profan. Relig.* (ed. Ziegler), p. 57, 14 f.

formed. A mystic formula has been preserved both by Firmicus Maternus (*op. cit.*, p. 43, 15) and Clement of Alexandria (I. p. 13, 12 f., ed. Stählin), which reminds us forcibly of the Eleusinian formula already quoted : ἐκ τυμπάνου βέβρωκα, ἐκ κυμβάλου πέπωκα, γέγονα μύστης Ἄττεως : "I have eaten out of the tympanum, I have drunk from the cymbal, I have become an initiate of Attis ".[1] This certainly seems to point to some sacred meal in which the participant entered into communion with the god. It is possible that the anointing of the lips of the votaries with holy oil ought to be compared with the rite of smearing the tongue with honey for a certain grade of initiation into the mysteries of Mithra, a rite which is by some regarded as pointing to the gift of immortality.[2] We have no means of dating the formula, but it has all the appearance of a high antiquity.[3] The mystic words are put by Firmicus into the lips of a man

[1] In Clement the formula is more elaborate: ἐκ τυμπάνου ἔφαγον, ἐκ κυμβάλου ἐκερνοφόρησα, ὑπὸ τὸν παστὸν ὑπέδυν. It is needless to discuss the additional details.

[2] So Dieterich, *Eine Mithrasliturgie*,[2] pp. 170, 171, 174.

[3] For a full description of the Attis-festival, see Eisele, *loc. cit.*, pp. 634-637 ; Hepding, *Attis*, p. 150 ff.

whom he describes as *moriturus*, "about to die". Dieterich interprets this in a sacramental sense, and finds confirmation for his opinion in an extremely compressed account of the Attis-festival given by Sallustius, an official under the Emperor Julian, in his περὶ θεῶν καὶ κόσμου. There (ch. 4) a description is given of "the cutting of the tree and the fast, as though we also were cutting off the further process of generation," and, at the next stage of the cult, the initiates are fed with milk, "as being born again" (ὥσπερ ἀναγεννωμένων).[1] Here again we are left in obscurity as to the age of the ritual. Plainly the conception points to a somewhat advanced step in the religious evolution of the cult. But if, as appears certain, these Phrygian rites sprang from a primitive nature-worship,[2] in which Attis was a tree-spirit who, as such, exercised power over the products of the earth, and especially the corn, it only required the purification of the crude, primal instinct of

[1] See Dieterich, *Eine Mithrasliturgie*,[2] p. 163.

[2] See, *e.g.*, the felling of the pine-tree. Mr. J. G. Frazer points out that Attis was addressed as "the reaped green (or yellow) ear of corn". He has collected conclusive evidence for Attis' rôle as a god of vegetation, *Adonis, Attis, Osiris*, pp. 174-177. For a deeper aspect of this idea which is possibly present, see G. Murray, *op. cit.*, pp. 46, 47.

sympathy with the fresh life of returning spring, by more spiritual aspirations which told of man's kinship with a higher order of being, to reach the notion, still dim and anthropomorphic, of a divine life which the grave could not quench. Eisele believes that the Cybele-Attis religion had undergone a process of this kind long before it spread over the Hellenic world. Many scholars, including Cumont and Dill, find the chief stimulus to purer and more profound religious ideas much later, in the contact of this Phrygian worship with the rapidly extending movement of Mithraism.[1] To such contact they would assign the extraordinary ceremony of *taurobolium*, the bath of blood, which, from the middle of the second century A.D., constituted perhaps the most impressive rite in the worship of the Great Mother. Here the notion of regeneration stands in the forefront. Various inscriptions describe the "baptised" as *in aeternum renatus*.[2] The rite seems originally to have belonged to the worship of a Persian goddess, Anâhita, closely associated with Mithra in the old religion of the Achæmenidæ,

[1] See Cumont, *op. cit.*, pp. 98-103; Dill, *op. cit.*, pp. 554-559.

[2] See Dill, *op. cit.*, p. 547, note 4.

and apparently assimilated to Cybele in Asia Minor, especially in Cappadocia.[1] How far the savage ritual had shaken off its grosser associations before its late emergence in the Cybele-cult of the Western world, it is impossible to say. But it would be rash to use it as evidence for a mystic doctrine of immortality within the first century of our era. The brief sketch we have given of the Cybele-Attis cult reveals with sufficient clearness the barbaric ritual by which its votaries sought to satisfy their religious needs. The picture could be heightened on its ruder side. And yet no unbiassed mind can fail to read between the lines almost pathetic indications of a craving for fulness of life, for a real and enduring σωτηρία. We may believe that some at least of the initiates could testify to a genuine experience in their ancient liturgical utterance: ἔφυγον κακόν, εὗρον ἄμεινον.[2]

In his famous treatise, *De Iside et Osir.*, 27,

[1] See Cumont, *op. cit.*, pp. 99, 332; Dill, p. 556. Hepding contests this on what seem to us quite inadequate grounds (*Attis*, p. 201).

[2] Apparently a formula of the Sabazius-cult: referred to in Demosth., *De Cor.*, 259. Used early in Attic marriage festivities (see Dieterich, *op. cit.*, p. 215).

Plutarch tells how Isis, unwilling that all the hardships she had endured and the heroic deeds she had done in avenging her brother and consort Osiris should be forgotten, wove them into a mystic ritual, "and established a doctrine of piety and a consolation for men and women who should fall into like misfortunes". His words reveal the influence of Isis-Mysteries at the close of the first century A.D. We have no definite evidence, indeed, for these mysteries earlier than the Imperial age, but so cautious an investigator as Cumont considers that "all the probabilities are in favour of a more ancient origin," and that "the Mysteries no doubt were linked to early Egyptian esoteric doctrine".[1] The circumstances in which the cult of Isis (and Osiris-Serapis) was brought into direct touch with the Greek world certainly favour this hypothesis. It was part of the far-seeing political outlook of the first Ptolemy to make religion one of his instruments in fusing together his Greek and Egyptian subjects. For this purpose he introduced into Alexandria the cult of Serapis. The origin of the god is still an unsolved problem. Many scholars have derived his name from the Egyptian

[1] *Op. cit.*, p. 335, note 4.

Osiris-Apis (*i.e.*, Apis of Memphis transformed into Osiris). Wilcken believes that it is non-Egyptian, and that the god was brought in from outside. In any case he was immediately identified with Osiris (-Apis).[1] An old tradition found in Plutarch reports that Ptolemy summoned one of the hierarchical aristocracy of Eleusis, the Eumolpid, Timotheus, to consult with him as to the character of the new divinity. Whether the tradition be genuine or not, it is true to the situation. The cult of Serapis was syncretistic. Osiris, the Lord of life and death, the final arbiter of human destiny, was surrounded with the halo of the Greek mysteries. But his fitness to be a mystery-divinity had long since been recognised. Plutarch describes (*De Iside et Osir.*, 39) a festival held when the Nile was receding, whose chief ceremonies plainly represented the search for the body of the slain Osiris and his restoration to life symbolised by a small image of vegetable mould mixed with spices. Similar celebrations seem to have been current in various parts of Egypt. In the temple of Isis

[1] Thus bilingual texts have in the Greek section Σαρᾶπις, in the Egyptian Osiris-Apis. See Wilcken, *Grundzüge d. Papyruskunde*, I., i., pp. 101, 102.

at Philæ, the body of Osiris is portrayed with corn springing from it, accompanied by the inscription : " This is the form of him whom one may not name, Osiris of the mysteries, who springs from the returning waters ".[1] It is easy to trace here the kinship with Eleusis and its sacred ear of corn, so prominent in the mysteries, as well as with Dionysiac legends belonging to the same cycle of nature-worship. Greeks of insight like Herodotus (ii. 49) and Plutarch (*De Iside et Osir.*, 35) discerned in him an intimate affinity with their own Dionysus. Thus no serious obstacles had to be overcome to commend the new syncretistic Mystery-cult to the Hellenistic world. From this time onward the Isis-Serapis worship had an extraordinarily wide range of diffusion. It is found at Athens at least as early as the third century B.C. ; at Pompeii about the end of the second ; in Rome by the time of Sulla.[2] Thence it spread wherever Roman influence penetrated. The fascination of the cult is not difficult

---

[1] See J. G. Frazer, *Adonis, Attis, Osiris*, pp. 257-263.

[2] See Drexler's masterly article, "Isis," in Roscher's *Lexikon*, vol. ii., spp. 383-386, 399, 401. Drexler gives a remarkable survey of the area of influence which belonged to the Isis-cult.

to understand. There was, of course, the imposing ritual, distinguished by its "contemplative devotion," which had all the splendid precision and order characteristic of Egyptian liturgical tradition. Still more appealing were the eschatological doctrines promulgated. Here Egyptian theology remained true to itself. There is a famous passage in an ancient Egyptian text relating to the worship of Osiris, which speaks of the loyal votary of the god after death : " As truly as Osiris lives shall he live : as truly as Osiris is not dead, shall he not die ; as truly as Osiris is not annihilated, shall he not be annihilated ".[1] In the reshaped Isis-Serapis cult this doctrine remains fundamental. The initiate is to share eternally in the divine life : nay, he does already share it. He becomes Osiris. Here is expressed with clearness the more dimly adumbrated hope of the Dionysiac-Orphic mysteries. The Isis Mystery-Religion exercised a peculiar attraction just because of its syncretism. Isis could be identified with innumerable deities. As queen of heaven, as Selene, as goddess of the cultivated earth, as Demeter, as giver of crops,

---

[1] See Erman, *Die ägyptische Religion*,[2] p. 111.

as mistress of the under-world, and also of the sea, as goddess of women and beauty and love, as queen of the gods assimilated to Hera and Juno, as goddess of salvation, and also of magical arts,[1] she will claim the adoration of a motley throng of worshippers. Thus " the great power of Isis ' of myriad names ' was that, transfigured by Greek influences, she appealed to many orders of intellect, and satisfied many religious needs or fancies ".[2]

A unique opportunity of understanding the significance of the Isis Mystery-Religion is afforded by the famous description in Apuleius of the initiation of Lucius at Cenchreæ.[3] The candidate for initiation had to remain within the precincts of the temple, until he was summoned (*vocatus*) by the goddess. Otherwise, he might pay the penalty of sacrilege by death. "For," says

---

[1] See Drexler, *loc. cit.*, *passim* ; Reitzenstein, *Poimandres*, pp. 162-164 ; and the notable passage in Apuleius, *Metam.*, xi., 5, where, in her revelation to Lucius, Isis says : *cujus numen unicum multiformi specie, ritu vario, nomine multijugo totus veneratur orbis*, and then recounts her various names.

[2] Dill, *op. cit.*, p. 569.

[3] *Metam.*, xi., chapp. 18-25. A graphic summary in Dill, pp. 576-579.

the high-priest, "the portals of the nether world and the guardianship of salvation are placed in the hand of the goddess, and the initiation itself is solemnised as the symbol of a voluntary death (*ad instar voluntariæ mortis*) and a salvation given in answer to prayer, for the goddess is wont to choose such as, having fulfilled a course of life, stand at the very threshold of the departing light, to whom nevertheless the great mysteries of religion can be safely entrusted; and after they have been, by her providence, in a sense born again (*quodam modo renatos*), she places them again on the course of a new life in salvation."[1] Lucius awaited the will of the goddess, giving himself up to prayer and fasting. When at length the wished-for day arrived, he was escorted by a band of Isis-worshippers and bathed by the high-priest in the sacred laver. Thereafter, in presence of the goddess, he receives mystic communications. Ten days of ascetic preparation follow, and then he is led into the innermost sanctuary. A mystic delineation is given of his culminating experience: "I penetrated to the boundaries of death: I trod the threshold of Proserpine, and after being

[1] Apuleius, *op. cit.*, xi., 21 (ed. van der Vliet).

borne through all the elements I returned to earth: at midnight I beheld the sun radiating white light: I came into the presence of the gods below and the gods above, and did them reverence close at hand ".[1]

The whole picture is of extraordinary significance both for the outer and inner aspects of Hellenistic Mystery-Religion. On the one hand there are the prescribed abstinences, the solemn baptism, the communication of mystic formulæ, and the overpowering scenes which formed the climax of initiation.[2] On the other, there is presented to us the preparation of heart, the symbol of cleansing, the conception of regeneration, and finally identification with the deity. The effect of the experience, as genuinely religious, is disclosed by the impressive prayer of thanksgiving offered by Lucius to the goddess

[1] *Op. cit.*, xi., 23.

[2] The description in Apuleius certainly implies something more than an ecstatic vision (so also Cumont as against De Jong), though of course a condition of ecstasy is implied in the ascent of the soul through the elements. This ascent typifies his assimilation to the deity, for next day he appears *duodecim sacratus stolis*, the *stolæ* symbolising the twelve spheres through which he has passed (see Reitzenstein, *Archiv f. Religionswiss.*, 1904, pp. 407, 408).

after initiation, a prayer no doubt taken from an actual liturgy: "Thou who art the holy and eternal Saviour of mankind, ever bountiful to the mortals who cherish Thee, Thou bestowest Thy gracious mother-love upon the wretched in their misfortunes. No day . . . no brief moment ever passes without Thy benefits. On land and sea Thou watchest over men and holdest out to them Thy saving right hand, dispelling the storms of life. Thou dost undo the hopelessly ravelled threads of Fate and dost alleviate the tempests of Fortune and restrainest the hurtful courses of the stars. . . . As for me, my spirit is too feeble to render Thee worthy praise, and my possessions too small to bring Thee fitting sacrifices. I have no fluency of speech to put in words that which I feel of Thy majesty. . . . Therefore will I essay to do that which alone a poor but pious worshipper can: Thy divine countenance and Thy most holy Presence will I hide within the shrine of my heart: there will I guard Thee and continually keep Thee before my spirit."[1]

When we pass to the Hermetic Mystery-literature, we are confronted with many complex

[1] Apuleius, *op. cit.*, xi., 25.

problems. To begin with, the *Corpus Hermeticum* is composed of various strata, some of which are by no means congruous with the rest. Even when we examine these strata separately, we discover a highly syncretistic blend of doctrine and ritual. It seems, therefore, illegitimate to speak of a Hermetic Mystery-Religion. Rather is this phase of religious thought valuable as embodying conceptions of Greek philosophy of the religious Stoic-Peripatetic type, relics of early Egyptian ideas, elements of the magical and alchemistic doctrines so prevalent in Egypt, and liturgic fragments which may belong to Hellenised Egyptian communities, but which at any rate reflect the syncretistic Mystery-cults between 300 B.C. and 300 A.D. It is not surprising to find such a product in Egypt, which might almost be called the religious clearing-house of the Hellenistic world. But the nature of the situation puts us on our guard against constructing any hard and fast theories as to the influence of Hermetic conceptions on non-Egyptian systems of thought. Even Reitzenstein himself, who argues strenuously for the essentially Egyptian character of Hermetic religion, admits that in many sections of the literature it is scarcely possible to distinguish between Egyptian and Greek conceptions.[1]

A few words must be said as to the origin and character of Hermetic literature : next we shall emphasise some of its leading ideas from the standpoint of Mystery-Religion, including in our survey the so-called Liturgy of Mithra : and, finally, we shall indicate the conflicting theories which prevail regarding it.

Reitzenstein believes that in the reign of Diocletian, about 300 A.D., an Egyptian priest made a compilation of eighteen sacred documents intended to show that the Hellenised religion of Egypt was uniform with that of the Empire as a whole. These documents belonged to different dates and to different religious communities, and they were arranged entirely to suit the various figures introduced in the dialogue. " Hermes, the herald of Egyptian religion, is summoned by the god Νοῦς, the Shepherd of men (Poimandres), to become Saviour of the whole

[1] See his article, "Hellenistische Theologie in Ägypten," *Neue Jahrb. f. d. klass. Alt.*, 1904, pp. 183, 184. This article forms the best introduction to his *Poimandres*, 1904, and *Die hellenistischen Mysterienreligionen*, 1910. An invaluable summary of results is given by Kroll in the article already quoted. These must be used to check some of Reitzenstein's conclusions.

world. He proclaims the new religion to his two disciples, Asclepios, son of the god Ptah, and his own son Tat: consecrates them at the close to be prophets, causing them to be born of God and united with Him, and then ascends again to heaven. The two prophets preach the new doctrine to King Ammon who adopts it, and thus the Egyptian religion is founded."[1] In addition to the Hermetic *Corpus*, various other fragments preserved in ancient authors may be assigned to this type of religion. It is important to note that the whole group of documents professes to be a revelation. Reitzenstein points out that this revelation is of two fundamental types. In the first, to which most of the purely theological documents belong, a god, Hermes or Æsculapius or Tat, describes what he has seen (*e.g.*, the Creation), or what has been communicated to him by his Divine Father and Teacher. In the second type, a man, who is of course a prophet, proclaims the revelation he has received either through drawing down by prayer a god who now dwells within him or by ascending to heaven with the help of a deity.[2] Reitzenstein would place the

[1] Reitzenstein, *loc. cit.*, p. 178.

[2] See Reitzenstein, *ib.*, pp. 179-181. The term νοῦς, so frequent in these writings, does not usually mean "understanding" but "the revealing God".

documents incorporated in this literature (whose dates cannot be accurately determined), roughly speaking, between the beginning of the first century A.D. and the end of the third.[1] But even if we did not find impressive parallels in other Hellenistic religions, it would be reasonable to assume that many of the incorporated conceptions belong to a much earlier date.[2]

Perhaps the most interesting document in the group, from the point of view of the Mystery-Religions, is the dialogue between Hermes and his son Tat on regeneration.[3] Tat reminds his father that he had told him that no one could be saved ($\sigma\omega\theta\hat{\eta}\nu\alpha\iota$) without regeneration ($\pi\alpha\lambda\iota\gamma\gamma\epsilon\nu\epsilon\sigma\iota\alpha$). Regeneration was only possible to one who had cut himself loose from the world. Tat has renounced the world and entreats his father, who has himself been regenerated, to communicate the secret. Hermes replies that this must be a revelation to the heart by the Divine Will.

[1] *Die hellenist. Mysterienreligionen*, p. 33.

[2] This consideration is not given an adequate place in Krebs' discussion, *Der Logos als Heiland*, p. 157. But G. Murray is rash in calling the Poimandres-revelation a "pre-Christian document," *op. cit.*, p. 143.

[3] The Greek text printed in the appendix to Reitzenstein's *Poimandres*, pp. 339-348.

By the mercy of God he had seen an immaterial vision (ἄπλαστον θέαν) inwardly, and had passed out through his own body into an immortal body. He is no longer what he was. Tat cannot discern his real being with bodily eyes. While Hermes speaks, Tat becomes conscious of a transformation. He is set free from the twelve evil propensities, which are replaced by the ten powers of God. He is now able by the Divine energy to have spiritual vision, and he feels himself one with all the elements. He only needs now to ascend into the Ogdoas, the abode of God. He asks to be taught the hymn of praise sung by the Divine powers present in the regenerate man when he reaches the Ogdoas. His father repeats the hymn, which is itself a very important document for Hermetic religion.[1] Tat can now declare: "My spirit is illumined . . . To Thee, O God, author of my new creation, I, Tat, offer spiritual sacrifices (λογικὰς θυσίας). O God and Father, Thou art the Lord, Thou art the Spirit (ὁ νοῦς). Accept from me the spiritual [sacrifices] which

---

[1] A good translation in Jacoby, *Die antiken Mysterienreligionen*, pp. 33, 34. With this should be compared the closing hymn of the Mithra-Liturgy, which also celebrates the regeneration of him who sings it. See *Eine Mithrasliturgie*,[2] p. 14.

Thou desirest." Hermes sums up the whole meaning of the experience in the suggestive words : νοερῶς ἔγνως σεαυτὸν καὶ τὸν πατέρα τὸν ἡμέτερον : " in the spirit thou hast come to know thyself and our Father ". It ought to be said that a large part of the dialogue is occupied with a blend of physical and ethical speculation of the later Stoic type. Various points of importance for Hermetic religion emerge from this dialogue. In this mystery of regeneration there is no external ritual. Tat experiences the psychical transformation as he listens to the revelation. Hence the revelation itself, the λόγος, may be said to constitute the Mystery : it produces the παλιγγενεσία. The chief result of the mystic experience is the true " knowledge " (γνῶσις) of God. This conception is prominent throughout Hermetic literature. Reitzenstein quotes a remarkable instance from the closing prayer of the Λόγος Τέλειος :[1] " We give thanks

[1] The Latin text found at the close of the *Asclepius* of Pseudo-Apuleius, proved by Bernays to be identical with the λόγος τέλειος of Hermes to Asclepius, mentioned by Lactantius. See Reitzenstein, *Archiv f. Religionswiss.*, 1904, p. 393, note 1. Reitzenstein discovered the Greek text in the magical Papyrus Mimaut (*c.* third century A.D.).

to Thee, most High, for by Thy grace we received this light of knowledge. . . . Having been saved by Thee, we rejoice that Thou didst show Thyself to us wholly, that Thou didst deify (ἀπεθέωσας) us in our mortal bodies by the vision of Thyself."[1] Here is a second idea of importance. The knowledge of God attained through the mystery of regeneration deifies. In *Poimandres* (*Hermetic Corpus*, i., § 26[2]) occur the words: "This is the blessed end for those who have attained knowledge, to be deified" (θεωθῆναι). We may compare the prayer in the Liturgy of Mithra (p. 12, 2 ff.): "Having been regenerated by Thee to-day, out of so many thousands called to be immortal (ἀπαθανατισθείς) in this hour, according to the purpose of the most gracious God". In the Liturgy of Mithra, it may be noted, the prayers are mingled with prosaic directions as to breathing, bellowing loudly, taking up prescribed postures, as well as with uncouth magical incantations. The observance of these instructions evokes strange supernatural visions. In the genuine

[1] See the whole prayer in Reitzenstein, *Die hellenist. Mysterienreligionen*, pp. 113, 114.

[2] See Reitzenstein, *Poimandres*, pp. 328-338.

Hermetic writings, however, it is plain that there has been a certain spiritualising of mystic cult, although the λόγος τέλειος, the " revelation which initiates," has marked affinities with the Egyptian conception of ritual, according to which the man who acquires a full knowledge of the liturgy can exercise immense influence upon the spiritual world.[1]

It is exceedingly difficult to estimate this highly syncretistic literature. Reitzenstein, as is well known, regards its fundamental strain as due to the evolution of ancient Egyptian ideas, and specifies the Hellenised doctrine of the priests of Ptah at Memphis. With this have been blended various constituents, such as the Stoic deification of the elements, a Hellenised non-Egyptian doctrine closely connected with astrology and the yearning for deliverance from εἱμαρμένη, and certain widely-diffused Hellenistic myths,[2] especially that of the Divine *Anthropos*. Cumont and W. Otto entirely dissent from Reitzenstein's belief

[1] Cumont, p. 343, refers to an article of Maspero, " Sur la toute-puissance de la parole " (*Recueil de travaux*, xxiv., 1902, pp. 163-175).

[2] See *Poimandres*, pp. 62-68, 71, 108, 109, 110, 114.

that the Hermetic literature is a typical expression of general piety in the second and third centuries A.D. Cumont regards " Hermetic " as the result of a long process whose aim was " to reconcile Egyptian traditions, first of all with Chaldaean astrology, then with Greek philosophy, and it shared in the transformation of this philosophy ".[1] Zielinski, in his searching investigation of *Hermetic*, irrefutably demonstrates the enormous preponderance of Greek philosophical elements in the syncretistic compound. He regards Peripatetic (-Stoic) cosmogonical speculations, which can be traced back to Arcadia and the Arcadian myth of Hermes (= Νοῦς) and his son Pan (= Λόγος), as the groundwork of the system, a system which certainly took shape in Egypt. On this foundation was built up a structure in which markedly Platonising and Pantheistic materials found a place. This he designates the *higher* Hermetic, and he regards the main error in Reitzenstein's theory as a failure to distinguish between the higher and lower types. The higher he considers to be purely Greek, the

[1] See Cumont, *Les Religions Orientales*,² p. 341 ; W. Otto, *Priester u. Tempel im Hellenistischen Aegypten*, ii., pp. 218-223.

lower, which has been incorporated, is a blend of Egyptian alchemy and magic.[1]

Probably each of these theories is partially true. To us it appears that Reitzenstein exaggerates the purely Egyptian character of this hybrid phase of religious thought and feeling. For Greek cosmogony is everywhere apparent. And yet the mystical conceptions of Hermetic literature can by no means be regarded merely as the outcome of these philosophical influences.[2] Rather do they appear as remarkable parallels to the doctrines we have examined in the other Mystery-Religions. They have been exposed, no doubt, to the influence of Greek religion in its Orphic-Dionysiac developments. But these developments themselves have been affected by Oriental beliefs. To find the Egyptian features of Hermetic only in what is magical, as Zielinski does, is to ignore the significance of Egypt in the history of Hellenistic Mystery-Religion. We believe that Reitzenstein is justified by the

[1] See his elaborate articles on "Hermes und die Hermetik," in *Archiv f. Religionswiss.*, 1905, 1906: especially the latter, pp. 25-27, 35-41, 56, 60. But *cf*. Kroll, *ut supr.*

[2] We do not forget that later Stoic cosmogony could be the medium of a mysticism like that of Posidonius (see chap. i.).

114 CHARACTER OF MYSTERY-RELIGIONS

prayers which appear in the extant documents in speaking of definite religious communities in Egypt, gathered around devout, prophetic leaders.[1]

In this sketch we have attempted to describe the leading ideas embodied in the Mystery-Religions and to indicate the range of their diffusion, giving instances, as occasion offered, of the religious terminology which they employed. We must next endeavour to estimate in detail the relation of St. Paul alike to their terminology and their ideas.[2]

[1] See, *e.g.*, *Neue Jahrb. f. d. klass. Alt.*, 1904, p. 182, and compare his estimate of the Liturgy of Mithra as revealing the *individual* expression of ancient and widely-propagated religious ideas: "The main thing about the Mithras-Liturgy is that one man from an approximately definable period had these ideas" (*Zeitschr. f. N.T. Wissensch.*, 1912, i., pp. 13, 14).

[2] We have omitted consideration of the Mithra-Mysteries, as these fall outside the scope of our discussion: see Cumont, *op. cit.*, p. xvi. Böhlig (*Die Geisteskultur von Tarsos*, 1913, pp. 89-92) contests Cumont's statement that in our period the Mysteries of Mithra "did not as yet possess any importance". But the evidence he adduces for their existence in Cilicia in Paul's time is utterly inadequate, and practically amounts to a single vague reference in Plutarch's *Life of Pompeius*, chap. xxiv., where mention is made of Cilician

CHAPTER IV

ST. PAUL'S RELATION TO THE TERMINOLOGY OF THE MYSTERY-RELIGIONS

In our last chapter enough has been said to establish the fact that in all the main centres of his missionary operations the Apostle Paul must have been brought into constant touch with the influences of the Mystery-Religions. The process of Hellenisation through which they had passed would impart to each a certain rough similarity of outline. Hence, although his sphere of work might frequently change, the Christian preacher would be confronted by a more or less stable complex of religious ideas. We are aware, indeed, of the emphasis laid by

pirates as "offering strange (or, foreign) sacrifices at Olympus and celebrating mysterious rites, of which that of Mithra is preserved up till now". Traces of Persian religious conceptions such as he cites are no valid proof of the currency of the Mysteries of Mithra. For the value of Plutarch's reference, *cf.* Wachsmuth, *Einleitung in d. Studium d. alten Geschichte*, p. 222.

early Christian apologetic on the repellent myths which lay in the background of various mystic cults. And such associations might seem once for all decisive against any openness on the part of the Apostle even to their profounder conceptions. But by this time their whole atmosphere was in process of being spiritualised. The Epistles give clear evidence that Paul did not shrink from deriving metaphors again and again from the Greek athletic festivals which equally came under the lash of ancient Christian writers. In vindicating the worship of the God who had revealed Himself in Jesus Christ against bondage to the elemental spirits ($\sigma\tau o\iota\chi\epsilon\hat{\iota}a$) he discloses some acquaintance with that astrological religion which we saw to be a potent force in contemporary Paganism. And the man who could write Philippians iv. 8 : "Whatsoever things are true, whatsoever things are reverend, whatsoever things are just, whatsoever things are pure, whatsoever things are lovely, whatsoever things are high-toned, if there be any virtue or anything praiseworthy, take account of these things," must surely have been sensitive to the higher aspirations of those whom he strove to win for the faith that had satisfied his own yearnings. Indeed it seems legitimate to cite

MYSTERY-TERMINOLOGY 117

his famous words: "I made myself slave of all that I might gain the more. . . . To all men I have become all things that at all events I might save some" (1 Cor. ix. 19, 22). And there is some significance for Paul's attitude in the position of Philo, also a Jew of the Diaspora, who, while manifesting a dislike of mystic cults,[1] has nevertheless been powerfully affected by some of their ideas.

When we attempt, however, to estimate the data presented in the Epistles, we soon realise how delicate is the problem. There is no doubt that Paul frequently employs terms which have received a more or less technical meaning in connection with the Mystery-Religions. These occur most prominently in the letters to Corinth and in the Imprisonment-Epistles, all of them addressed to communities which must have had intimate contact with mystery-brotherhoods. Side by side with these terms are found far-reaching conceptions to which there are at least thought-provoking analogies in Pagan religion. Restricting our discussion, meanwhile, to terminology, we must emphasise certain cautions which ought to

---

[1] See Bréhier, *Les Idées philosoph. et relig. de Philon*, pp. 244, 245.

be observed. To begin with, it seems highly precarious to postulate, as Reitzenstein does, an acquaintance on Paul's part with Hellenistic religious literature.[1] The description itself is nebulous. Probably it means for Reitzenstein documents of the type embodied in the Hermetic *Corpus* and the magical papyri. But this could scarcely be asserted even for Philo, who no doubt reflects many ideas belonging to the religion of ancient Egypt. And due weight must be assigned to Cumont's view, that the theology of the Egyptian Mysteries rather followed the general movement of ideas than stimulated it.[2] It is sheer hypothesis, therefore, to ascribe to Paul any direct acquaintance with Mystery-ideas through the medium of literature. It is altogether different when we think of liturgical formulæ and the technical terms of ritual in common circulation. We may grant at once that many of these would be familiar to the Apostle. No great stretch of imagination, for example, is required to picture the situation at Corinth or Ephesus. Without venturing on details we may admit that

[1] *Die hellenistischen Mysterienreligionen*, pp. 209, 210. For convenience' sake we shall refer to this work as *H.M.R.*

[2] *Les Religions Orientales*,[2] p. 135.

the Corinthian brotherhood of Christians would have many links of connection with the mystic guilds to which some of its members may, in all probability, have formerly belonged. In such passages as 1 Corinthians vii. 11 ("I give charge, yea not I but the Lord, that the wife depart not from her husband—but should she depart, let her remain unmarried, or else be reconciled to her husband—and that the husband leave not his wife"), and xii. 14 ff. ("For the body is not one member but many," etc.), we see, as Heinrici has instructively pointed out, the Christian community "in danger of stooping to the level of a pagan cult-association".[1] And the somewhat perplexing exordium of chapter xii. ("You know how, when you were Gentiles, you were forcibly carried away [by demons] to voiceless idols") gives us a dim glimpse of the heathen background.

But the interesting question arises: How far does the use of mystic terminology involve the adoption of the ideas which it expresses? Are we to assume that terms can be transferred from one phase of religious thought to another without suffering serious alteration? It must be recog-

[1] *Zeitschr. f. wiss. Theol.*, 1876, p. 509.

nised that many of the Mystery-conceptions, and many of the terms in which they are set forth, spring directly from that strain of Mysticism which seems to be everywhere latent in humanity and only requires favouring conditions to reveal itself.[1] Here Christianity and Pagan religion were bound to manifest affinities. The problem in such cases will be that of determining how far a more or less naïve realism has been subdued to finer intuitions of spiritual truth. Room will have to be left for the presence of symbolism, a factor which must certainly be reckoned with in the thought of Paul.[2] On the other hand, there is real force in Reitzenstein's contention that cult, conception, and language hang closely together.[3] To what extent, then, must the terminology of the Mystery-Religions carry with it its original significance? And how far are we to suppose a unique religious thinker like Paul to be conscious of this? May we adopt as a rough criterion his demonology? This, indeed, is to a large extent

[1] *Cf.* E. Underhill, *Mysticism*, p. 126.

[2] Wendland shows how the value of the symbolic in religion was recognised by the higher Greek thought as far back as Socrates (*Die hellenistisch-römische Kultur*,[2] p. 103).

[3] *Zeitschr. f. N.T. Wiss.*, 1912, i., p. 17.

already part of his inheritance from Judaism. But it bears the clear stamp of foreign influences. Now it admittedly shows traces of primitive popular conceptions. Are we to suppose that his mind would be receptive of similarly primitive ideas in more central spheres of thought? These are questions which cannot be hastily answered. And dogmatic statements are utterly irrelevant. But it is of further interest to notice that here and there in the Pauline Epistles we have more than isolated terms and ideas of the type in question. In certain contexts, as, *e.g.*, 1 Corinthians ii. 6 ff., we light upon *groups* of conceptions which have associations with the Mystery-Religions.[1] This cannot be accidental. It lets us see the connections of thought in the Apostle's mind. And these constitute important evidence for the influence of Mystery-Religion. But their significance can easily be exaggerated. Take a familiar example from our own time. Many cultivated religious writers of to-day are fond of using analogies and illustrations from the field of biology. And these often appear in rather elaborate groupings. Yet if they are analysed with care,

[1] Reitzenstein has emphasised this, *H.M.R.*, pp. 53, 210. See also Wendland in *G.G.A.*, Sept., 1910, p. 655.

they will be found to be anything but rigidly scientific. Terms like "evolution," "heredity," "struggle for existence," "variations," "acquired characters," etc., are in the air. Hence they may be used singly or in series as little else than convenient channels of appeal to the popular interest. Such a possibility must certainly be allowed for in the case of a great preacher like Paul, who would make it his business to find common ground with his audiences, without necessarily accepting the precise interpretations which they might put upon his terms. In any case, an individuality like Paul could not borrow without transforming.[1] "If we are to speak of Mystery-piety in Paul's case," says Reitzenstein, "we must never forget that the mystery is for him only the symbol (*Bild*) of an actually experienced μεταβολή, a conversion."[2] It is wholly a question of his precise relation to his environment. That we can

[1] See an admirable paragraph by Reitzenstein in *Zeitsch. f. N.T. Wiss.*, 1912, i., p. 23.

[2] *Ib.*, p. 27. Wendland attractively suggests that Paul stood towards the religion of the Mysteries, as Plato towards Orphism. It in no sense constitutes the centre of his religious life, but it yields him effective forms of expression for his Christian experience (*Die hellenistisch-römische Kultur*,[2] p. 185).

only estimate by a careful examination of the facts.

Let us begin with the important term μυστήριον. It occurs more than a dozen times in the Pauline Epistles,[1] and it certainly suggests some affinity with ethnic religious usage. But that usage is itself flexible. Probably the notion of "something kept secret" always belongs to it, including such ideas as the hidden sense of a passage and the mystic meaning of a word. It stands, of course, for any ritual or magical action. Thence it develops such senses as the document which contains a revelation, or a divinely taught prayer, which is of necessity believed to be effectual.[2] In trying to determine the shades of meaning involved in any Pauline term, it is self-evident that the usage of the LXX must be examined. There are, roughly speaking, about a dozen instances of μυστήριον in the LXX, and

[1] We include Ephesians, as the only argument which appears to us really valid against Paul's authorship is that of the *style*, and in this respect there seems to be a far closer affinity between Ephesians and Colossians than between Colossians and any of the other Epistles. The hypothesis which accounts for this affinity by a process of borrowing fails to do justice to the essentially Pauline spirit of the Epistle.

[2] See Reitzenstein's valuable note, *H.M.R.*, pp. 95-97.

with the exception of two, in which it is combined with τελετή in the technical sense (Wisd. of Sol. xiv. 15, 23), it seems invariably to mean "secrets" or "secret plans," once or twice of God, usually of men. In Daniel ii. 18 (LXX) it stands for the dream which the king had forgotten. In the one passage where it occurs in the Gospels (Matt. xiii. 11 = Mark iv. 11 = Luke viii. 10), in the phrase τὰ μυστήρια (Mark, τὸ μ.) τῆς βασιλείας τοῦ θεοῦ (Matt., τῶν οὐρανῶν), it suggests the secret purposes or plans of God concerning His kingdom which are coming to light in the work and teaching of Jesus, and which appeal only to sensitive hearts. When we turn to the Pauline Epistles, we at once discover that some of the instances directly tally with the usage of the LXX and Synoptics. To this class belongs Romans xi. 25 : "For I do not wish you, brethren, to be ignorant of this μυστήριον . . . that callousness has, in part, fallen upon Israel until the fulness of the Gentiles come in, and so all Israel shall be saved". Paul here deals with what has been for him a serious problem, the rejection of the Gospel by the chosen people, and its glad acceptance by the heathen. The one explanation he can find is a *secret purpose* of God whereby the ingathering of the Gentiles shall finally prove a compelling force to attract Israel also. In 1 Corinthians xv. 51 he describes the transformation of believers at the Parousia as a μυστήριον, *i.e.*, as a Divine plan which has been revealed to him, the knowledge of which could not have been reached in any other way. His standpoint here is made plain by 1 Corinthians xiii. 2: " If I have the gift of prophecy, and know all μυστήρια and all γνῶσις ". The prophet is for the Apostolic Age, as for the Old Testament (and we may include the Mystery-Religions), the man who is able to declare to his fellows the secret mind of God. So Paul, in 1 Corinthians iv. 1, can speak of himself and his fellow-labourers as " ministers of Christ and stewards of the μυστήρια of God ". Their function is to reveal the Divine " secrets ". The " speaking with tongues " Paul estimates at a lower value than " prophesying," yet that also is a gift of the πνεῦμα, and presupposes a certain contact with the Divine. Hence he who speaks " in a tongue " may be described (1 Cor. xiv. 2) as speaking by the Spirit.

One secret purpose of God, however, overshadows all others for the Apostle's mind, and in its various bearings seems to fill his thought predominantly as he lies a prisoner at Rome. It is described most explicitly in Ephesians iii. 1 ff. : "For this cause I Paul, the prisoner of Christ Jesus on behalf of you Gentiles, if as a matter of fact ye heard of the stewardship of the grace of God granted to me with a view to you, how that by revelation was made known to me the μυστήριον . . . which was not made known in other generations . . . that the Gentiles are fellow-heirs and fellow-members of the body, and fellow-partakers of the promise in Christ Jesus through the Gospel". It is magnified also in Colossians i. 25 ff. : "According to the stewardship of God granted to me with a view to you, to fulfil the word of God, the μυστήριον hidden from ages and generations : but now it has been manifested to his saints, to whom God was pleased to make known what is the wealth of the glory of this μυστήριον among the Gentiles, which is Christ in you (*i.e.*, Gentiles), the hope of glory". The same overpowering fact is referred to, a few verses lower down, in ii. 2, a passage in which the text is far from certain, but which on any reading connects the μυστήριον of God with "Christ, in whom are all the treasures of wisdom and knowledge hidden". In Colossians iv. 3 and Ephesians vi. 19, Paul describes himself as a prisoner on account of this μυστήριον. A wider aspect of the significance of the great truth is unfolded in Ephesians i. 9 ff. : "Having made known to us the μ. of his will, according to his good pleasure which he purposed in him for the dispensation of the fulness of the times, to sum up all things in Christ". The notion of a hidden process to be revealed in its true character at the Parousia, when all restraints shall be removed, is apparent in 2 Thessalonians ii. 6-8 (τὸ μ. τῆς ἀνομίας). Ephesians v. 32 stands by itself. In admonishing husbands and wives as to their mutual relationships, he enforces his precepts by the illustration of Christ and the Church. He cites Genesis ii. 24 on the unity of man and wife, and then adds : "This μ. is important; I declare it with reference to Christ and the Church". The instances quoted by Hatch from Justin Martyr,[1] in which μυστήριον is interchanged with παραβολή, σύμβολον, and τύπος, justify in this passage the translation "symbol".

Before we deal with the only remaining

[1] *Essays in Biblical Greek*, pp. 60, 61.

passage,[1] let us briefly collect the implications of Paul's use of μυστήριον. It is remarkable that it is mostly found, paradoxically, in close connection with verbs of revelation (ἀποκαλύπτειν, φανεροῦν, γνωρίζειν). That wholly accords with Paul's favourite idea of his own function of κηρύσσειν (*e.g.*, 1 Cor. i. 23 : "we proclaim Christ crucified"; *cf.* 2 Cor. v. 20 : "on Christ's behalf, therefore, we are ambassadors as though God were beseeching you through us : we entreat you on Christ's behalf, be reconciled to God"). It most commonly refers to that transforming discovery which Paul had reached along the lines of his own Christian experience, that the Gospel of Christ was intended for Gentiles on the very same terms as for Jews. Often it has a distinctly eschatological outlook, as in Romans xi. 25 ; 1 Corinthians ii. 7 : "We speak the wisdom of God in a mystery . . . the wisdom which God fore-ordained for our glory" (εἰς δόξαν ἡμῶν); 1 Corinthians xv. 51 ; Ephesians i. 9 ; Colossians i. 26 : "to fulfil the word of God, the

---

[1] We have omitted Rom. xvi. 25, as we entirely agree with Dr. Denney's judgment on the passage : "It is very difficult to believe that such mosaic work is the original composition of Paul" (*E.G.T.*, *ad loc.*).

mystery hidden from the ages—but now it has been manifested to the saints, to whom God was pleased to make known what is the riches of the glory of this mystery among the Gentiles, which is Christ in you, the hope of glory" (ἡ ἐλπὶς τῆς δόξης); 2 Thessalonians ii. 7.[1] Hence there is no ground for Prof. Percy Gardner's assertion that for Paul "the Christian mystery lies in a relation between the disciple and his heavenly Master," or that "the mystery of Paul was a sacred but secret belief in the existence of a spiritual bond holding together a society in union with a spiritual lord with whom the society had communion".[2] Evidence for such a position is completely lacking. Indeed Prof. Gardner passes by the most significant feature in the passage which he takes as his starting-point, 1 Cor. ii. 1-10, a section which we must now consider. Here Paul distinguishes between the usual subject of his preaching, "Jesus Christ and him as crucified" (ver. 2), and "a wisdom," a more difficult ele-

[1] It is putting the matter too strongly to say, as J. Weiss does (on 1 Cor. ii. 7), that μυστήριον "is concerned as a rule with eschatological matters," but there is some ground for the statement.

[2] *The Religious Experience of St. Paul*, pp. 78, 79.

ment in his teaching, which he declares τοῖς τελείοις, "a Divine wisdom ἐν μυστηρίῳ (vers. 6, 7), which has been hidden". The following clauses show that this is concerned with the glorious future of the redeemed. We shall examine the meaning of τέλειος immediately, but this passage certainly has a suggestion of the Mysteries; the Apostle speaks of a more advanced stage of Christian instruction which demands a higher grade of understanding. The same background appears in the continuation of the passage, in which emphasis is laid upon the revelation of the deep things of God through the Spirit to the πνευματικός. Here, however, as we have seen, Old Testament conceptions must be allowed for, and even in the former case we cannot, on the basis of our data, decide how far Paul identifies himself with the Mystery point of view. We are warned against straining his language by the phrase employed quite casually in Philippians iv. 12: "I have been initiated into the secret of being filled and of being hungry".

We have just noted that Paul refers in 1 Corinthians ii. 6 to a σοφία, a higher stage of instruction, which he imparts to the τέλειοι. How much is involved in the content of the word? It is possible that there is an allusion in both these expressions to arrogant claims made by adherents of the Apollos-party. We know that Alexandrian Judaism laid great stress on a superior knowledge (σοφία) which was the privilege of elect souls, bestowed by God. The personified σοφία is described as μύστις . . . τῆς τοῦ θεοῦ ἐπιστήμης (Wisd. viii. 4). Philo, in expounding certain Old Testament passages, speaks of "instructing in divine mysteries (τελετὰς . . . θείας) the initiates (μύστας) who are worthy of such sacred mysteries" (*De Cherub.*, 42). He himself has been μυηθεὶς τὰ μεγάλα μυστήρια (*ib.*, 49). It is probable that τέλειος belongs to this circle of mystery-ideas. Plato uses the phrase τὰ τέλεα καὶ ἐποπτικὰ [μυστήρια] to denote the higher initiation (*Sympos.*, 210 A), and describes the man who rightly uses the recollections of what his soul once saw in fellowship with God (συμπορευθεῖσα θεῷ) as "being ever initiated into perfect mysteries" (τελέους ἀεὶ τελετὰς τελούμενος) and alone becoming "truly perfect" (τέλεος ὄντως : *Phædr.*, 249 C). Some scholars, *e.g.*, W. Bauer, hold that τέλεος (= τέλειος) here cannot mean "fully initiated," that sense being involved in τελούμενος, and τέλεος, which is suggested by a play upon words, having its ordinary significance.

But when we find μυστικοῦ τέλους (= mystic rite) in Æsch. Fr., 387 (Nauck, ed. 2), and the plural τέλη (e.g., Eur., *Hipp.*, 25, τέλη μυστηρίων) constantly employed with this meaning, it is surely hazardous to say that τέλειος cannot be used with this technical connotation. In the Hermetic literature, those who have received the baptism of the Divine νοῦς become τέλειοι.[1] Only the τέλειος, who has shared in the Divine γνῶσις, can make another τέλειος.[2] Hence arises the phrase λόγος τέλειος used as a title for one of the Hermetic documents, the revelation which initiates into the knowledge of God.

But other aspects of τέλειος must not be ignored. Of the seven passages in which the word occurs, two definitely contrast τέλειος with νήπιος (1 Cor. xiv. 20 ; Eph. iv. 13, 14). Here the word must mean " grown-up," " mature," as opposed to " childish ". This is the stage of ripe knowledge as contrasted with rudimentary attainment. As we shall find πνευματικοί used as equivalent to τέλειοι in the context of the passage from which we started (1 Cor. iii. 1 ff.), and there put in antithesis to νήπιοι, there seems a good deal to

[1] See Reitzenstein, *H.M.R.*, p. 165 ; Kroll, *op. cit.*, sp. 811.
[2] See Reitzenstein, *Neue Jahrb. f. klass. Alt.*, 1904, p. 188.

be said for this significance. The term "mature" would, roughly speaking, suit all the Pauline passages. A further possibility, however, is emphasised by J. Weiss in the excellent note on τέλειοι appended to his commentary on 1 Corinthians iii. 3. He points out that in the later Stoics and Philo τέλειος is constantly used of the culminating stage of the good life, which the philosopher is called to strive after. Philo (*Leg. Alleg.*, iii., 159) places it after the two earlier phases of ὁ ἀρχόμενος and ὁ προκόπτων. And a passage in Epictetus (*Enchir.*, li., 1 f.) aptly illuminates τὸ τέλειον which Paul contrasts with τὸ ἐκ μέρους in 1 Corinthians xiii. 10, and still more the difficult οἱ τέλειοι of Philippians iii. 15. In the latter verse, as in 1 Corinthians ii. 6, τέλειος seems to have an anticipatory sense. For Paul has just spoken of himself as "not having yet reached the goal" (τετελείωμαι, Phil. iii. 12), and that implication may certainly be read between the lines in 1 Corinthians ii. 6 ff. Epictetus (*loc. cit.*) warns the τέλειος of the danger of making no progress (οὐ προκόψας) and remaining in life and death an ordinary man. Thus for him the term applies already to the man who has set out on the true path and is still advancing.

This accords admirably with Paul's usual standpoint, from which he sees in his converts the end in the beginning, and can think of them as ideally "saints" because they have received the new life, although that life has to develop in the face of many obstacles. It is extremely difficult to decide between these various shades of meaning. And in this case the LXX sheds little light on Paul's usage. There τέλειος usually translates תָּמִים (and תָּם), "sound," "healthy" (of sacrificial animals), or "having integrity" (of men), as well as שָׁלֵם and שָׁלֶם, denoting "submission to God" and "peace-offerings". Wellhausen finds the root-idea in שָׁלֵם to be fellowship between God and His worshippers, and this suggests an early ritual connotation which is perhaps implied in τέλειος as used in the LXX. In one passage (1 Chron. xxv. 8) it occurs in the phrase τελείων καὶ μανθανόντων, translating מֵבִין = "teachers". This recalls the contrast in Paul between τέλειοι and νήπιοι. It seems quite possible to combine the sense of "mature" with that of "complete attainment" for which J. Weiss argues. And in view of the earlier associations of the communities which Paul addresses, we cannot certainly rule out the suggestion that the Mystery-atmosphere is to some extent present,[1] although plainly no conclusion can be drawn from this term as to Paul's personal attitude towards the Mystery-conceptions.

It is universally admitted that Paul's use of πνευματικοί in 1 Corinthians iii. 1 ("As for me, brethren, I could not speak to you as 'spiritual' men") implies its equivalence to τέλειοι in ii. 6. And whatever differences may arise in the interpretation of details, it is obvious from ii. 10-16 that the basal significance of πνευματικός is "one who has received 'the spirit that is from God,'" as Paul puts it (ver. 12). He applies the adjective to spiritual gifts, such as prophecy and speaking with "tongues" (1 Cor. xiv. 1 ff.), to the law as a Divine ordinance (Rom. vii. 14), to the future organism (σῶμα) of believers divinely given (1 Cor. xv. 44 f.), and in the vague phrase τὰ πνευματικὰ τῆς πονηρίας, to "spiritual powers of evil" (Eph. vi. 12). A more abnormal use appears in 1 Corinthians x. 3 f., where, as epithet of βρῶμα, πόμα, and πέτρα, it seems to mean "having spiritual significance". Characteristic of Paul's standpoint is 1 Cor-

[1] So even Lightfoot on Colossians i. 28.

inthians xiv. 37 ("If any one presumes to be a prophet or spiritual, let him clearly recognise that what I write to you is the commandment of the Lord"), from which it is evident that προφήτης and πνευματικός are alternative descriptions of the same type of person. "Endowed with πνεῦμα" expresses the content of the term. We can without much difficulty determine what this involves for the Apostle. Out of some 150 instances of πνεῦμα in his Epistles, all, except perhaps about thirty, refer to the direct influence of God. The πνεῦμα for Paul is, in these cases, the Divine response to faith, faith in Christ crucified, risen, and alive for evermore. For the present we shall pass by the relation of the πνεῦμα to Baptism. But it may be said that, as a matter of practical religious experience, Paul identifies the πνεῦμα with the indwelling Christ. Romans viii. 9, 10, is decisive: "But ye are not in the flesh but in the spirit, that is if the Spirit of God dwells in you. Now if any one have not the Spirit of Christ, he does not belong to him. But if Christ be in you, the body is dead because of sin, but the spirit is life because of righteousness." Possession of the πνεῦμα neutralises the evil ten-

MYSTERY-TERMINOLOGY

dencies of the σάρξ,[1] the "flesh," which the Apostle has discovered as an actual fact of experience, but which he never analyses metaphysically. The last clause of the passage just quoted illustrates about one-half of the remaining uses of πνεῦμα in Paul. The gift or accession of the Spirit transforms the inner life so that it becomes assimilated to the life of Christ, which is Divine. Hence the new life of the Christian can be designated πνεῦμα as contrasted with σάρξ, as, *e.g.*, in Romans viii. 10, or i. 9: "God, whom I serve ἐν τῷ πνεύματί μου in the Gospel of his Son". Sometimes he distinguishes between the indwelling πνεῦμα and the life which it controls, as in Romans viii. 16: "The Spirit itself bears witness with our spirit that we are children of God". Elsewhere, the distinction falls into the background: *e.g.*, 1 Corinthians vi. 17: "He that is joined to the Lord is ἓν πνεῦμα". Rather more than a dozen passages occur in which πνεῦμα is more colourless and seems to stand simply for the inner life of man

[1] Apparently σάρξ was used in a disparaging sense of the body by the Orphics, and later, by Plato and Platonising thinkers. See esp. Seneca, *Ep.* 92, 110, qu. by Capelle in his instructive art., "Body (Greek and Roman)," *Encycl. of R. and E.*, Vol. 2.

without special reference to Divine inspiration, *e.g.*, 1 Corinthians ii. 11 : "What man knows the things of man, except the spirit of man which is in him?" Here πνεῦμα is virtually the equivalent of ψυχή, the ordinary life-principle of humanity, the correlative of σάρξ, man's material nature discovered in experience to be sinful. So Paul can speak, in 2 Corinthians vii. 1, of cleansing themselves "from all defilement of flesh and spirit (σαρκὸς καὶ πνεύματος)," a passage which proves that he has no really dualistic theory of σάρξ and πνεῦμα. He very rarely employs ψυχή, and only in the sense we have mentioned; but in three interesting passages he contrasts ψυχικός with πνευματικός to describe man apart from the Divine influence of the πνεῦμα (1 Cor. ii. 14; xv. 44, 46). His exact meaning is brought out by Jude 19 : οὗτοί εἰσιν . . . ψυχικοί, πνεῦμα μὴ ἔχοντες. It is more difficult to define the precise relationships of the term νοῦς which Paul occasionally uses in this circle of ideas, but, generally speaking, it seems to have the meaning given it in the popular philosophy of the period (= λογικὴ ψυχή), the power of judging which belongs to the inner life as such. When this judgment is true to itself, it will decide for the Divine law, as, *e.g.*, Romans vii. 25 : "So therefore I for myself (*i.e.*, as apart from Divine influence) with my νοῦς serve the law of God". But so long as the νοῦς is not invigorated by the Divine πνεῦμα it will be hampered by its fleshly associations, so that he has to add : "but with my flesh the law of sin". The νοῦς is a purely natural capacity which none the less provides as it were the basis for the operations of the Divine πνεῦμα. Hence, in Romans xii. 2, Paul can speak of the "renewing" (ἀνακαίνωσις) of the νοῦς (*cf.* Eph. iv. 23). And in his graphic description of ecstatic experiences in 1 Corinthians xiv. 13 ff. he still distinguishes between τὸ πνεῦμά μου and ὁ νοῦς μου, πνεῦμα denoting his inner life on its inspired side, while νοῦς represents the cool, critical judgment which regulates unique spiritual experiences with a view to practical utility.[1] In two important passages (Rom. xi. 34, and 1 Cor. ii. 16 : "who hath known the mind of the Lord?") the Apostle, quoting from the LXX of Isaiah xl. 13, retains the expression νοῦν κυρίου, νοῦς being here the LXX translation of the Hebrew *ruach*, ordinarily rendered by πνεῦμα.

[1] J. Weiss' note on 1 Cor. xiv. 14 appears to miss the whole point of the passage.

Probably the translators must have known of a use of νοῦς equivalent to πνεῦμα. At any rate it is impossible to make a distinction between the two in 1 Corinthians ii. 16.

Now Reitzenstein, in his famous researches into the Hermetic literature and its parallels in magical papyri and contemporary Pagan mystery-cults, asserts that Paul's various uses of πνεῦμα are all to be found in Hellenistic religious documents; that his antithesis between πνευματικός and ψυχικός was current before Paul's time; that πνευματικός was a fixed religious conception in the sphere of the mystic faiths of Paganism; and that νοῦς had already become an important religious term, the direct equivalent of πνεῦμα. "It is in any case noteworthy," he declares, "that all the passages in Paul can be explained from Hellenistic usage (particularly those in which we cannot decide whether he is speaking of the πνεῦμα of man or of a Divine πνεῦμα, as, e.g., 1 Cor. v. 4, 5). Whether all may be as easily understood from the Hebrew use of *ruach* and *nephesh*, or from that of πνεῦμα in the LXX, the theologian must determine."[1] We shall attempt briefly to examine and estimate the evi-

[1] *H.M.R.*, p. 140.

MYSTERY-TERMINOLOGY 141

dence which he adduces, and then to analyse the relevant phenomena in the Old Testament.

1. The use of πνεῦμα in Hellenistic mystery-documents. (*a*) πνεῦμα contrasted with σῶμα and σάρξ: Kenyon, *Greek Pap.*, i., p. 80 : ἐπικαλοῦμαί σε τὸν κτίσαντα ... πᾶσαν σάρκα καὶ πᾶν πνεῦμα; *Pap. Berol.*, i., 177 : σοῦ τὸ σῶμα περιστελεῖ [ὁ θεός], σοῦ δὲ τὸ πνεῦμα ... ἄξει σὺν ἑαυτῷ.[1] (*b*) Used of God : Wessely, *Zauberpap.*, i., p. 72 (l. 1115) : "Hail, Spirit that enters into me ... according to the Divine will, in graciousness"; i., p. 284 : "And straightway enters the Divine Spirit" (τὸ θεῖον πνεῦμα).[2] *Cf.* the prayer in the Liturgy of Mithra (p. 4, l. 13 f.) : "that I may be initiated and that the holy Spirit (ἱερὸν πνεῦμα) may blow within me".[3] The materialistic character of the latter passage is obvious. An interesting example is found in the prayer of the prophet Urbicus (*Pap. Lugd.*, v., col. 10, 12, publ. by Dieterich) : "My spirit (πνεῦμα) was heard by all the gods and demons". This is expounded in detail : "My spirit was heard by the spirit of heaven ... by the spirit of earth," etc. πνεῦμα is the link between earth and heaven.[4]

---

[1] *H.M.R.*, p. 136.   [2] *H.M.R.*, pp. 137, 136.
[3] Ed. 2 (Dieterich-Wünsch).   [4] *H.M.R.*, p. 138.

(c) Identification of πνεῦμα with ψυχή. Here Reitzenstein confines himself to a group of striking instances from Philo. He holds that in more philosophical circles, while the description of the higher life as πνεῦμα is known, the conception of ψυχή as the antithesis of σῶμα has taken root so firmly that it cannot be displaced. But it is impossible to mistake the significance of such sentences as *De Abrah.*, 236 : " All those who are able to behold things in a bodiless and naked form, who live rather for the soul (ψυχῇ) than for the body ". Here and in numerous other places ψυχή stands for the spiritual life. A very suggestive example occurs in a prayer of the Liturgy of Mithra (p. 14, 24 f.) : "Abide with me in my soul (ψυχῇ), forsake me not ". Obviously in this utterance no sharp distinction could be drawn between ψυχή and πνεῦμα.

2. πνευματικός and ψυχικός in the Mystery-literature. The form in which Reitzenstein has presented his material on this point makes it difficult to distinguish between the actual data and his bold inferences from them. In our last paragraph we noted the conception of the Divine Spirit (πνεῦμα) as entering the human personality. This being so, we might expect to find the corre-

sponding adjective to describe the condition of the spirit-possessed person. As a matter of fact, only one instance is adduced, from Wessely, *Zauberpap.*, i., p. 89 (l. 1778), where Eros is addressed as "lord of all *spiritual* perception (πνευματικῆς αἰσθήσεως) of all hidden (*i.e.*, Divine) things".[1] The contrasted term ψυχικός seems only to occur once in the extant fragments, but the passage is very suggestive. In the opening prayer of the Liturgy of Mithra, the aspirant after the vision of God makes supplication: "For to-day I, a mortal born of mortal womb, exalted by Almighty power and incorruptible right hand, with immortal eyes shall behold by immortal spirit the immortal Aeon and Lord of the crowns of fire, I who have been sanctified by sacred rites, while, for a little, my human natural powers (ἀνθρωπίνης μου ψυχικῆς δυνάμεως) stay behind. . . . Stand still, mortal nature of man."[2] Obviously ψυχικῆς here describes human nature as apart from πνεῦμα. The other examples to which Reitzenstein refers come from Gnostic documents of post-Christian date. He asserts without argument that the well-known Gnostic categories,

[1] *H.M.R.*, p. 139.
[2] *Eine Mithrasliturgie*,² p. 4, 18 ff.

σαρκικοί, ψυχικοί, and πνευματικοί cannot have had their origin in Paul's usage (*e.g.*, 1 Cor. iii. 1), but must be due to the Hellenistic Mystery-Religions, which recognised three classes, unbelievers, proselytes (*religiosi*), and τέλειοι (or, πνευματικοί). He seems to base his position largely on the fact that in the Gnostic classification the use of ψυχικός for an intermediate group reveals the persistence of the more philosophical idea of ψυχή, so that no sharp division had to be made. But in Paul also there are various instances, as we have seen, in which no clear distinction is drawn between ψυχή and πνεῦμα. And at this point it may be worth while to remind ourselves of a possibility which cannot be summarily ruled out. The Hellenistic documents from which quotations have been made cannot be dated with any confidence. In chapter ii. we noted the remarkable influence of certain Jewish conceptions on Egyptian magical papyri. When we remember how fluctuating were the boundary-lines between various phases of Gnosticism and Pagan religious communities, it is by no means impossible to believe that semi-Christian Gnostic influence filtered into these Hellenistic Mystery-brotherhoods, leaving its mark both upon ideas and terminology. We must return to the subject in the course of our discussion. Meanwhile it may be noted that parallel phenomena occur in this highly syncretistic period. For example, H. Graillot, in an article on the epithet *omnipotentes*, as used of Cybele and Attis (*Revue Archéol.*, 1904, 1), is disposed to attribute the usage to Christian influence. This may be doubtful. But Cumont's observation regarding Judaism must surely with equal force apply for a later date to Christian influence :[1] "Scholars have not attempted . . . to determine up to what point Paganism was modified by an infusion of Biblical ideas. This transformation must necessarily have operated to some extent."

But without pressing this point, let us glance at Reitzenstein's parallels between what he calls the "double-being" of Paul and corresponding phenomena in the Mystery-Religions. Here we must guard against clear-cut definitions and rigidly logical inferences. For we move in an extraordinarily elusive sphere. "If it be asked," says Dr. Inge, "which is our personality, the shifting *moi* (as Fénelon calls it) or the ideal self, the end or the developing states? we must

[1] *Les Religions Orientales*,[2] pp. 95, 96.

answer that it is both and neither, and that the root of mystical religion is in the conviction that it is at once both and neither."[1] Hence we dare not isolate such an affirmation as Paul's bold words in Galatians ii. 20: "I live, yet not I, but Christ liveth in me". Indeed, the very sentence which follows reveals that Paul's is as far as possible from a disintegrated life: "that which I now live *in the flesh* I live by faith, faith in the Son of God who loved me and gave himself for me". That is to say, the relation of the human individual Paul to Jesus the historic Person is never lost in a vague and impalpable experience. Reitzenstein lays great stress on what he regards as a sort of two-fold personality in the initiates of the Hellenistic Mystery-Religions. Thus in the Liturgy of Mithra the suppliant exclaims: "It is not possible for me, a mortal born, to rise up on high with the golden radiance of the immortal light," and he bids his human nature be still, while he attains the vision of God with his Divine.[2] In the vision of the alchemist Zosimus, who reflects the

[1] *Christian Mysticism*, p. 33.
[2] *Eine Mithrasliturgie*,[2] p. 4, 27-29.

MYSTERY-TERMINOLOGY 147

popular Mystery-theology, such sentences occur as this: "The men who desire to reach virtue enter in here and become spirits (πνεύματα), escaping from the body".[1] Reitzenstein believes that various expressions in the poets of the period indicate a quickening of the religious sense in this direction, as, *e.g.*, Lucan, *Phars.*, v., 167, 168, of the inspiration of the Pythia: the god, who takes possession of her, *mentemque priorem expulit atque hominem toto sibi cedere jussit pectore* ("drove out her former inner life and bade the human being yield to him wholeheartedly"). Here he takes *mens* as equal to ψυχή. That is driven out and replaced by the presence of the god himself, so that for the time a new being arises.[2] To such instances as we have quoted Reitzenstein adduces parallels from Paul, more especially the antithesis between πνευματικός and ψυχικός. On the basis of 1 Corinthians ii. 6-iii. 4, he asserts that for Paul the ψυχικός is "man pure and simple," the πνευματικός "no longer man at all". But the parallels are irrelevant. So far as we can judge, the

[1] See Berthelot, *Les alchimistes grecs*, p. 109, 12, cited by Reitzenstein, *H.M.R.*, p. 141.

[2] *H.M.R.*, p. 150.

"pneumatic" condition in the Mystery-literature seems always to be associated with states of ecstasy. There is no evidence that Paul regards the πνευματικός as having in any sense ceased to be true man. For possession of the πνεῦμα is in Paul's eyes the normal, abiding condition of the Christian. Of course we do not forget his descriptions of special "pneumatic" experiences, such as glossolalia and prophecy. We know the extraordinary value placed upon them in the early Church, as represented for instance by the Christian community at Corinth. Probably this was mainly due to their "ecstatic" character, which was especially manifest in the phenomenon of speaking with "tongues". The affinities of "prophecy" are discernible from the fact that the "prophets" prepared themselves for revelations by seasons of fasting and prayer.[1] But by Paul they are always subordinated to the permanent "fruit" of the Spirit, "love, joy, peace, long-suffering, gentleness," etc. (Gal. v. 22 f.). Nothing, therefore, could be more irrelevant than to take the phrases κατὰ ἄνθρωπον (1 Cor. iii. 3 : "whereas there is among you

[1] *Cf.* Hermas, *Vis.*, ii., 2 ; and see H. Achelis, *Das Christentum in d. drei ersten Jahrhunderten*, i., p. 91.

MYSTERY-TERMINOLOGY 149

jealousy and strife, are you not carnal, and do you not walk after the manner of man?") and ἄνθρωποι (iii. 4: "when one says, I am of Paul, and another, I am of Apollos, are you not men?") as Reitzenstein does, in a baldly literal sense.[1] The πνευματικοί are still liable to temptations and spiritual perils (Gal. vi. 1 f.). But as those who possess the pledge of the Spirit (2 Cor. v. 5) they are destined for the eternal life of God.

3. We have seen that in one or two instances Paul adopts from the LXX a use of νοῦς as virtually equivalent to πνεῦμα. Probably this implies, as Reitzenstein urges, that the usage was not unfamiliar to the Apostle and his readers. It would be unsafe to dogmatise, but it is certainly suggestive to find that in the Hermetic mystical literature νοῦς often appears to be a synonym for πνεῦμα. Thus in the famous Λόγος τέλειος, extracted by Reitzenstein from the Papyrus Mimaut,[2] thanks are given to the Highest because He has graciously bestowed "spirit, revelation, and knowledge" (νοῦν, λόγον, γνῶσιν). In document XII. (XIII.) of the Hermetic *Corpus*, ὁ νοῦς is described as

[1] *H.M.R.*, p. 168.

[2] See *Archiv f. Religionswissenschaft*, 1904, p. 393 ff.

the "soul" (ψυχή) of God, which rules over everything.[1] This conception is freely used in *Poimandres*. Doubtless it began with markedly philosophical affinities,[2] but it has filtered down into popular religion. Very significant is a passage in the Κρατὴρ ἢ Μονάς: "All who were baptised in the νοῦς, these partake of γνῶσις and become τέλειοι ἄνθρωποι, having received the νοῦς" (§ 4).[3] It is evidently a Divine gift. We may compare the *Mithras-liturgy*, p. 4, 13: "in order that I may be regenerated by νόημα," which we are almost bound to translate by "spirit". It lies outside our present purpose to deal with the intimate connection between νοῦς and λόγος, the Thought being regarded in Hermetic philosophical mythology as the father of the Word. But the hypothesis maintained by Reitzenstein that the syncretistic religion of Hellenistic Egypt, as embodied in the Hermetic Mystery-literature, had really become the religion of νοῦς, not in the sense of "understanding," but of a revealing

---

[1] Reitzenstein, *Poimandres*, p. 102, note 1.

[2] See, *e.g.*, Zielinski, *Archiv f. Religionswissenschaft*, 1906, pp. 25 f., 35, 56.

[3] See *H.M.R.*, p. 165.

deity, receives a good deal of corroboration from the documents which have come down to us.

Before going further, let us try to ascertain the positions which may be taken as established. Reitzenstein has certainly shown that in documents of the Hellenistic Mystery-Religions πνεῦμα and νοῦς are used to denote the Divine life or spirit in itself, or that life or spirit as imparted to those who fulfil certain religious conditions, and especially some prescribed initiation. They become, in short, religious terms. It is also evident that a distinction can now be drawn between πνεῦμα and ψυχή, the principle of Divine life being contrasted with that of merely human. But instances are exceedingly uncommon, and Reitzenstein himself admits that ψυχή has been so firmly entrenched as the antithesis of σῶμα that it could with difficulty be used in a disparaging sense. It need scarcely be observed that the usages in question reveal a marked departure from the ordinary Greek use of πνεῦμα or νοῦς. Reitzenstein would attribute their appearance mainly to Oriental influence, a realm in which a man like Paul would easily find himself at home. But the instance which he cites from Lucan has surely distinct affinities with earlier Hellenic thought: *cf.*, *e.g.*, Æsch., *Prom.*, 902 f.: ἔξω δὲ δρόμου φέρομαι λύσσης πνεύματι μάργῳ, where the "raging spirit of frenzy" is the visitation of a god. When we remember how prevalent was the conception of the ἔνθεος, the person filled with the god, and recall the derivation of πνεῦμα from πνέω, to "blow" or "breathe," it seems precarious to restrict the emergence of such ideas to a period dominated by its contact with Oriental religions. One question should here perhaps be touched upon. Reitzenstein, Heitmüller and others lay stress on the notion that Paul, like his Stoic contemporaries and the devotees of the Mystery-Religions, conceived the πνεῦμα to be substance as well as power. Thus in the Liturgy of Mithra one of the instructions runs: "Take up your stand and draw the πνεῦμα from the Divine . . . and say, Come to me, O Lord" (p. 10, 23 ff.). That is typical of the πνεῦμα-conception in Hellenistic religious literature. Traces of a similar "animism" may be found in Hebrew thought. But there, as Volz shows, with the ethical deepening of religion the conception of power in *ruach* as the Spirit of God comes to

MYSTERY-TERMINOLOGY 153

overshadow that of an imparted substance.[1] It is from this standpoint, as we shall discover, that Paul's thought must in the main be estimated. We should frankly admit that the processes of ancient psychology are so far removed from our habits of thought that it is unsafe to deny the survival of realistic notions side by side with such profoundly ethical conceptions as those most prominent in Paul's use of πνεῦμα. We must recognise that he lived in an atmosphere in which everything causal was regarded as substantial, in which "force" and "body" constituted no antithesis.[2] But it is difficult to find unmistakable traces of such a view even in Paul's speculations on the σῶμα πνευματικόν. If his conception of πνεῦμα was highly animistic, he has succeeded even there in concealing it. To interpret 1 Corinthians vii. 14, where Paul speaks of an unbelieving husband being sanctified by his believing wife, as referring to a physical process by which the πνεῦμα is transmitted (so Heitmüller),[3]

[1] See *Der Geist Gottes im A.T.*, pp. 76, 77.

[2] *Cf.* Seneca, *Ep.*, 106 : *quod facit corpus est*. It is remarkable to find the blending of these ideas in recent scientific speculation on matter and energy.

[3] *Taufe und Abendmahl bei Paulus*, p. 19.

is grossly to caricature the Apostle's entire meaning.

In view of these conclusions, we must now return to Reitzenstein's original inquiry as to whether Paul's use of the terms πνεῦμα, ψυχή, νοῦς, πνευματικός, and ψυχικός is more easily explained from Hellenistic religious usage or from the Old Testament. Our examination of Reitzenstein's material discloses an interesting affinity between conceptions of the indwelling Divine spirit belonging to the Mystery-Religions, and Paul's central idea of the gift of the πνεῦμα. But one omission is noteworthy. Nothing adduced is strictly relevant to the profoundly ethical contrast which Paul draws between σάρξ, "flesh" (not σῶμα), and πνεῦμα, "spirit".[1] Further, on Reitzenstein's own showing, the antithesis between πνεῦμα and ψυχή, so fundamental for Paul, is exceedingly rare, inasmuch as ψυχή is always apt to retain its significance as the higher part of man, in opposition to σῶμα.

What light is thrown on the situation by the Old Testament? Practically every leading conception in this sphere of Paul's religious thought may be said to have its roots definitely laid in

[1] This may be asserted even in the face of Capelle's evidence cited on p. 137, note 1.

that soil. In a number of Old Testament passages *bāsār*, "flesh," like many of the physical organs of man (*e.g.*, liver, kidneys), has a psychical connotation (*e.g.* Job. iv. 15 ; Ps. lxxxiv. 2 ; Ezek. xxxvi. 26) : and " in an important group of cases 'flesh' is used of man, or man's essential nature, in contrast with God, or with 'spirit' to emphasise man's frailty, dependence, or incapacity " (Isa. xxxi. 3, xl. 6 ; Ps. lvi. 4 ; Jer. xvii. 5, etc.).[1] Here is the palpable foundation for Paul's conception of σάρξ, a factor which he had discovered in his own experience as making for evil, although he affords no evidence for the hypothesis of an inherently evil matter. This σάρξ, with its evil affections, can be overcome by πνεῦμα. We have already seen that for Paul πνεῦμα in an overwhelming number of instances means the Divine gift to faith in Christ, the indwelling Spirit of God, or the indwelling Christ. Again his thought links on directly to the Old Testament. There, the conception of the *ruach* of God, developing with that of God Himself, came to be regarded as the source of prophetic inspiration (Ezek. ii. 2), the instrument of Divine

[1] See the admirable discussion in Prof. Wheeler Robinson's *The Christian Doctrine of Man*, pp. 22-25, a work to which we are deeply indebted at this point.

revelation generally (Zech. vii. 12), and, most notably, the endowment for special functions (Isa. lxi. 1 f.) and for character (Ps. li. 11). The Old Testament had conceived man's relation to God "along two principal lines, namely, that of the Spirit of God as acting more or less intermittently and externally upon man, and that of spiritual fellowship with God, which sought realisation in many ways".[1] These lines converge in Paul, and are fused together through his personal experience of the risen Christ. The relation of $\pi\nu\epsilon\hat{\upsilon}\mu\alpha$ to $\psi\upsilon\chi\acute{\eta}$ and of $\pi\nu\epsilon\upsilon\mu\alpha\tau\iota\kappa\acute{o}s$ to $\psi\upsilon\chi\iota\kappa\acute{o}s$ in Paul finds its direct explanation in Old Testament usage. We noted that occasionally the Apostle makes no apparent distinction between the Divine $\pi\nu\epsilon\hat{\upsilon}\mu\alpha$ as imparted, and the resultant human life which he designates $\pi\nu\epsilon\hat{\upsilon}\mu\alpha$, *e.g.*, Romans vii. 10. So also in Ezekiel xi. 19, xxxvi. 26, no line of cleavage can be drawn between the Divine and the (renewed) human *ruach*.[2]

Of special interest is the connection of Paul's terminology with the relationships of *ruach* ($\pi\nu\epsilon\hat{\upsilon}\mu\alpha$ in LXX) and *nephesh* ($\psi\upsilon\chi\acute{\eta}$ in LXX)

[1] Wheeler Robinson, *op. cit.*, p. 125.
[2] See Volz, *op. cit.*, p. 76, note 1.

in the Old Testament. A group of passages in Paul has been referred to, in which πνεῦμα seems to denote the inner life of man, apart from any emphasis on its Divine elements. This usage has often complicated the exegesis of the Epistles, but it is only another proof of Paul's fidelity to Old Testament terminology. After the Exile, *ruach* encroaches on the sphere of *nephesh*, with which it has always been akin, and comes to denote " the normal breath-soul as the principle of life in man " ;[1] see especially Isaiah xxvi. 9 : " with my *nephesh* I desired thee in the night, yea, with my *ruach* within me, I sought longingly for thee " ; and compare the exact parallel in Psalm lxxvii. 2, 3 (" my *nephesh* refused to be comforted. I remember God, and am disquieted : I complain and my *ruach* is overwhelmed "). Finally, the use of *nephesh* (ψυχή) in the Old Testament to signify the life-principle both in itself and as the basis of individuality, and further in connection with a wide range of states of consciousness (particularly emotional),[2] supplies a luminous background (*a*) for Paul's religious use of πνεῦμα, (*b*) for the sharp antithesis between

[1] See Wheeler Robinson, *op. cit.*, pp. 19, 110 f.
[2] Wheeler Robinson, *op. cit.*, pp. 16, 17.

πνευματικός and ψυχικός, which rests essentially on normal Old Testament usage.

A word must be said as to the Old Testament affinities of νοῦς. Following Old Testament practice, Paul frequently uses καρδία (= lēb), "heart," as a more or less general description of the inner life of man, occasionally emphasising its emotional, intellectual, or volitional character, all these being aspects of lēb which receive separate prominence in the Old Testament (e.g., Judges xviii. 20; 1 Kings iii. 9; 1 Sam. ii. 35).[1] But the range of καρδία as denoting intellectual activities is curtailed by Paul's employment of νοῦς. And the existence beside it, in a scarcely distinguishable sense, of the term συνείδησις, which belongs to Greek (popular) philosophy, may suggest that this is the point in his psychological terminology at which Paul was chiefly affected by contemporary usage. At the same time it must be observed, as Bonhöffer has pointed out,[2] that the specifically Christian and Jewish use of συνείδησις in the sense of our conception of "conscience" without further determination, "has no analogy in Stoicism," for Stoic thought has

[1] See Wheeler Robinson, op. cit., p. 22.
[2] Epiktet u. d. Neue Testament, p. 157.

no idea corresponding to the notion of "a personal God towards whom man recognises his responsibility". Böhlig, who attempts (*Die Geisteskultur von Tarsos*, p. 123) to modify this verdict, is obliged after all to admit (p. 126) that Paul has remoulded the idea by the force of his religious genius.[1] As we have seen, his employment of νοῦς as the equivalent of πνεῦμα, the phenomenon singled out by Reitzenstein in this connection for comparison with the Mystery-terminology, depends on quotations from the LXX, and cannot therefore be made the basis of any general hypothesis.

We have sought to prove that Paul's religious use of πνεῦμα, ψυχή, and cognate terms, has its roots in the soil of the Old Testament. Endowment with the Spirit was never lost sight of, even in the most barren periods of Judaism. But the exuberance of religious feeling in the early Christian community brought the phenomenon into the forefront of experience. And one of Paul's most notable spiritual achievements was the regulation of all that was uncontrolled in these manifestations, in order that the spiritual energy which lay behind them might

[1] An admirable note on the history of the term συνείδησις in Norden, *Agnostos Theos*, p. 136, n. 1.

be conserved for the edification of the Church. Now it is abundantly clear that parallel phenomena existed in the ethnic religions. There also the πνευματικός, by whatever name he might be called, was a familiar figure. As possessed by the god, or partaking of the Divine πνεῦμα or νοῦς, he too burst forth into mysterious ejaculations and rapt utterances of the kind described in the New Testament as γλώσσαις λαλεῖν. The experience is as widespread as the sway of intense religious feeling. It is found to a greater or less degree in all revival movements, from Wales to the hill-tribes of India, and reveals among other elements the influence of the collective consciousness of the crowd. It may be difficult to determine the precise sense which Paul or his readers assigned to the term γλῶσσα, but we have no right to find the origin of the experience, as J. Weiss does, "in the soil of Hellenistic ecstasy and mysticism". Nor are the later instances of it due to "suggestion" from the Biblical narratives.[1] It belongs to the very essence of spiritual ferment. Its psychological significance, up to a certain point, can be analysed. But here as elsewhere the tree is

[1] *Erster Kor.-Brief* (Meyer⁹), p. 339.

known by its fruit. The one criterion of religious ferment is its ethical productivity.

It is interesting to note that Paul himself distinctly recognises the existence of such experiences in his pagan environment, experiences belonging to the sphere of the Mystery-Religions. In the difficult passage (1 Cor. xii. 1 ff.) in which he introduces his discussion of πνευματικοί (or πνευματικά) he refers to ecstatic conditions known to his readers in their pre-Christian days, and supplies a test (ver. 3) for distinguishing these from their new Christian enthusiasm. And then among the gifts of the Spirit, he specifies that of διακρίσεις πνευμάτων, the power of discerning between the Spirit of the true God, the Holy Spirit, and other spiritual manifestations of an ecstatic kind which he regards as having no moral value. In the same paragraph he singles out an important endowment of the Spirit, the λόγος γνώσεως or "word of knowledge," which he classifies with such gifts as faith, power to heal, prophecy, glossolalia, and others. The salient fact about γνῶσις for our purpose is its prominence in the terminology of the Mystery-Religions.

No better illustration of the meaning of γνῶσις

in the Hermetic Mystery-literature could be given than that contained in the closing prayer of the Λόγος τέλειος of the Papyrus Mimaut, the Greek text of which has been reconstructed by Reitzenstein with the help of the very valuable Latin translation found in the *Asclepius* of Pseudo-Apuleius.[1] Here the worshippers give thanks to the Highest that by his grace they have received "the light of knowledge". This γνῶσις has been bestowed upon them "in order that knowing thee truly (ἐπιγνόντες) we may rejoice". Then the prayer proceeds: "Having been saved by thee, we rejoice that thou didst reveal thyself to us wholly, we rejoice that while in our bodies thou didst deify us by the sight of thyself". After further thanksgiving comes the closing petition: "Having thus worshipped thee, we have made no request of thy goodness (?) but this: be pleased to keep us in the knowledge (γνῶσις) of thee: hear our supplication that we should not fall away from this manner of life". With this may be com-

[1] See Reitzenstein in *Archiv f. Religionswissenschaft*, 1904, pp. 393-397; *H.M.R.*, pp. 113, 114. The papyrus probably belongs to the third century A.D., but the condition of the text suggests that it goes back to a much earlier original.

pared the concluding prayer in *Poimandres*, 32 (ed. Reitz., p. 338): "Listen to me when I pray that I may not fall away from knowledge . . . and strengthen me and [fill me] with this grace that I may enlighten (φωτίσω) those in ignorance". It is plain from the connection of sentences in the first of these extracts that γνῶσις means that apprehension of God which results in salvation or, in its more concentrated description, deification. This is made quite clear by a remarkable sentence in *Poimandres*, § 26 (ed. Reitz., p. 336): "This is the blessed issue for those who have attained γνῶσις, to be deified (θεωθῆναι)". Hence it may be said that γνῶσις in the Hermetic Mystery-religion is the direct pathway to the highest point which can be reached by the initiate. It is essentially a supernatural gift, not to be attained by any mere process of intellectual reflection. Its associations in the Hermetic literature are very significant. In *Corp. Hermet.*, ix. (x.), 4, εὐσέβεια, piety, is defined as γνῶσις τοῦ θεοῦ. In xiii. (xiv.), 8, the coming of γνῶσις is accompanied by the impartation of the "powers" of God. So, when in the hymn of regeneration the initiate calls on these δυναμεῖς to join in the praise he offers, he appeals to γνῶσις ἁγία as the source of his illumination (xiii. 18). Akin to this conception is that of ἐξουσία, which belongs to the man endowed with γνῶσις, and enables him to become holy like God (*Poim.*, § 32). Now the term ἐξουσία is used in magical literature for the supernatural power which depends on a supernatural knowledge.[1] And so we need not be surprised to find γνῶσις itself appearing in magical formulæ. Thus a magician in supplicating the god whose powers he desires to have at his command, says: "I am he to whom . . . thou didst grant the γνῶσις of thy mighty name, which I shall keep secret, sharing it with no one".[2] Occasionally γνῶσις is associated with cosmological mysticism, and seems to be attained by the ascent of the soul through the elements.[3]

[1] See Reitzenstein, *H.M.R.*, p. 183; *Poimandres*, p. 48, note 3. It is extremely doubtful whether Paul's use of ἐξουσία (as, *e.g.*, in 1 Kor. viii. 9, ix. 3) is to be explained from this atmosphere, as Reitzenstein suggests. The passage which he cites from Porphyrius (*de Abst.*, i., 41, 42) can scarcely be regarded as valid evidence (*Z. f. N. T. Wiss.*, 1912, i., 19-21).

[2] Quoted by Reitzenstein from a Leiden Papyrus published by Dieterich (*Jahrb. f. klass. Phil.*, Suppl., xvi., p. 799, l. 19), *H.M.R.*, p. 123.

[3] *H.M.R.*, p. 121.

This is its more philosophical aspect, which came to be accentuated in the speculations of Christian Gnosticism.

It is worth noting that emphasis is laid upon the converse of γνῶσις, ἀγνωσία. Thus in *Poimandres*, § 27, an appeal is made to " earth-born " men, "who have given themselves over to drunkenness and slumber and to ἀγνωσία τοῦ θεοῦ," to be sober (νήψατε) and to cease from debauchery and the spell of unthinking sleep. It is inevitable that with this we should compare 1 Corinthians xv. 34 : "Awake to soberness (ἐκνήψατε) righteously and sin not : for some have wilful ignorance of God ". Reitzenstein, who aptly observes that ἀγνωσία, both in *Poimandres* and in 1 Corinthians, is a positive rather than a negative conception, infers from Paul's use of the term in the same context with the exhortation to be sober, that he must here depend on the ideas of Hellenistic mysticism because ἀγνωσία and νήφειν occur together in a single section of *Poimandres*. But there is nothing extraordinary in Paul's juxtaposition of the two words. There is indeed a very close parallel in 1 Thessalonians v. 4 ff. : "You, brethren, are not in darkness, that that day should overtake you as a thief. . . . Let us therefore not sleep, as do the rest, but let us watch and be sober. For they that sleep sleep by night, and they that are drunken are drunken by night. But let us, who are of the day, be sober." Although the term ἀγνωσία is not found here, the same idea of ignorance is expressed by σκότος, darkness, and combined with the metaphor of drunkenness. Further, ἀγνωσία occurs in Wisdom of Solomon xiii. 1, in precisely the sense which Paul gives to it, and in a context with which he shows many points of contact in Romans i. 18-32 : " Being punished in these creatures which they supposed to be gods, they saw and recognised as the true God him whom before they refused to know : wherefore also the last end of condemnation came upon them. For verily all men by nature are vain, who had wilful ignorance (ἀγνωσία) of God, and from the good things that are seen were not able to know him that is" (Wisd. xii. 27-xiii. 1). The term appears to be similarly used in 1 Peter ii. 15, where Christians are reminded that it is by their high standard of conduct that they can bridle the wilful ignorance (ἀγνωσία) of senseless men. Here there is certainly implied a distinct prejudice which they have to live down. Reitzenstein quotes, as illustrating the condition or period of ἀγνωσία, a passage from a doctrinal treatise of the Ophite sect of the Peratæ, preserved by Hippolytus, which begins : ἐγὼ φωνὴ ἐξυπνισμοῦ ἐν τῷ αἰῶνι τῆς νυκτός ("I am the voice of awaking from sleep in the æon of the night"). We venture to believe that this Gnostic passage and also that which is so closely akin to it in *Poimandres* are directly coloured by the Pauline sayings to which we have referred. This appears to us to be one of the many places in which the Hermetic literature reveals the influence of a semi-Christian Gnosticism which was thoroughly at home in the Pauline Epistles.[1]

The brief conspectus of evidence presented suffices to indicate that in this literature γνῶσις belongs to the same circle of ideas as πνεῦμα and νοῦς. Perhaps Reitzenstein does not exaggerate in saying that γνῶσις θεοῦ as an influence which transforms into πνεῦμα is a fundamental conception in the phase of religion under review.[2]

On the strength of the affinities between Paul and the Mystery-Religions in the "pneumatic"

---

[1] See also Krebs, *op. cit.*, p. 147. Norden (*Agnostos Theos*, pp. 5, 6) would associate the theme of ἀγνωσία with a stereotyped form of missionary discourse belonging to Hellenistic religion. But much of his argument seems a begging of the question.   [2] *H.M.R.*, p. 133.

group of ideas, Reitzenstein finds the clue to the Apostle's use of γνῶσις in the influence of Mystery-conceptions. The term is used with considerable elasticity in the Epistles, but certain fixed ideas lie in the background. Paul undoubtedly regards γνῶσις as a supernatural χάρισμα. Thus in 1 Corinthians xii. 8, where it is grouped with ἐνεργήματα δυνάμεων, προφητεία, and other "gifts". Its connection indeed with προφητεία is specially intimate, e.g., 1 Corinthians xiii. 2: "If I have prophecy and know all μυστήρια and all γνῶσις," and verses 8 and 9, where, in contrast to love, γνῶσις, προφητεῖαι, and γλῶσσαι are described as vanishing, in view of a complete γνῶσις which is to come. "Knowledge," therefore, in Paul's view, is the result of possessing the Divine πνεῦμα. In passages like Romans ii. 20, "having the outline of knowledge and truth in the law," γνῶσις may appear to have a more general sense, but we are inclined to agree with Reitzenstein that for Paul it never means merely "rational knowledge".[1] A most suggestive glimpse of the Apostle's conception is afforded by 1 Corinthians viii. 1-3. In consulting Paul about their conduct with regard to flesh which has been offered to idols, the "stronger"

[1] *H.M.R.*, p. 126.

MYSTERY-TERMINOLOGY 169

Christians at Corinth assert the claim : " We all have γνῶσις ". Obviously they mean the application of that γνῶσις which they possess, as having the πνεῦμα, to this special case, and the words have a tone of contempt for the " weaker " brethren. Paul, as in chapter xiii., subordinates "knowledge" to love.[1] And then come the important words : " If any one presume to have attained a measure of knowledge, he has not yet come to know in the manner in which he ought. But if a man love God, he is known by him." Here is a surprising turn of thought. Love is the condition of mutual understanding between God and man. And clearly such an understanding means far more than intellectual comprehension : it is really fellowship of spirit. The same sense of γνῶσις appears in 1 Corinthians xiii. 12 : " At present I know partially, but then I shall know completely as already I am completely known (*i.e.*, by God) ". Galatians iv. 9 is parallel : " But now having come to know God, or rather having been known by God, how do you turn again to the weak and beggarly elemental spirits ? " Reitzenstein has omitted to notice the most important passage of all, Philippians iii. 8-10 : " I count

[1] In chap. xiii. all manner of spiritual χαρίσματα are similarly made subordinate.

all things but loss on account of the surpassing worth of the γνῶσις of Christ Jesus my Lord . . . that I may win Christ and be found in him . . . in order to know (γνῶναι) him and the power of his resurrection and the fellowship of his sufferings . . . if haply I may attain to the resurrection from the dead ". Plainly γνῶσις and γνῶναι here refer to the most intimate fellowship conceivable between the soul and Christ. We may compare with these passages *Corp. Hermet.*, x., 15 : " For God does not ignore man, but thoroughly knows (γνωρίζει) and desires to be known by him. For this alone is salvation for man, the γνῶσις of God." While γνῶσις in Paul, as in the Mystery-literature, is repeatedly emphasised on its intellectual side, its inherently religious significance is quite obvious.[1] Hence the question arises : Was Paul's use of γνῶσις shaped by the Mystery-terminology, or can we trace it back to a strain of thought in the Old Testament ?

In chapter ii. we pointed out that for the

[1] Norden has collected a large amount of valuable material to show the central place of γνῶσις in Hellenistic tradition, as denoting a religious experience rather than an intellectual process. This significance he assigns to the influence of the East (*Agnostos Theos*, pp. 95-109). But his conclusions are not all equally valid (see Bousset and Pohlenz in *Theol. L.Z.*, 1913, 7, sp. 195).

MYSTERY-TERMINOLOGY 171

prophets the "knowledge of God" was something experimental, a revelation of God in the inner being. Thus, in Hosea ii. 20: "I will betroth thee unto me in faithfulness, and thou shalt truly know (ἐπιγνώσῃ) the Lord" (*cf.* v. 4);[1] Isaiah xi. 2: "The spirit of the Lord shall rest upon him, the spirit of wisdom and understanding, the spirit of counsel and might, the spirit of knowledge (LXX, γνώσεως) and of godly fear (εὐσεβείας)". *Cf.* Proverbs ii. 5: "Then shalt thou understand the fear of the Lord [virtually = piety, εὐσέβεια] and find the knowledge (ἐπίγνωσιν) of God," where the parallel clauses describe a practical relationship to God. These and other instances suggest a close affinity between the Old Testament conception and that of Hellenistic religion. In view of Paul's intimate connection with the prophetic thought it is scarcely possible to doubt that his use of γνῶσις is affected by the דַּעַת יְהוָה of the Old Testament. But it seems equally certain that in employing the term and the idea it embodies, he presupposed his hearers' acquaintance with these through the medium of the Mystery-

[1] Is it possible that this *intimate* significance of ירע may be the spiritual expansion of the earlier sexual application of the term? *Cf.* 1 Cor. vi. 15-17.

Religions, and at least to some extent adopted the current usage.[1]

There are several noteworthy utterances in which Paul hints at a direct relationship between γνῶσις and ἀποκάλυψις, "revelation". In 1 Corinthians xiv. 6 glossolalia is said to be unprofitable unless accompanied by ἀποκάλυψις or γνῶσις or προφητεῖα or διδαχή. In verses 29, 30, the προφήτης appears as the recipient of ἀποκαλύψεις. In Ephesians i. 17 he prays that God may grant his readers the spirit of wisdom and ἀποκάλυψις in the full knowledge (ἐπιγνώσει) of Him.[2] Obviously ἀποκάλυψις signifies for the Apostle a special Divine communication of spiritual truth, the illumining by the πνεῦμα of some matters of spiritual moment,[3] and it depends on fellowship with God in Christ. Now Paul himself closely associates ἀποκαλύψεις with

[1] See further an admirable excursus on 1 Corinthians xii. 10, by J. Weiss (Meyer⁹), and Lietzmann's note on 1 Corinthians viii. 3.

[2] Dr. Armitage Robinson, as against Lightfoot, Hatch, and others, endeavours to prove that ἐπίγνωσις is not an intensified γνῶσις, but rather means "knowledge directed towards a particular object" (*Comm. on Ephes.*, pp. 248-254). But his arguments are unconvincing.

[3] *Cf.* Galatians i. 12, ii. 2; Ephesians iii. 2.

ὀπτασίαι "visions," in 2 Corinthians xii. 1. And the description there given furnishes a definite instance of an experience which is appealed to as a proof of his inherent sympathy with the phenomena of the Mystery-cults. The breathlessness and brokenness of the sentences reflect the intense emotion with which Paul defends himself against unscrupulous opponents. But an unprejudiced exegesis of 2 Corinthians xii. 1-5 must conclude that this was an experience in which the Apostle gloried (vers. 1, 5), and which he regarded as a momentous event in his spiritual history. The abrupt fashion in which he breaks off his narrative, combined with the plurals used in verse 1, suggests that he could have recounted other occurrences of the same kind. The motive of his reticence is clear from verse 6: "I hold back (*i.e.*, from dwelling on experiences of this kind), lest any one should place to my credit anything beyond what he sees me to be or hears from me". "His authority must not rest on any trafficking in mysteries which cannot be controlled, but only on that which the Corinthians can see and hear—namely, the 'weakness' of Paul, *i.e.*, his sufferings for Christ's sake and the courage with which he faces them " (Lietzm., *ad loc.*). The occurrence described evidently belongs to the "ecstatic" type. It is dated exactly "fourteen years ago," like the analogous events in the lives of Old Testament prophets.[1] It was a time of spiritual crisis for Paul, apparently some seven years after his conversion. The main details of the description are characteristic of Jewish Apocalyptic. In the original recension of the *Testament of Levi* (ii. 9, 10, iii. 1, 4, ed. Charles), God dwells in the third heaven, and there *Slavonic Enoch* (ch. viii.) places Paradise. The narrative as a whole is closely parallel to accounts of the ascent of the soul to heaven in Hellenistic Mystery-Religions,[2] in Jewish Apocalypses, in Rabbinic mysticism, in Philo, Plotinus, Suso,[3] and later mystics. Suso's account of his ecstasy is peculiarly suggestive. "Being there alone, and devoid of all consolations—no one by his side, no one near him—of a sudden his soul was rapt in his body or out of his body. Then did he see

[1] *Cf.* Isaiah vi. 1; Jeremiah i. 1; Ezekiel i. 1.

[2] An excellent summary in Wendland's *Die hellenistisch-römische Kultur*, ed. 2 (much enlarged and completely revised), 1912, pp. 170-176.

[3] See especially E. Underhill, *Mysticism*, pp. 225-227.

MYSTERY-TERMINOLOGY 175

and hear that which no tongue can express. That which the Servitor [his description of himself] saw had no form neither any manner of being; yet he had of it a joy such as he might have known in the seeing of the shapes and substances of all joyful things. . . . This ecstasy lasted from half an hour to an hour, and whether his soul was in the body or out of the body he could not tell. But when he came to his senses it seemed to him that he returned from another world."[1] We noted in an earlier chapter the ecstatic accompaniments of Ezekiel's prophetic work, and corresponding conditions in Judaism.[2] "Mystics of all ages," says Miss Underhill, "have agreed in regarding such ecstasy as an exceptionally favourable state: the one in which man's spirit is caught up to its most immediate vision of the Divine. . . . Clearly this apprehension will vary with the place of the subject in the spiritual scale. The ecstasy is simply the psycho-physical agent by which it is obtained."[3]

[1] *Mysticism*, p. 226.

[2] Similar states are recorded of themselves by such sober geniuses as Wordsworth and Tennyson. See Inge, *Christian Mysticism*, p. 14.

[3] *Mysticism*, p. 428. See the very valuable examination of ecstasy on pp. 427-452.

It is futile to regard such phenomena as pure hallucinations. But their worth can only be tested by the effect produced upon the spiritual life and activity of their subjects. St. Paul has nothing to fear from the application of such a test.

In the light of established facts, it is evident that no conclusions can be drawn as to the Apostle's relation to the Mystery-Religions on the strength of his ecstatic experiences. Yet it cannot be doubted that these would afford him important points of contact with men and women who had grown up in the atmosphere of mystic cults. The peculiar sensitiveness of temperament which made the great missionary "theopathetic" in this special sense was an integral part of his equipment for the work to which he was consecrated. We need not dwell on Paul's further reference to ecstasy in 2 Corinthians v. 13 : εἴτε γὰρ ἐξέστημεν, θεῷ· εἴτε σωφρονοῦμεν, ὑμῖν ("if we were out of our senses it was to God : if we have self-control it is for you"). Here, as in chapter xii., he will make no boast of his experiences of ecstasy. These were, like the glossolalia (1 Cor. xiv. 2, "He that speaks with a tongue speaks not to man but to God"), a matter between him and God. His ordinary disciplined life is what concerns them, and with that he is not afraid to confront his enemies, for it has been absorbed in the faithful preaching of the Gospel.[1] It is illegitimate for Reitzenstein to connect ἐκστῆναι and σωφρονεῖν directly with ἐκδημοῦντες and ἐνδημοῦντες of verse 9, as if there were any indication in his writings that the Apostle equates the condition of ecstasy with death (a notion which Reitzenstein finds in Hellenistic religious literature), and then, on the basis of this assumption, to infer that σωφρονεῖν has the significance of "living on earth". Nor is it admissible to translate verse 13 as Reitzenstein does : " our ecstasies occurred and still occur for God, are a service to Him, a cult ". This expansion is foisted upon the text in order to find a mystery-conception in Paul.[2] There is no trace of such a notion in his words.

As we propose in our next chapter to discuss the two central doctrines of the Mystery-Religions, regeneration and communion with the Divine, we must defer till then our examina-

[1] See Heinrici's admirable notes *ad loc.* σωφρονεῖν is the technical antithesis to ἐκστῆναι. The evidence in Heinrici.

[2] *H.M.R.*, p. 193,

tion of ἀναγεννᾶσθαι, παλιγγενεσία, σωτηρία, ἐν Χριστῷ εἶναι, and cognate expressions. Meanwhile we shall consider certain terms which indeed touch these doctrines, but admit of separate treatment. It has already been indicated that for the Mystery-cults γνῶσις was the pathway to a transformation finally resulting in deification. From *Corp. Hermet.*, x., 4, we learn that when the knowledge and vision (γνῶσις καὶ θεά) of the Divine light is attained, all the bodily senses are lulled into silence. The initiate is oblivious of all bodily perceptions and movements. That which is beheld illumines the whole inner life, drawing the soul out from the body and transforming (μεταβάλλειν) it into οὐσία ("the Divine or supra-sensible," Reitzenstein). "For it is impossible that the soul which has contemplated the beauty of the good should be deified ἐν σώματι ἀνθρώπου." Compare the direction given in the Liturgy of Mithra (p. 14, 26 ff.) : " Gaze upon the God . . . and greet him thus : ' Hail, Lord, ruler of the water . . . potentate of the spirit. Born again, I depart, being exalted : and having been exalted I die : born through that birth which gives life, dissolved into death, I go the way which thou hast appointed.' " Here the transformation is compared to dying. In a magical papyrus [1] the following occurs : " I was united with thy sacred form ($\mu o \rho \phi \hat{\eta}$), I was strengthened by thy holy name ". The new $\mu o \rho \phi \acute{\eta}$ appears as the consequence of initiation. Reitzenstein refers to a remarkable passage in Seneca (*Ep.* vi. 1), where he tells his friend Lucilius that he is not only improved (*emendari*) but transformed (*transfigurari*), and speaks of the sudden change. For Seneca, this of course means an inward experience.[2] But Reitzenstein believes that the metaphor is derived from the terminology of the Mystery-Religions, perhaps through Posidonius. We are unable to see the relevance of the parallels which Reitzenstein finds in the use of *reformare* and *reformatio* in the initiation-experience of Lucius (Apul., *Metamorph.*, xi., 16, 27), for these surely refer to his restoration to human form.[3] But it is pertinent to note certain ex-

[1] Wessely, *Zauberpap.*, i., p. 48, l. 179 ff. ; quoted by Reitzenstein, *H.M.R.*, p. 69.

[2] See Wendland, *Die hellenistisch-römische Kultur*,[2] p. 85, note 4.

[3] *H.M.R.*, p. 105. Possibly there may be some cogency in Apul., *Metamorph.*, xi., 30 : *Osiris in alienam quampiam personam reformatus.*

pressions in the vision of the alchemist Zosimus, who seems to have preserved a much older stratum of Mystery-theology. He speaks of a priest who, in his vision, "renewed" him (καινουργῶν με) so that he became πνεῦμα. This process he describes later as μετασωματούμενος, exchanging body for spirit.[1]

The material with which we have been dealing recalls Paul's language in 2 Corinthians iii. 18 : "We all with unveiled face beholding (or, reflecting) as in a mirror the glory of the Lord are transformed (μεταμορφούμεθα) into the same image from glory to glory, as from the Lord, the Spirit". Romans viii. 29 declares that "those whom God foreknew he also predestined to be conformed (συμμόρφους) to the image of his Son". And in Philippians iii. 21 it is said of Christ that He "will transform (μετασχηματίσει) the body of our humiliation so as to be conformed (σύμμορφον) to the body of his glory". With these passages we may connect Romans viii. 23 : "We ourselves also who have the first-fruits of the Spirit [*i.e.*, the πνεῦμα as pledge of what is to be], we also groan within ourselves,

[1] Berthelot, *Les alchimistes grecs*, p. 108, 5, 17 ; quoted in *H.M.R.*, p. 141.

earnestly awaiting our sonship, the redemption of our body ". Obviously Philippians iii. 21 and Romans viii. 23 refer to the transformation of the σῶμα ψυχικόν (1 Cor. xv. 44), the ordinary body of flesh and blood, into the σῶμα πνευματικόν, the organism which is the fit expression of the πνεῦμα. These two statements refer the transformation to the Parousia. But the mention of the "firstfruits consisting in the πνεῦμα" at least suggests that Paul may have regarded the process as having in some sense already begun. It is possible to find that idea implied in 2 Corinthians v. 4, 5 : "Those of us who are in the body (τῷ σκήνει)[1] groan under our burden, not that we desire to strip ourselves of it (ἐκδύσασθαι), but to put on another over it (ἐπενδύσασθαι), that what is mortal may be swallowed up by life. Now he that prepared us for this very experience is God, who gave us the pledge of the Spirit." The germ of the future σῶμα is somehow connected with the indwelling πνεῦμα. How are we to estimate the crucial statement, 2 Corinthians iii. 18, in view of all the

---

[1] A typically Hellenistic term : cf. Corp. Hermet., xiii., 15 : καλῶς σπεύδεις λῦσαι τὸ σκῆνος.

facts? The key to it is surely found in the expression πολλῇ παρρησίᾳ in the introductory sentence of the paragraph. Paul has been accused of concealing something (iv. 2, 3). He repels the charge indignantly and emphasises the openness of his Gospel. This he contrasts with the veil on Moses' face (iii. 13), the veil on the heart of Israel (ver. 15), and the veiling of the Gospel in the minds of unbelievers (iv. 3, 4). Hence the prominent idea in verse 18 is the "unveiled face". Here we are plainly moving to some extent among metaphors, yet the occurrence of the terms εἰκών and δόξα warns us against a merely metaphorical interpretation. No doubt in Romans xii. 2 μεταμορφοῦσθαι is used of a purely inward "renewal". But the combination of συμμορφιζόμενος with γνῶναι in Philippians iii. 10 suggests a background for the Apostle's conception akin to that of the Mystery-terminology. In 2 Corinthians iv. 16, the very context in which the "spiritual organism" is introduced, there occur the pregnant words: "If our outward man is being destroyed, yet our inward is being renewed day by day". It is natural to connect this "renewal" with the growth of a "pneumatic" life in the believer, which ultimately issues in the σῶμα πνευματικόν.¹ And some colour is lent to the influence of the Mystery-conceptions upon this whole group of ideas by the doctrine of the σῶμα πνευματικόν itself which we must proceed briefly to investigate. But before doing so, we would point out that, whatever links of contact may be here detected between Paul's thought and the Mystery-idea of transformation by the vision of God, there is a difference in the point of emphasis. In the Mystery-Religions the chief stress is laid upon a quasi-magical transmutation of essence. The very nature of Paul's conception of the πνεῦμα sets in the forefront the *moral* significance of the process. And so it is difficult even to surmise the nature of any "metaphysical" speculation on the experience, which may have found a place in Paul's mind.²

[1] Reitzenstein refers to a conception of the alchemist Zosimus which assigns to the inner life of every man a φωτεινὸς καὶ πνευματικὸς ἄνθρωπος (*H.M.R.*, p. 177). But this is probably a late development.

[2] Little light is shed on Paul's conception by Schweitzer's remark that for the Apostle renewal, spirit, ecstasy, gnosis, etc., are all dependent on the entrance of the individual into a "new cosmic process" (*Geschichte d. Paulin. Forschung*, p. 175).

This difficulty is not lessened by his statements regarding the σῶμα πνευματικόν. The most lucid of them all is Philippians iii. 21. There two things are said. Christ, at His Parousia, is by His almighty power to transform the earthly bodies (σάρξ καὶ αἷμα, 1 Cor. xv. 50) of believers. The result will be assimilation to His own σῶμα, the characteristic of which is δόξα. In 1 Corinthians xv. 49 Paul affirms : "Even as we wore the image of the earthly (*i.e.*, Adam), so shall we wear the image of the heavenly (*i.e.*, Christ)".[1] Plainly, the idea of the σ. πν. is modelled on his conception of the mode of existence of the exalted Christ. And it seems to us impossible to doubt that this conception is intimately associated with the Damascus vision.[2] In the obscure passage, 2 Corinthians v. 1, 2, the σ. πν. is described as the "building from God," the "house not made with hands, eternal in the heavens" (*cf.* 1 Cor. xv. 38). The impression that

[1] The reading φορέσωμεν, although so widely attested, is plainly an error. The whole context demands φορέσομεν, which is read by B. This common interchange in MSS. between ο and ω, due to pronunciation, appears also in Romans v. 1.

[2] See some valuable paragraphs in Feine, *N.T. Theologie*, pp. 362, 501, 502.

the transformation is a definite and sudden act of God is confirmed by 1 Corinthians xv. 51 : "we shall all be changed in a moment". In 2 Corinthians v. 1 ff. the suggestion is of a sudden event (ἐπενδύσασθαι). It is difficult to regard this passage as denoting something which already belongs to the constitution of the believer's life. Reitzenstein argues strongly for the thought of the ἔσωθεν ἄνθρωπος as the nucleus which, as in a certain sense an ἔνδυμα or garment, is to be clothed over (ἐπενδ.) with the σ. πν.[1] His argument, however, depends largely for its validity on the very doubtful reading ἐκδυσάμενοι (for ἐνδυσάμενοι) in 2 Corinthians v. 3. And it reads into Paul a crassness of idea which we fail to trace in the passages adduced. Probably on the basis of our data it is impossible to determine how Paul conceived the relation of the πνεῦμα in the believer to the σ. πν. To say, as J. Weiss does, that "Paul evidently pictures it as an 'ethereal,' light, pure, heavenly material" gives us but little aid in grasping the conception.[2] He is following a far more important clue when he urges that what concerned the Apostle

[1] *H.M.R.*, pp. 177, 178.
[2] *Erster Kor.-Brief* (Meyer⁹), p. 373.

above all else was the persistence of his individuality.

Reitzenstein holds that the notion of the σ. πν. has its roots in Hellenistic Mystery-Religion. The passages to which he refers are of a highly philosophical character. The one (*Corp. Hermet.*, vii., 2, 3) speaks of the necessity of "tearing off the tunic which you are wearing, the robe woven of ignorance," but there is no hint of the Pauline conception. The other (*ib.*, xvii.)[1] deals with σώματα ἀσώματα, "incorporeal bodies," but a glance at the context shows that we are moving in the region of abstract metaphysics, from which there appears to be no path to the realm of Pauline speculations. Two extracts quoted by J. Weiss give more promise. In *Corp. Hermet.*, xiii., 14,[2] Tat, who has just been regenerated, asks if his transfigured σῶμα will ever suffer dissolution. His father assures him that the former body was subject to disintegration, but that which has come from the birth of true being is indissoluble and immortal. "You do not recognise that you are now θεός and a child of the One." In the opening prayer of the

[1] *Poimandres* (ed. Reitz.), p. 354, 12 f.
[2] *Ibid.*, p. 344, 17 ff.

Liturgy of Mithra, the initiate, after addressing the various elements, appeals to " my perfected body . . . formed by a glorious arm . . . in the world which is unlighted and in that which is full of light ".[1] In the first passage, apart altogether from its philosophical substratum, the notion of a completely transformed essence, which makes the subject already a god, is utterly alien to Paul's thought. Weiss himself admits that he is unable to explain the sentence from the Liturgy, but believes that at any rate we find here the notion of a " supra-earthly body ". An examination of the context will show that we have in the passage a curious blend of Stoic speculation and cosmological tradition.[2] And it is noteworthy that the appeal of the prayer is made before the regenerating process begins. There is surely a wide gulf between these notions and the thought of St. Paul.

Some scholars, notably Reitzenstein[3] and Wendland,[4] bring the Pauline conception of the

[1] *Eine Mithrasliturgie*,[2] p. 4, 3 ff.

[2] See Dieterich's notes on the passage, *Eine Mithrasliturgie*,[2] pp. 58, 59.

[3] *H.M.R.*, pp. 106, 159, 175 ff.

[4] *Die hellenistisch-römische Kultur*,[2] p. 172, note 2; *G.G.A.*, September, 1910, p. 657.

σῶμα πνευματικόν into direct connection with the idea of the heavenly garments, which, in various phases of Oriental religion, purified souls receive in their ascent through the spheres towards their abode in the infinite light.[1] Traces of the idea appear in the account of the initiation of Lucius given by Apuleius.[2] But even if primitive imagination has left its impression on the Apostle's conception, the picture of the beatified soul in shining raiment is much too obvious to require explanation by any process of borrowing. If we had to postulate such a process, it would be more relevant to refer to parallels in the Apocalypses, *e.g.*, *Eth. Enoch*, lxii., 15 (ed. Charles): "The righteous and elect will have risen from the earth . . . and will have been clothed with garments of glory".[3] Paul's metaphor of "putting on Christ" (Gal. iii. 27) cannot be regarded as a true parallel to his speculations on the "spiritual organism," but must rather be

[1] See Cumont, *Les Religions Orientales*,[2] pp. 235 f., 391, note 54.

[2] Especially *Metamorph.*, xi., 23.

[3] See Charles's notes, the parallel in *Slav. Enoch*, 22, 8 (with references), and Bousset, *Die Religion d. Judentums*,[2] p. 319.

compared with such Old Testament passages as Psalm cxxxii. 9 : " Let thy priests be clothed with righteousness " (*cf.* 2 Chron. vi. 41 *et al.*), and with remarkable phrases such as Judges vi. 34 : " The spirit of Jehovah clothed itself with Gideon " (*cf.* Job xxix. 14, etc.).

In discussing γνῶσις we pointed out that for the Mystery-Religions its ultimate issue was deification. We must reserve our discussion of this conception for a later chapter. Meanwhile, let us briefly examine the terms εἰκών and δόξα, which have intimate affinities with the σῶμα πνευματικόν. They are linked together in the important passage, 2 Corinthians iii. 18, which has already been discussed. In connection with 1 Corinthians xv. 49 we saw that " the εἰκών of the heavenly " was virtually equivalent to the σ. πν. And Philippians iii. 21 is evidence that the character of the σ. πν. is δόξα. It may therefore be said that δόξα is that by which the εἰκών expresses itself. Where are we to look for the background of these ideas ? Paul's use of εἰκών is very instructive. In 1 Corinthians xi. 7 he describes man as the εἰκὼν καὶ δόξα θεοῦ, and in Colossians iii. 10 he speaks of the " new man " as being " renewed with a view to complete knowledge κατ' εἰκόνα τοῦ κτίσαντος αὐτόν". Obviously these passages are an echo of Genesis i. 27 (LXX): "And God created man, κατ' εἰκόνα θεοῦ created he him" (*cf.* v. 1). The idea is emphasised both in Palestinian and Hellenistic Judaism, *e.g.*, Sirach xvii. 3 : "He endowed thee with strength befitting thee and made thee according to his own image (εἰκόνα)"; Wisdom ii. 23 : "God created man for incorruption and made him an image (εἰκόνα) of his own proper being". Alongside of this usage in Paul is that which designates Christ as the εἰκών of God (2 Cor. iv. 4 ; Col. i. 15), and regards believers as destined to be conformed to that εἰκών (Rom. viii. 29). This combination is precisely parallel to his conception of the first and second creations (Rom. v. 12-21 ; 1 Cor. xv. 44-49). The εἰκών of God which was lost in the first creation through sin is to be restored in the second through Christ, in whom sin's power has been broken. Hence in spite of Clemen[1] it is impossible to doubt that Paul's use of εἰκών has an intimate connection with the Old Testament through the medium of the LXX. We believe that this holds good also of δόξα.

[1] *Religionsgeschichtliche Erklärung d. N.T.*, pp. 262, 263.

MYSTERY-TERMINOLOGY 191

The term is extraordinarily common in the Epistles with varying shades of meaning, from that of the radiance of a heavenly body to the energy which is exerted by the Divine nature, in addition to such senses as "honour" and "praise" as well as the eschatological idea of the "glory" which awaits the redeemed. Now δόξα is almost invariably the LXX translation of *kabod*, which occurs an immense number of times in the Old Testament with a considerable flexibility of signification ; and as expressing or interpreting *kabod*, a most important religious term, it must have been thoroughly familiar to all Jews of the Diaspora. To discuss the conception in the Old Testament and in Judaism would require a treatise. A somewhat careful investigation has convinced us of the validity of Prof. Buchanan Gray's conclusions :[1] "The glory of J". was originally used to express the manifestations of J".'s power and might, or more generally of His nature : through Isaiah the phrase became enriched and deepened in meaning, and subsequently continued to express this idea. . . . The phrase first unmistakably expresses a physical phenomenon in Ezekiel, who uses it to express

[1] Art. "Glory" (in Old Testament), *H.D.B.*, ii., p. 185.

the form under which *in his visions* he realises the movement of J". . . . It is not till we come to P. in the fifth century that the phrase is used of a physical phenomenon actually supposed to have been visible to the natural eye."[1] This requires to be supplemented only as regards the fact, put with some exaggeration by Stade[2] and Von Gall,[3] that more especially in the Psalter the glory of J". is closely associated with the Messianic Age.

Paul's use of δόξα corresponds remarkably to its Old Testament background and also to its usage in Apocalyptic writings, which ordinarily emphasise its more "physical" aspect.[4] From what has already been said, its close kinship with πνεῦμα is evident. Faithful to its Old Testament atmosphere, it denotes the manifested

---

[1] See also Duhm, *Die Theologie d. Propheten*, pp. 170, 171, 279; Dillmann, *Handbuch d. A.T. Theologie*, 1895, p. 283 f., where *kabod* is defined as "the majesty of a self-revealing Being". For its connection with holiness, see Cheyne on Isaiah vi. 3.

[2] *Ausgewählte Reden*, p. 49.

[3] *Die Herrlichkeit Gottes*, pp. 32-47. This discussion contains much that is suggestive for the New Testament.

[4] See, *e.g.*, 4 Ezra vii. 78, 91; Eth. Enoch, lxi. 8, lviii. 3; Apoc. Baruch, xlviii. 49, etc.

life or energy of the living God, *e.g.*, Romans vi. 4 : " As Christ was raised from the dead through the δόξα of the Father"; Colossians i. 11 : " strengthened with all power according to the might of his δόξα ". A second group of instances are distinctly eschatological, *e.g.*, Romans viii. 18 : " the glory destined to be revealed εἰς ἡμᾶς " ; Colossians i. 27 : " Christ in you, the hope of glory " ; 1 Thessalonians ii. 12 : " Who calleth you into his own kingdom and glory ". This usage seems to be parallel to the Old Testament notion of " glory " as characteristic of the Messianic Age. Finally there are passages which may be directly linked to Old Testament pictures of theophanies, *e.g.*, 2 Thessalonians i. 9 : " who shall suffer punishment . . . from the face of the Lord and from the glory of his might " ; Philippians iii. 21 : " the body of his (*i.e.*, Christ's) glory " ; 2 Corinthians iii. 8 : " if glory (*i.e.*, the reflection of the Divine on the face of Moses) belonged to the ministry of condemnation ". Obviously it will be difficult to draw a distinction between these examples and the eschatological group. For they have usually in view the unveiled Divine Presence, the sphere of the Divine existence. We have indicated that

Paul's conception of the σῶμα πνευματικόν was largely due to his vision on the Damascus road. Now the essential characteristic of the σ. πν. for him was δόξα. Hence δόξα, in its sense of the radiant self-expression of the (Divine) πνεῦμα, probably reflects a certain impression belonging to his conversion-experience, and this impression has given it a quasi-physical significance.[1] But already in the Old Testament and the Apocalypses a "sensible" element belonged to the conception. So that Paul has only followed his usual practice of remoulding the earlier idea in the light of his personal experience.

In view of these facts, it is quite irrelevant, with Reitzenstein, to refer the "peculiar association of the conceptions δόξα and πνεῦμα of necessity to Egyptian-Hellenistic Mysticism".[2]

---

[1] See Sokolowski, *Geist u. Leben bei Paulus*, pp. 63, 64, 162, 163. Sokolowski is inclined to exaggerate the "materiality" of δόξα, but it is true that Paul "was not accustomed to distinguish between the physical and the spiritual in our fashion".

[2] *H.M.R.*, p. 180. Böhlig (*Die Geisteskultur von Tarsos*, 1913, pp. 97-101) attempts to show that the root of Paul's conception of δόξα is to be found in Persian religion. Various points in his argument he admits to be hypothetical: *e.g.*, "how Paul arrived at his peculiar conception of δόξα can only

But we must glance at the interesting parallels to Paul's use of δόξα which he adduces from the Mystery-literature. In a magical papyrus, edited by Dieterich,[1] it is said of the Creator: "Thou didst give to the sun its δόξα and all its might," where δ. evidently means "radiance," a sense unknown in ordinary Greek literature.[2] Similarly in other parts of this document, and in a papyrus published by Wessely (i., p. 74, l. 1200): "I addressed thine unsurpassable δόξα". In a curious alchemistic treatise ascribed to Komarios, dealing with chemical processes in terms derived from the Mystery-religions, the

be conjectured" (p. 100); "one may therefore *perhaps* say, with his δόξα-conception Paul took over Persian ideas in Hellenistic dress" (p. 101). But the precariousness of his basis is evident from the statement that the notion of δόξα as "sensible" is "foreign to the LXX" (p. 98). A careful examination of *kabod* in the Old Testament would have prevented such a dictum.

[1] *Abraxas*, p. 176, 5. Krebs points out that this papyrus belongs to the third century A.D., *op. cit.*, p. 162.

[2] Deissmann, in his pamphlet, *Die Hellenisierung d. semit. Monotheismus*, pp. 5, 6, suggests that this may have been an ancient realistic meaning which survived in the popular language of the environment of the LXX translators, and points to Δόξα as a name of women and ships as perhaps retaining this significance.

phrase ἐνδύσασθαι δόξαν occurs repeatedly, but the evidence, it seems to us, proves nothing, as Reitzenstein himself admits that this work has undergone Christian revision.[1] Founding on this passage, he is inclined to ascribe the sense of "radiance" belonging to δόξα to the influence of an Egyptian verb, meaning "to shine," with a corresponding noun signifying "advantage," from which he attempts, without any data, to derive the meaning of "glory". This would connect the LXX use of δόξα with Egyptian Mystery - terminology. Deissmann's suggestion, quoted above, appears to us far more probable. A notable parallel occurs in *Corp. Hermet.*, x., 7, in which the transformed soul is represented as "joining the chorus of the gods," and then it is said: "this is ἡ τελειοτάτη δόξα of the soul". Here we are reminded of various Pauline passages. Perhaps the most remarkable instance is in Wessely, *Zauberpap.*, ii., p. 37, l. 512, where a magician prays to Isis: δόξασόν με, ὡς ἐδόξασα τὸ ὄνομα τοῦ υἱοῦ σου Ὥρου.[2] Probably the prayer is one for Divine

[1] *H.M.R.*, p. 142.

[2] *H.M.R.*, pp. 100, 170. Reitzenstein's interpretation of the whole passage, Romans viii. 30, is quite arbitrary.

power, an idea characteristic of the Pauline δόξα, while the second clause contains the notion of "glory" in the stricter sense. Reitzenstein aptly compares the ἐδόξασεν of Romans viii. 30.

Paul's use of the terms φωτίζειν, "illumine," and φωτισμός, "illumination," has a history parallel to that of δόξα and δοξάζειν. They are used again and again in the LXX of spiritual illumination, as translations of Hebrew אוֹר or its derivative מָאוֹר. Instances are Psalm xviii. (xix.) 8: ἡ ἐντολὴ κυρίου τηλαυγὴς φωτίζουσα ὀφθαλμούς ("the commandment of the Lord is clear, illumining the eyes"); Psalm xxvi. (xxvii.) 1: κύριος φωτισμός μου καὶ σωτήρ μου, τίνα φοβηθήσομαι; ("the Lord is my illumination and my saviour, whom shall I fear"). Closely akin to our first example is Ephesians i. 18: πεφωτισμένους τοὺς ὀφθαλμοὺς τῆς καρδίας ὑμῶν ("the eyes of your heart being illumined"). In Ephesians iii. 9 φωτίσαι is parallel to εὐαγγελίσασθαι, and directly recalls the interesting use of φωτίζειν in 2 Kings xvii. 27, 28 (LXX) as = "teach". Equally significant is φωτισμός which is found in Paul only in 2 Corinthians iv. 4, 6. He plainly uses the word in a wholly spiritual sense, as in the one case the φωτισμός is that of the Gospel, and in the other the φωτισμὸς τῆς γνώσεως τῆς δόξης τοῦ θεοῦ is described as a process taking place ἐν ταῖς καρδίαις. Reitzenstein explains the Pauline passages from the Hermetic use of φωτίζειν as the action of γνῶσις. The vision of God who is in essence φῶς illumines (φωτίζει) in a quasi-physical sense. He compares the occurrence in Apuleius' description of the Isis-Mysteries of the term *illustrari*, applied to the initiate, and sums up by remarking that the usage is non-Jewish.[1] In view of the evidence given above, comment on this is needless. And the evidence we have adduced from the Old Testament makes it wholly superfluous to seek for the explanation of Paul's use of any of these terms in Hellenistic Mystery-Religion. What we do learn from the parallels is the ability of many of his readers to catch the meaning of a more or less technical terminology, due not merely to a course of instruction in the Old Testament, but to their acquaintance with a religious vocabulary already current among the Mystery-associations.

[1] *H.M.R.*, pp. 119, 120.

CHAPTER V

ST. PAUL AND THE CENTRAL CONCEPTIONS OF
THE MYSTERY-RELIGIONS

In the light of the evidence we have sought to exhibit in the preceding chapters it is not difficult to give a rough account of the chief aims of the Mystery-Religions. They may be said to offer salvation (σωτηρία) to those who have been duly initiated. And salvation means primarily deliverance from the tyranny of an omnipotent Fate, which may crush a human life at any moment. Death, with its unknown terrors, will be Fate's most appalling visitation. Hence the element prized above all others in σωτηρία is the assurance of a life which death cannot quench, a victorious immortality. This boon is reached by the process of regeneration (ἀναγεννᾶσθαι, παλιγγενεσία). A genuinely Divine life is imparted to the initiate in a transformation of essence, which in many, if not in all, instances is conceived more or less physically, though at least occasionally a psychical element is quite manifest. The full significance of the process becomes clear from its being frequently described as deification ($\theta\epsilon\omega\theta\hat{\eta}\nu\alpha\iota$, $\dot{\alpha}\pi o\theta\epsilon\omega\theta\hat{\eta}\nu\alpha\iota$). And it always seems to depend on some kind of contact with Deity. In order to reach a standpoint from which a comparison with St. Paul's conceptions can be profitably made, we must examine with some care the prevalent ideas of communion with the god, through which, for the Mystery-Religions, the process of regeneration or deification becomes possible.

The first thing that strikes us about these ideas is that they reflect the various phases of primitive belief which emerge in the Mystery-cults, from the crudest up to those which have become spiritualised in the course of a gradual development. We touch a very ancient stratum of thought in the idea that communion with a deity can be gained through partaking of him. This conception is found in early Egyptian texts, and seems to be involved in the rites which circled round the mystic figure of Dionysus-Zagreus, in which the bull, representing the god himself, is torn asunder and devoured. His life passes into his votaries.¹ A more refined form of this idea, which perhaps meets us in the usage of sacramental meals, must be discussed in a later chapter in connection with Paul's view of the Lord's Supper. Less crass in its associations, but perhaps scarcely less corporeal in its implications, is that contact with deity described in Greek religion as ἐνθουσιασμός. This condition was induced by all kinds of sensuous stimuli. It might mean the entrance of the god into the human personality as it was. A remarkable instance, belonging somewhat incongruously to an elevated plane of Mysticism, occurs in a prayer to Hermes:² "Come to me, O Lord Hermes, ὡς τὰ βρέφη εἰς τὰς κοιλίας τῶν γυναικῶν". Here the corporeal background is evident enough. Closely akin, although nearer the sphere of the spiritual, is the prayer of the Liturgy of Mithra: "that I may be initiated, and that the holy spirit may blow

¹ See Dieterich, *Eine Mithrasliturgie*,² pp. 105, 106; Rohde, *Psyche*,³ ii., pp. 15, 117, 118, with the notes. The scholion on Clem. Alex., *Protrept.*, i., p. 433, quoted by Dieterich, is specially significant: "those initiated into the mysteries of Dionysus ate flesh raw, this initiation symbolising the mangling of his body which Dionysus endured at the hands of the Titans".

² Quoted by Dieterich from Kenyon, *Greek Papp.*, i., p. 116.

within me ".[1] But ἐνθουσιασμός was often virtually synonymous with ἔκστασις. Here the soul is regarded as leaving the body and becoming one with the deity. In many mystic cults, such as that of Dionysus and the Great Mother, a state of wild delirium is produced, and the subject of it becomes conscious of impressions and powers completely alien to his normal experience.[2] As Proclus expresses it: "Going out of themselves, they are wholly established with the gods and possessed by them ".[3] But ecstasy is found in a large variety of phases. It has no necessary connection with frenzy. The ascent of the soul into the sphere of the Divine is often conceived of, as apart from all sensuous excitements. We have seen, *e.g.*, how the condition of γνῶσις, or the vision of deity, transforms the soul which has left behind the hampering associations of the body into οὐσία, the Divine essence. The astral mysticism, so dear to Posidonius, employs the

[1] *Mithrasliturgie*,[2] p. 4, 13 f.

[2] *Cf.* Plato, *Ion*, 434 B : πρὶν ἂν ἔνθεός τε γένηται καὶ ἔκφρων καὶ ὁ νοῦς μηκέτι ἐν αὐτῷ ἐνῇ.

[3] On *Republ.*, p. 59, 19 (ed. Schöll). See Rohde's important discussion, *Psyche*,[3] ii., pp. 18-21.

method of absorbing contemplation. By its means, communion with the divinity is possible of attainment. To the same sphere of more "spiritual" modes of achieving union with the gods belongs one described in the Hermetic literature, in which external ritual plays a very subordinate part. Here the communication of a revelation produces the mysterious change. The revelation regenerates. The soul is enabled to pass upwards into the Divine abode, and to become one with deity as having received the ten powers ($δυνάμεις$) of God. A close kinship may be traced between this representation and the $ἀπαθανατισμός$ or process of deification which appears in the Liturgy of Mithra. But the latter is accompanied by a variety of ritual postures and gestures. Thus the aspirant is enjoined to inhale the Divine breath (or spirit), in which case he will behold himself being raised into the upper air. As he sees the gods rushing at him, he is to place his forefinger on his mouth and exclaim, "Silence, silence, silence". Thereupon he must emit a whistling sound, and utter some mystic vocables, and then he will behold the gods looking upon him graciously. The Liturgy abounds in similar directions. A still more spiritual foundation for the *unio mystica* is traceable in that pantheistic Element-mysticism, resulting partly from ancient physico-religious speculations, partly from Pythagorean and Stoic versions of these, which teaches that men reach the vision of God which deifies by means of the "elements" in them, of which the first principles exist in the deity.[1] This is a favourite doctrine of Hellenistic religion. Sextus Empiricus (vii., 93) quotes a saying of Posidonius that "light is apprehended by the light-like power of vision, sound by the air-like hearing, and similarly the nature of the universe must be apprehended by reason which is akin to it". To the same effect is the Orphic verse: τῷ λαμπρῷ βλέπομεν, τοῖς δ' ὄμμασιν οὐδὲν ὁρῶμεν : "by brightness we see, with the eyes we perceive nothing".[2] Cornford ingeniously suggests that the conception goes back to "that old magical doctrine which grouped things into classes of kindred, united by a sympathetic continuum".[3] Nothing could more strikingly reveal the continuity of mystic thought

[1] See Dieterich, *Abraxas*, pp. 58, 59.

[2] Numerous exx. in Dieterich, *Eine Mithrasliturgie*,² pp. 56, 57.

[3] *From Religion to Philosophy*, p. 133.

than a comparison of this element-mysticism with the words of Ruysbroek: "All men who are exalted above their creatureliness into a contemplative life are one with this Divine glory—yea, *are* that glory, and they see and feel and find in themselves, by means of this Divine light, that they are the same Ground as to their uncreated nature. . . . Wherefore contemplative men should rise above reason and distinction . . . and gaze perpetually by the aid of their inborn light, and so they become transformed, and one with the same light by means of which they see, and which they are."[1]

Some further ideas of a more or less primitive character must be noted. Traces exist in obscure mystical formulæ of the conception of union with the god under the guise of the marriage relationship. The terms employed disclose how grossly sensuous were the early forms of the notion.[2] While hints of a survival of the ceremonial of the ἱερὸς γάμος appear here and

[1] Quoted by Inge, *Christian Mysticism*, p. 189.

[2] *E.g.*, the description of the sacred snake (associated with the Dionysus-Sabazius mysticism) as ὁ διὰ κόλπου θεός. The mystic drama corresponded to the designation. See Dieterich, *Eine Mithrasliturgie*,[2] pp. 123, 124.

206 ST. PAUL AND CENTRAL CONCEPTIONS

there, it is probable that fairly early the conception came to be little more than a metaphor. The symbol was one which must inevitably take its place in all mystical self-expression.[1] In the last chapter it was pointed out that regeneration in the Liturgy of Mithra is compared to dying: "Born again I depart, being exalted [*i.e.*, into the Divine sphere], and having been exalted I die : born through that birth which gives life, dissolved into death, I go the way . . . which thou hast appointed" (p. 14, 31 ff.). Brückner remarks that this prayer might just as appropriately come from the lips of a worshipper of Attis or of Serapis.[2] For one of the most arresting aspects of the idea of regeneration in the Mystery-Religions is that which is associated with the death and restoration to life of a Divine person, a process through which, by a mystic sympathy, the initiate obtains the guarantee of undying life for himself. It is of supreme im-

---

[1] *Cf.* E. Underhill, *Mysticism*, p. 496 : "The mystic for whom intimate and personal communion has been the mode under which he best apprehended Reality, speaks of the consummation of this communion, its perfect and permanent form, as the *Spiritual Marriage* of the soul with God".

[2] *Der sterbende und auferstehende Gottheiland*, p. 11.

portance for our purpose to notice that the central deities in this sphere of religion, Osiris (-Serapis), Attis, and Dionysus,[1] are intimately connected with the growth and decay of vegetation. Isis and Cybele are each represented as mourning her beloved, just as Demeter at Eleusis mourns for her daughter Kore, with whom at a later period Dionysus (Iacchus) was brought into close affinity. The real significance of the myths becomes clear when it is observed that the festivals of these deities were held either in early spring, when the blackness of winter began to give place to a luxuriant life, or in autumn, after the fruits of the earth had been gathered in, and when the cornseed (as in Egypt) was buried in the soil. In the case of both Attis and Osiris the mourning and the rejoicing were celebrated at the same festival. The ancient formula of

[1] Cornford makes the interesting observation that "the seasonal round of vegetation" symbolised in such deities as Dionysus "is a larger transcript of the phases of human existence, birth and death, and rebirth in the wheel of reincarnation". Hence Mystery-Religion "holds fast to the sympathetic principle that all life is one, and conceives nature under that form which seems to keep her processes most closely in touch with the phases of human experience" (*op. cit.*, pp. 111, 112).

the Attis-ritual, quoted in chapter iii., reveals the significance for the initiates of the god's restoration to life: "Be of good cheer, initiates, the god has been saved: thus for you also shall there be salvation from your troubles". It is difficult to determine by what actual process, previous to the institution of the *taurobolium*,[1] the votaries of Attis were assured of their immortality. Perhaps it is sufficient to emphasise what Mr. Cornford calls that "passionate sympathetic contemplation (θεωρία) in which the spectator is identified with the suffering God, dies in his death, and rises again in his new birth" (*op. cit.*, p. 198). The early formula, quoted on page 92, suggests a sacred meal in which the participant entered into communion with the living deity. But this is no more than hypothesis.[2] We have also seen that in the Osiris-cult, the worshipper, as becoming one with the god who lives, must share eternally in his Divine

---

[1] See Hepding's clear discrimination between an earlier *taurobolium* which was simply a sacrifice, and the later (the earliest epigraphical evidence for which belongs to 305 A.D.) which was the initiation of individuals (*Attis*, pp. 199, 200).

[2] Dieterich makes assertions on this question which go beyond the data, *e.g.*, *Mithrasliturgie*,[2] p. 174.

life. Of the mystic ritual by which this process was symbolised in the Hellenistic period we know little beyond some obscure indications which may be gathered from Apuleius.

Certain remarkable hints, however, have been handed down to us of a death issuing in life through which the initiated had to pass. These have often been exaggerated, and treated as full-fledged doctrines. But we must beware of going beyond our data. The clearest evidence of the conception is found in Apuleius' description of the initiation of Lucius into the Isis-Mysteries, which was succeeded after an interval by that into the rites of Osiris. There the initiation is described by the high priest as "the symbol of a voluntary death" (*voluntariae mortis*) which is followed by a new birth (*quodam modo renatos*). Probably this explains Lucius' account of what befell him in the innermost shrine : " I penetrated to the boundaries of death ". How much of a genuinely religious experience was involved, and what precisely it meant, it is hard to determine. There was of course an impressive sensuous ritual. Perhaps we ought to interpret in the light of this passage the designation by Firmicus Maternus of an initiate of Attis as *moriturus*, "about to die". And Dieterich would assign to the same group of ideas a reference of Proclus, in his work on the theology of Plato, to "priests who in the most mysterious of all initiations give orders to bury the body as far up as the head". Dieterich regards this as a symbolic burial, and believes it to belong to Dionysiac-Orphic ritual.[1] There is a further description by Sallustius, in his treatise *Concerning the gods and the world*, of Attis-initiates as "cutting off the further process of generation". To this scanty evidence must be added the passage from the Liturgy of Mithra quoted above. The extract which Reitzenstein makes from *Corp. Hermet.*, xiii., 3, and supports from the visions of Zosimus, in which regeneration is depicted as an experience of death and burial, apart altogether from its relevance, depends far too much upon conjectural emendation to be used as valid testimony.[2] One or two survivals of mystic ritual seem to bear upon the conception before us. Sallustius speaks of those newly initiated into the Attis-mysteries as receiving the nourishment of milk, "as born

[1] *Op. cit.*, p. 163.
[2] See *Poimandres*, pp. 368-370.

anew" (ὥσπερ ἀναγεννωμένων). With this Dieterich would compare the Dionysiac-Orphic formula found in Southern Italy: "a kid I lighted upon the milk," ἔριφος denoting the "newly born" in the mystic sense.[1] But the formula is so obscure that it is precarious to make it the basis of argument. Nor is it legitimate to adduce the barbarous ceremony of the *taurobolium*, the bath of bull's blood, associated with the ritual of the Great Mother and Attis, in which the descent into the pit seems to have symbolised the burial of the old life, and the votary, coming up from his bloody baptism, was feasted as a god, and described as "born again for eternity". For Cumont has shown that this was a comparatively late development of the cult.[2]

We have dwelt on these meagre data because they have been made the foundation of extraordinarily bold assertions. Thus Loisy gives the following summary of St. Paul's conception of Jesus Christ: "He was a saviour-god, after the manner of an Osiris, an Attis, a Mithra. Like them, he belonged by his origin to the

[1] *Op. cit.*, p. 171.
[2] *Les Religions Orientales*,[2] pp. 98-105; see also Hepding, *Attis*, 199 f.

celestial world; like them, he had made his appearance on the earth; like them, he had accomplished a work of universal redemption, efficacious and typical; like Adonis, Osiris, and Attis, he had died a violent death, and, like them, he had been restored to life; like them, he had prefigured in his lot that of the human beings who should take part in his worship, and commemorate his mystic enterprise; like them, he had predestined, prepared, and assured the salvation of those who became partners in his passion".[1] This paragraph implies that Paul's whole conception of salvation through Christ is exactly parallel to the central ideas of the Mystery-Religions. Before we examine the question more closely, we may offer the preliminary caution that nothing is more misleading than an inaccurate use of terminology.[2] Paul never speaks

[1] *Hibbert Journal*, October, 1911, p. 51. *Cf.* Brückner, *op. cit.*, pp. 36, 37; Dieterich, *op. cit.*, p. 175 ff.; Lake, *Earlier Epistles of St. Paul*, pp. 233, 234. G. Murray accepts some very precarious theories of Bousset as to pre-Christian "Redeemers" (*op. cit.*, pp. 143, 144).

[2] "We may speak of 'the vespers of Isis' or of a 'Last Supper of Mithra and his companions,' but only in the sense in which one talks of . . . 'the socialism of Diocletian'. . . . A word is not a demonstration" (Cumont, *op. cit.*, p. xiii.).

of Jesus as a "saviour-god". For him there is one God, "the Father of our Lord Jesus Christ". In Jesus the redeeming love of God is brought near to men (Gal. ii. 20 ; iv. 4, 5). Nor is it legitimate to call Osiris or Attis " saviour-gods" in the sense in which "Saviour" was applied by Paul to Jesus. Paul knew Jesus as an historical Person who, as the result of boundless devotion to the good of His brethren, suffered a shameful death, from which He did not flinch, in loyalty to His Father's purpose, so that this death became to men the very pledge of the unspeakable love of God and the forgiveness of sins. Osiris and Attis were originally mythological personifications of the processes of vegetation. The legends of their deaths have nothing to do with a purpose of spiritual redemption. There is no parallel between the New Testament narrative of the Incarnation, which meant so much for Paul, and the myths which recount their history. It is a caricature to compare the story of the murder of Osiris or the self-destruction of Attis with that of the self-sacrificing death of Jesus. Nor is any real comparison possible

See also some vigorous paragraphs in Schweitzer, *Gesch. d. Paulin. Forschung*, pp. 151, 152.

between the New Testament view of the resurrection of Jesus and the restoration to life of these mythical divine persons. In the one case, the disciples of Jesus were raised from despair to a victorious joy a few days after the crucifixion which had blighted all their hopes, by an experience of their risen Lord which, however much it may elude attempts at explanation, can never be resolved into a subjective fancy of Peter's, gradually kindling the hearts of his companions, and finally constituting the basis of the Christian Church. The world-transforming effect demands a more elemental cause. And only such a cause is in harmony with the Jesus of the Gospels. The return to life of Osiris and Attis is embodied in grotesque myths, and these become the centre of an elaborate ritual, through which there is conveyed to their votaries the hope of immortality. There is no true analogy, moreover, between the New Testament idea of a fellowship in the sufferings of Christ and that ritual sympathy with the goddesses who mourned the loss of Osiris and Attis, or with the woes of these deified beings themselves. In the former, self-sacrificing devotion which shrinks from no hardship is the core of the experience. Those

OF THE MYSTERY-RELIGIONS 215

who are constrained by the love of Christ dedicate their lives to His obedience. But this is not ritual. It means a new moral attitude to the world and to God. It is an assent of the will to that estimate of things which is involved in the cross of Christ. It is an identifying of themselves with the position of the Crucified who triumphed over human sin in its most awful manifestation, without faltering in loyalty to His redemptive mission. The latter is the result of sensuous impressions more or less artificially produced. It is stimulated by the blare of exciting music, by frenzied dances, and by orgies of savage self-mutilation. It depends on an elaborate machinery of pompous processions, ascetic prescriptions, a ceremonial celebrated at dead of night, when the darkness was suddenly illuminated by the flashing of a torch. Hence a foundation is wholly lacking for Loisy's conclusion: "These are analogous conceptions, dreams of one family, built on the same theme with similar imagery".[1]

But we must now attempt to discover what relationship, if any, exists between Paul's standpoint and the central Mystery-doctrine of Re-

[1] *Loc. cit.*, p. 52.

generation (involving salvation or deification) through communion with deity. To begin with, we are not at liberty to identify their respective ideas of salvation. For the Mystery-Religions σωτηρία has primarily in view the pressure of those burdens (such as fate, necessity, etc.) which are involved in the limitations of earthly life, and especially the dark shadow of death. In the Osiris-cult, at least, the immortal life beyond the grave is pictured in the precise form of the bodily life,[1] as was that of Osiris himself. What the conception of the eternal future meant for the Cybele-Attis cult it is impossible to determine. The deification which was the goal in the Hermetic doctrine seems certainly to have been clothed in a more spiritual guise. But it is important to note that σωτηρία was invariably assured " by the exact performance of sacred ceremonies ".[2] Hence it was invariably conceived as a *character indelebilis*.[3] Above all, it did not necessarily involve a new moral ideal. " We have no reason to think," says Prof. Percy Gardner, " that those who claimed

[1] See, *e.g.*, Brückner, *op. cit.*, p. 29.
[2] Cumont, *op. cit.*, p. xxii.
[3] *Cf.* Anrich, *Das antike Mysterienwesen*, p. 54.

salvation through Isis or Mithras were much better than their neighbours. They felt secure of the help of their patron-deity in the affairs of life and in the future world; but they did not therefore live at a higher level."[1]

Paul's conception of σωτηρία is many-sided. Like all his regulative ideas it has direct connections with the Old Testament, and denotes that Messianic salvation which is the consummation of God's redeeming purpose for His people. Again and again in the LXX σωτηρία is the translation of יְשׁוּעָה or תְּשׁוּעָה, which was a current Messianic idea. The term includes deliverance both from material and spiritual ills. In Paul, along with its cognate verb σώζω (which he uses far more frequently than the noun), it is always spiritual,[2] and associated with the good news of God in Christ. But as the Apostle made no distinction between physical and spiritual in his conception of death as the consequence of sin, σωτηρία involves immortal life in the profoundest sense of the phrase, an ethical quite as distinctly

[1] *Religious Experience of St. Paul*, p. 87.

[2] Probably Phil. i. 19 means acquittal for Paul in his trial, but that also he regards as ultimately the working of God.

as a metaphysical reality, a sharing in the Divine life which for him is primarily love and holiness. The best illustration of the meaning of the idea for Paul occurs in Romans v. 8-10: "God proves his own love towards us because while we were still sinners Christ died for us. Much more, therefore, having been justified now by his blood, we shall be saved from the wrath [the final eschatological reaction of the Divine nature against sin] through him. For if when we were enemies we were reconciled to God by the death of his Son, much more, having been reconciled, we shall be saved by his life." The atmosphere of σωτηρία in Paul is the love of God revealed to men in the Cross of Jesus Christ. Everything in it goes back to that. And this background reveals the essential difference between it and the σωτηρία of the Mystery-Religions. Further, σωτηρία, in Paul's usage, is from the very nature of the case charged with moral implications. The mercy of God in Christ lays claims upon men. They are under obligation (ὀφειλέται) "not to live according to the flesh" (Rom. viii. 12). "The love of Christ constrains us . . . that they who live should live no longer to themselves, but to him who died

OF THE MYSTERY-RELIGIONS 219

for them and was raised" (2 Cor. v. 14, 15). Here again we move among a different group of ideas from those of the Mystery-Religions. We are far from denying all moral influence to initiation. There is at least some evidence to the contrary. But, as we have seen, there was no necessary connection between the mystical experiences and a changed ethical standard. A further point must be emphasised. In Romans i. 16, Paul declares that his Gospel, the good news of God's forgiveness in Christ the crucified, is "the power of God resulting in salvation for every one that believes". Salvation is given to faith. And faith for Paul means personal surrender to the "Son of God who loved me and gave himself for me" (Gal. ii. 20).

How, then, does Paul conceive this salvation to be mediated to the believer? His words in Romans v. 5 are decisive: "Our hope [*i.e.*, of the final salvation, which he has described as ἡ δόξα τοῦ θεοῦ] cannot put us to shame, because the love of God has been poured out in our hearts through the Holy Spirit which has been given to us". Another way of expressing the same fact occurs in Romans viii. 16: "The Spirit himself bears witness with our spirit that we are children of God". The gift of the Spirit is the Divine response to faith.[1]

Here we are brought into the heart of Paul's conception of the New Life. For him, as for the Mystery-Religions, regeneration is intimately related to communion with the Divine. He does not happen to use the term ἀναγεννᾶσθαι (or cognates). But there is scarcely even a difference of metaphor in his affirmation: "If any one is in Christ, he is a new creation (καινὴ κτίσις): old things have passed away, behold, new things have come into being" (2 Cor. v. 17; similarly, Gal. vi. 15, "Neither circumcision is of any value nor uncircumcision but a new creation"). But before we look briefly at Paul's idea of communion with Christ, it must be noted how this, like everything else in the sphere of salvation, stands out against the background of the Cross. The words we have just quoted rest on the judgment that "one died for all" (ver. 14). And the very next affirmation is: "Now all this

---

[1] *Cf.* Weinel, *Biblische Theologie d. N.T.*, p. 318: "We can see clearly that this doctrine of the Spirit and of Christ in the believer is not mere theory, not an imitation of Mystery-doctrine, but inmost personal experience metaphysically interpreted after the manner of his time".

comes from God who reconciled us to himself through Christ" (ver. 18). So that in Paul we dare not isolate the thought of communion with Christ from the demonstration of the Divine Love in the Crucified. The significance of the living Lord for the Apostle lies in the fact that this is He who loved men and gave Himself for them. Dr. Denney does strict justice to Paul's standpoint when he says that for him Christianity "consists, first and last, of experiences generated in the believer by the Cross. . . . Whatever it may be proper to say of the Holy Spirit, or of union to Christ, or incorporation in Him, must be said on the basis of such experiences and within their limits."[1] This reveals at a glance the impassable cleft between Paul and the Mystery-Religions in their central experiences.

It is almost needless to say that Paul's most characteristic description of the believer's relation to Christ is ἐν Χριστῷ εἶναι. It is really only a variant expression when he speaks of Χριστὸς ἐν ἡμῖν. And often a distinction can scarcely be drawn between this and τὸ πνεῦμα ἐν ἡμῖν. The phrase is sufficiently indefinite to

[1] *Expositor*, vi., 4, pp. 310, 311.

permit a large freedom of interpretation. Not to speak of the purely sensuous explanation of Dieterich,[1] or Heitmüller's elusive designation of the relation as "physical-hyperphysical,"[2] it seems to us precarious to go even as far as Deissmann has gone in emphasising the "local" element in the thought.[3] The Apostle is surely using the language dear to mystics of all ages, which transcends spatial categories. The key to the meaning of the phrase is found in some of Paul's most passionate words, *e.g.*, Galatians ii. 20: "No longer do I live, but Christ lives in me: as for the life I now live in the flesh, I live by faith, faith in the Son of God who loved me"; and Philippians iii. 8 f.: "Christ Jesus my Lord, for whom I suffered the loss of all things, and do count them but refuse that I may win Christ and be found in him, not having a righteousness of my own, that which is from the law, but that which is through faith in Christ, the righteousness which is from God on

[1] *Op. cit.*, pp. 109, 110.

[2] *Taufe und Abendmahl bei Paulus*, p. 20.

[3] "Dwelling in a pneuma-element which may be compared to the air" (*Die neutestamentliche Formel "in Christo Jesu,"* p. 98).

the ground of faith". These passages, and many others which might be adduced, make it clear that Faith, in Paul's far-reaching sense of a personal surrender of the life, is the proper basis of this unspeakably intimate relation of the soul to Christ.[1] In the Mystery-Religions there is no conception which can be compared with this.[2] Not only so; it recalls the thoroughly ethical character of Paul's mysticism. This is no vague absorption in the suprasensible Reality. It is a personal relationship established by adoring trust in and devotion to Him in whom Paul has reached the possibility of a life which shall be "right" with God. The passage we have just quoted from Philippians is a striking testimony to that aspect of his religion.[3]

[1] So also Pfleiderer, in the *first* edition of his *Paulinism*, E. Tr., i., p. 199. In our judgment, Pfleiderer shows a much surer insight into Paul's thought in this early work than in any of his later writings.

[2] Reitzenstein's brief note on the Hellenistic conception of πίστις (*H.M.R.*, p. 85) does little more than reveal its meagreness.

[3] But Paul's mysticism seems to mean something more than "a relation of ethical harmony," in which Prof. Pringle-Pattison finds the real truth of the mystical ex-

We do not require to dwell on the assertion, often made, that Paul's is a Christ-mysticism rather than a God-mysticism. The distinction must count for little in view of a statement like Colossians iii. 3: "Your life is hid with Christ in God". Of more importance is the relation of the Spirit to this experience. As we have seen, the Apostle seems here and there at least to use Christ and the Spirit as synonyms. The most notable case is 2 Corinthians iii. 17: "Now the Lord is the Spirit: and where the Spirit of the Lord is, there is liberty". Perhaps the most direct application of this idea to our subject is 1 Corinthians vi. 17: "He that is joined (κολλώμενος) to the Lord is one spirit". But in this aspect also, the moral implications of the mystic fellowship are made prominent: the "life" and "power" which are the tokens of the Spirit's presence are essentially ethical. Possession of the Spirit means the free, unhampered relation of the child to the Father, *e.g.*, Romans viii. 15: "You did not receive the spirit of bondage again resulting in fear [the characteristic of their religious experience as pagans],

perience (art. "Mysticism," *Encyc. Brit.*, ed. 9, vol. xvii., p. 129).

but you received the spirit of adoption by which we cry, Abba, Father" (*cf.* Galatians iv. 6). That relationship by its very *raison d'être* forbids any compromise with evil; Galatians v. 16-24 is decisive: "Walk by the Spirit and you shall not fulfil the lusts of the flesh," etc. In this connection Paul lets us see clearly what he means by "life"; *e.g.*, Romans viii. 13: "If you by the Spirit put to death the deeds of the body (= "the works of the flesh," Gal. v. 19), you shall live". These positions once more reveal the difference of atmosphere between Paul and the Mystery-cults.

It is in this light that we must briefly examine his statements regarding death and resurrection with Christ, on which so much stress has been laid by those who find in Paul the direct influence of Mystery-conceptions. The passages usually selected to establish this influence are those which speak of "being baptised into the death of Christ," or, "being buried with him in baptism". There are, however, only two which are really relevant: Romans vi. 3, 4, and Colossians ii. 12. We must consider these, along with 1 Corinthians xii. 13, and Galatians iii. 27, which are closely akin to them, in our next chapter on Baptismal Rites. But the great bulk of Paul's utterances concerning death with Christ have no reference whatever to baptism. Thoroughly typical is Galatians ii. 19: "I through the law died to the law that I might live to God. I have been crucified with Christ." The same conception appears in Romans vii. 4: "You also were made dead to the law through the body of Christ". So also Romans vi. 6: "Knowing this, that our old man was crucified with him that the body of sin might be done away, that so we should no longer be in bondage to sin";[1] and Galatians vi. 14: "God forbid that I should glory save in the cross of our Lord Jesus Christ, through which (or, whom) the world has been crucified unto me, and I unto the world". The thought occurs with different expression in Colossians i. 21, 22: "You, being in time past alienated and enemies in your mind in your evil works yet now hath he reconciled in the body of his flesh through death, to present you holy and without blemish". Colossians ii. 20 is also important: "If you died with Christ from the elements ($\sigma\tau o\iota\chi\epsilon\hat{\iota}a$) of the world, why, as

[1] This passage is quite independent of the reference to baptism which occurs earlier in the chapter.

though living in the world, do you subject yourselves to ordinances?" We do not, of course, deny the connection between this passage and the reference to baptism in ii. 12. But its true explanation is found in ii. 14, 15: "Having blotted out the bond written in ordinances that was against us . . . and he hath taken it out of the way, nailing it to the cross, having despoiled (or stripped off himself) the principalities and the powers". Whatever be the significance of baptism for Paul, the conspectus of passages before us plainly shows that when he speaks of the believer as "dying with Christ," he has the quite definite idea of identification with the relation toward sin of the crucified Redeemer, the identification which he sums up in the memorable words of Philippians iii. 10, συμμορφιζόμενος τῷ θανάτῳ αὐτοῦ. There is not a suggestion of baptism in the whole context of the verse. The correlative to this idea is, of course, living with Christ, rising with Christ, or (as in Philippians iii. 10), "knowing the power of his resurrection".

Now, so far as we can judge, the central Pauline conception which we have just examined has no real equivalent in the Mystery-

Religions. Even if we ventured to assert, with some scholars, on the basis of the very meagre extant evidence, that the initiates in the mystic cults regarded themselves as having died with the Divine persons whose restoration to life they celebrated, it is perfectly obvious that the death of which Paul speaks is something wholly different. It is exclusively a death to sin, and its correlative is a life to holiness in the most ethical sense conceivable. The ceremonial dedication to a deity whose ritual, based on the revival of life in the world of nature, suggests the soul-kindling prospect of a life beyond the grave, could very naturally be described as a dying to the ignorant past, and the entrance on a new life of hope. But it requires an unusually daring imagination to fill these terms in the Mystery-cults with the profound ethical content which they held for St. Paul. We admit a certain kinship in the imagery, but this imagery has been the common property of mystics and philosophers and preachers throughout the ages.

CHAPTER VI

BAPTISMAL RITES

RITES of purification were common to all ancient religions. One of the best-known features in the Eleusinian Mysteries was the bath of cleansing in the sea (ἅλαδε μύσται). The Orphic rule of life was based on an elaborate cathartic ritual. In the account of the initiation of Lucius into the Mysteries of Isis (Apul., *Metamorph.*, xi., 20), an ablution precedes the central rites. Part of this ceremony consisted in sprinkling the neophyte. The ritual of sprinkling was apparently current in Egypt. A similar ceremonial is mentioned in Livy's description of the Bacchanalia. No doubt the idea of regeneration was associated with these lustrations, as, indeed, Tertullian (*De Bapt.*, 5) distinctly affirms. But our knowledge of the baptismal rites of the Mystery-Religions is meagre in the extreme. One or two significant facts may be noted. No trace remains of the baptism of the initiated "into the name" of any of the Mystery-deities, although the cult-action may have formed part of a definite acknowledgment of the deity in question. Nor is there any hint that the influence of the Divine πνεῦμα, a feature which we have seen to be current in mystic doctrine, was ever connected with the ritual of lustration. Lietzmann, Heitmüller, and others have laid strong emphasis on the fact that Paul links the rite of baptism to the experience of death and resurrection with Christ, and would refer the connection to the hints of a dying to live which they profess to find in the Mystery-cults.[1] We have already examined the evidence in detail, and have noted its scantiness. And we have endeavoured to show that the background and atmosphere of the Pauline conceptions of death and resurrection with Christ are so incongruous with the Mystery-ritual as to rob of their validity any parallels which may be adduced. The ceremony of the *taurobolium*, by far the most striking analogy that can be cited, we found, on the authority of experts like Cumont and Hepding, to be inadmissible as evidence for our period. We must deal with Paul's view of Baptism in detail. It may be noted that one

[1] See Lietzmann's excursus, *Römerbrief*, pp. 30, 31.

BAPTISMAL RITES 231

remarkable passage has been found in a Paris Papyrus (No. 47), in which it is possible to connect ἀποθανεῖν directly with βαπτίζεσθαι. The words occur in a letter from Apollonius, a novice in the temple of Serapis at Memphis, to his spiritual director Ptolemæus. He reproaches Ptolemæus and the gods for delaying his full initiation, and apparently quotes some expressions that Ptolemæus had used in reference to a warning dream which had come to him. The closing words of the quotation are : καὶ οὐ δυνάμεθα ἀποθανεῖν, κἂν ἴδῃς ὅτι μέλλομεν σωθῆναι, τότε βαπτιζώμεθα. The mingling of Ptolemæus' words with the writer's own has made the sentence read clumsily. In *Die hellenistischen Mysterienreligionen*,[1] Reitzenstein interpreted "we cannot die" of Ptolemæus' warning that death is the penalty of premature initiation. Then Apollonius speaks in person : "If you see [*i.e.*, in a dream] that we are destined to attain salvation, then we may proceed to baptism". Reitzenstein pointed out the exact parallel between this and the experience of Lucius at Cenchreæ. There his spiritual father, Mithras, informs Lucius that death is the punishment for those who go

[1] Pp. 77 f.

forward to initiation without the call of the goddess. When he has seen in a dream that salvation is destined for Lucius, he admits him to initiation, of which baptism is a preliminary stage. Now,[1] however, Reitzenstein takes ἀποθανεῖν as synonymous with βαπτιζώμεθα, admitting, indeed, that this is the only trace of such a conception of baptism in Hellenism, and illustrating the idea from Herodotus' account of the sacred honours paid to the bodies of those drowned in the Nile. His earlier interpretation appears to us far more probable from the whole character of the passage and the striking parallels which can be adduced from the Isis-Mysteries. In any case, it is obvious that the later hypothesis rests on the slenderest of foundations. Reitzenstein himself allows that the words cannot be explained with any certainty.[2]

Prof. Lake, in his recent *Earlier Epistles of St. Paul*, holding that the average Gentile

[1] *Zeitschr. f. N.T. Wiss.*, 1912, 1, p. 9 f.

[2] The passage is interpreted on totally different lines by Prof. Milligan in his *Greek Papyri*, p. 22. He translates βαπτιζώμεθα by "immersed in trouble". But Reitzenstein's rendering seems more intelligible for the context as a whole.

Godfearer regarded the Christianity presented to him by Paul and his fellow-workers as a Mystery-Religion, goes the length of attributing the antinomianism which the Apostle has to combat to the Gentile-Christian's view of baptism "as an *opus operatum* which secured his admission into the Kingdom apart from the character of his future conduct,"[1] and he credits Paul himself with a similar magical conception.[2] Now as to the nature of the antinomianism which caused the great missionary such sore anxiety, we have his own testimony, and it takes a wholly different direction from Prof. Lake's hypothesis. Thus, in Romans iii. 5-8, the antinomian argues for his own unrighteousness that it "commends the righteousness of God": the truth of God, through his falsehood, redounds to the Divine glory. His watchword is: "Let us do evil that good may come," and his whole position is summed up in Romans vi. 1: "Shall we remain in sin *in order that grace may abound?*" What Paul means by grace is perfectly clear from the discussion in chapter v. It is certainly not baptism, but the forgiveness of sins through faith in Christ Jesus. And the tendency of the

[1] *Op. cit.*, p. 46.   [2] *Ibid.*, p. 385.

antinomian is to take advantage of the mercy of God, because it is utterly inexhaustible. We believe that Prof. Lake is equally wide of the mark in asserting that, for Paul, baptism was "a mystery or sacrament which works *ex opere operato*". And we must now investigate the available data.

We venture to think that one of the chief impressions left upon the careful reader of the Epistles must be that of the Apostle's detachment from ritual in every shape and form. If "sacramental teaching is central in the primitive Christianity to which the Roman Empire began to be converted,"[1] it is certainly astonishing to find such scanty references to it in letters, some of the most important of which were addressed to Christian communities which Paul had never visited. It is absurd to suggest that the reason for this silence lies in the fact that "Baptism and its significance was common ground to him and all other Christians".[2] This is not in accord with Paul's practice. His delight is to come back again and again to all the crucial elements in his own religious experience, an experience which was fundamental in shaping his

---

[1] Lake, *op. cit.*, p. 385.   [2] *Op. cit.*, p. 384.

BAPTISMAL RITES 235

doctrine. Hence we are in no way surprised to find that in his first Epistle to the Christians at Corinth, a community whose "main feature," according to Prof. Lake, was that "they all accepted Christianity as a Mystery-Religion," and regarded Jesus as "the Redeemer-God, who had passed through death to life, and offered participation in this new life to those who shared in the mysteries [Baptism and the Eucharist] which He offered,"[1] Paul thanks God that he had only baptised a few of them. "For," he declares, "Christ sent me not to baptise, but to preach the Gospel, and that not with wisdom of words, so that the cross of Christ might not be annulled" (1 Cor. i. 17). It is "the word of the cross" which is "the power of God to those who are being saved" (1 Cor. i. 18), not a "mystery" of Baptism or anything else. Prof. Lake attaches high importance to 1 Corinthians x. 1 ff., where Paul compares the experiences of Israel in the wilderness to Baptism and the Lord's Supper, as indicating their central importance for Christianity at Corinth.[2] We must examine the passage carefully in our next chapter on Sacramental Meals. We may remark, how-

[1] *Op. cit.*, p. 233.   [2] *Ibid.*, p. 233, note 1.

ever, at this point, that the analogy chiefly reminds us of the allegorical fancies of Philo. It occurs in a context dealing with sacrificial meals, so that it lay ready to hand. It certainly cannot sustain the weight of the argument which Prof. Lake has built upon it, that "it is a warning against the view that Christians are safe because they have been initiated into the Christian mysteries".[1] For it is a sheer begging of the question to assume that Paul associates with the actual food some supernatural nourishment. He merely interprets it, quasi-allegorically, as spiritual fare, in the sense of being a special Divine gift, belonging to a history which is supernaturally ordered. The curious statement that "all were baptised into Moses" tells against the magical significance which Lake and others read into the Pauline idea of baptism, for we cannot conceive the implication of some mystic relationship established between the people and Moses by these events in their history. "All that can properly be asserted is that, as the crossing of the Red Sea definitely committed the people to follow Moses as their divinely appointed head, so baptism is a definite committal and consecra-

[1] *Op. cit.*, p. 177 f.

BAPTISMAL RITES

tion to the following of Christ."[1] And we agree with the writer just quoted that the whole point of Paul's argument lies in the uselessness of sacraments apart from that ethical obedience to which believers have pledged themselves in these sacred ordinances.

Accordingly, it is a true instinct for facts which leads Weinel, in spite of his emphasis on the Mystery-element in Paul's religion, to the somewhat exaggerated assertion that "for Paul the sacrament was an alien body," and he very suggestively notes that in the entire Epistle to the Romans, "that document in which he sets forth and defends his own conception of Christianity, only once does baptism enter his mind (vi. 3 ff.), and the Lord's Supper not even once".[2] Similarly Holtzmann, from the same general standpoint, finds an irreducible contradiction between the mysterious virtue of the sacrament of baptism in Paul and his conception of the life-giving Spirit with its free activities, bound to no action which can be assigned to a given point of time.[3] And Heitmüller can only account for the incongruity

---

[1] Lambert, *The Sacraments in the New Testament*, p. 159.
[2] *Biblische Theologie d. N.T.*, p. 330.
[3] *N.T. Theologie*,[2] ii., p. 198.

by explaining that Paul had not himself instituted the sacrament of baptism but found it already existing in the Christian society.[1] Yet while we are far from confining the outlook of any great thinker within the bounds of a rigid logic, this theory of glaring contradictions in his mind is always apt to make us suspect the legitimacy of crediting him with the positions on which the judgment is based. It is so easy to isolate a conception from the general context of his thinking, and thus to lay the emphasis on the wrong elements. Let us try to estimate Baptism in its relations to those features which Paul seems to regard as fundamental in Christian experience.

It will be universally admitted that for St. Paul, possession of the Spirit is the indispensable condition of the Christian life, *e.g.*, Romans viii. 9 : "If any one have not the Spirit of Christ, he does not belong to him". Again and again throughout the Epistles he refers to this experience as crucial. Now if, as Lake and Heitmüller suppose, he regarded the baptismal rite as the actual vehicle by which salvation was conveyed to the Christian, it would seem inevitable

[1] *Taufe und Abendmahl bei Paulus*, 1903, p. 23.

BAPTISMAL RITES

that it should be given a prominent place in his many references to the gift of the Spirit. As a matter of fact, there is only one passage in which they are brought into close connection (1 Cor. xii. 13), and it occurs quite incidentally in his discussion of diversities of spiritual gifts. "For as the body is one and has many members, but all the members of the body, although many, are one body, so also is Christ. For by (or in) one Spirit we were all baptised into one body, whether Jews or Greeks. . . . And we were all made to drink of one Spirit." The emphasis here is placed on the one community into which they were admitted on being baptised. The unity of Christians is the idea which stands before his mind. Baptism is a visible pledge of this unity in Christ. It has for Paul, as Holtzmann says, "social significance".[1] It is of course, as we shall presently see, something more than a mere symbol. And probably the difficult phrase, πάντες ἓν πνεῦμα ἐποτίσθημεν, does refer to the spiritual experiences associated with baptism. If we interpret the vague expression, ἐν ἑνὶ πνεύματι, in the light of its context, it seems most natural to explain it by means of verse 11: "all these (the

[1] *N.T. Theologie*,[2] ii., p. 199.

various gifts) are wrought by one and the same Spirit, distributing to each separately according to his will". That is to say, the Spirit is regarded as active in the ordinance of baptism. But there is no suggestion of the "unmediated and naked sacramental conception," which some scholars attribute to the Apostle.[1]

When Paul speaks of the reception of the Spirit, he is in the habit of connecting it with a quite definite group of experiences. Particularly instructive is Galatians iii. 2, where this is the very question at issue: "Did you receive the Spirit as the result of keeping law, or was it the consequence of the hearing of faith?" The compressed phrase is elaborated in Romans x. 17: "So then faith comes from hearing, and hearing through the word of Christ". Similar in tenor is Ephesians i. 13: "in whom [Christ] you also, having heard the word of truth, the gospel of your salvation,—in whom, having also believed, you were sealed with the Holy Spirit of promise". We doubt whether there is any reference to baptism in the word ἐσφραγίσθητε. But if there were, it is obviously not the experience of regeneration

---

[1] See a peculiarly crass statement in Schweitzer, *Geschichte d. Paulin. Forschung*, p. 166.

which is referred to, but the joyful assurance of the new status in Christ Jesus. In 1 Corinthians ii. 4, 5, he emphasises the manifestation of the power of the Spirit which accompanied his preaching as contrasted with that lack of σοφία for which some of the Corinthians censured him, "that your faith might rest not on the wisdom of men but on the power of God". Again, in 1 Thessalonians ii. 13, he associates the Divine working in those that believe with their willing reception of his message. And in the remarkable words of 1 Corinthians iv. 15 ("In Christ Jesus I begat you through the Gospel") he directly attributes their new life to the power of Christ operating in the Gospel.

If we turn to his profound conception of fellowship with Christ, we find ourselves in the same atmosphere. There are indeed one or two important passages in which Baptism appears as a primary element in the experience. These we shall examine immediately. Meanwhile, it is worth noting that the clearest affirmation of communion with the risen Lord which ever fell from Paul's lips gives the same prominence to *faith* as do his statements on the Spirit. "I through the law died to the law that I might live unto God. I have been crucified with Christ, and no longer do I live, but Christ lives in me. And the life which I now live in the flesh, I live by faith, faith in the Son of God who loved me and gave himself for me " (Gal. ii. 19, 20). But this passage is also of importance as showing that death with Christ, which Lietzmann, Heitmüller, and others identify with the baptismal experience, is something quite independent of that.

Here we enter the province of Paul's thought in which justification, forgiveness of sins, and the cross of Christ are the ruling ideas. And we venture to say, in flat contradiction of Heitmüller,[1] that these, and not " effects of a mystic-enthusiastic nature," are " the foci of Pauline piety ". It is needless to quote passages which prove that the new life, which means for Paul a right relation to God, is reached along the pathway of faith in Christ crucified and risen as the demonstration of the holy love of God in its bearing on sinful men. Romans v. 1 is typical: " Therefore, having been justified by faith, we have peace with God through our Lord Jesus Christ, through whom also we have obtained access into that grace in which we stand ".

[1] *Op. cit.*, p. 14.

Everything fundamental for salvation is to be found there. But Paul's conception of union with Christ, which is supposed, by Heitmüller for example, to belong to the "physical-hyperphysical" atmosphere of baptism, turns out to be embedded in the stratum of thought which we are examining ; see, *e.g.*, Philippians iii. 9 ff. : "That I may win Christ and be found in him, not having mine own righteousness which is of the law, but that which is through faith in Christ, the righteousness which is of God on account of ($\epsilon\pi\iota$) faith". To be in Christ, that is to say, is for Paul virtually identical with "having the righteousness of God," *i.e.*, being justified, forgiven. Plainly, therefore, the central experiences of the Christian life are for the Apostle primarily associated with faith. Now the first of these central experiences is the breaking off of relations with sin. Paul frequently relates it to fellowship with the death of Christ. "You died to the law [the régime in which sin is active] through the body of Christ" (Rom. vii. 4). This is expanded in Romans vi. 10 ff. : "In that he died, to sin he died once for all : but in that he lives, he lives unto God. So also do you reckon yourselves to be dead to sin but alive to God in

Christ Jesus." And the meaning is elucidated by Colossians ii. 11 : "In whom you also were circumcised with the circumcision not made with hands in the stripping off of the body of flesh, in the circumcision of Christ". This inward circumcision means union with Him who on the cross abjured the flesh and all its implications. Obviously the metaphor is the same as that in Romans ii. 29 ($\pi\epsilon\rho\iota\tau o\mu\grave{\eta}$ $\kappa\alpha\rho\delta\iota\alpha s$), and it seems impossible to identify it with baptism, because it is deliberately described as "not made with hands". But here and in a few other places, Paul brings baptism into connection with this death to sin, the distinctly Christian attitude. What does the connection mean ?

Prof. Lake has no difficulty in reaching a conclusion. "The Pauline doctrine of Baptism," he says, "is that on the positive side it gives the Christian union with Christ, which may also be described as inspiration with the Holy Spirit, while on the negative side it cleanses from sin. This is accomplished by the power of the name of the Lord Jesus Christ, and by the sacramental effect of water, according to the well-known idea that results could be reached in the unseen spiritual world by the performance of analogous acts in the visible

BAPTISMAL RITES 245

material world."[1] This explanation (which is also that of Heitmüller) stands in manifest antagonism to Paul's unvarying emphasis upon faith as the primary factor in salvation, on the human side. Indeed Heitmüller asserts that it is not easy to see "that, or how far, faith can play a really essential part in the process,"[2] an admission which, in the light of the Epistles, seems to us little less than a *reductio ad absurdum* of his hypothesis.[3] Let us briefly examine the crucial passages.

Of fundamental importance is Romans vi. 1 ff. : " What shall we then say ? Shall we continue in sin that grace may abound ? God forbid. We who died to sin, how shall we continue to live in it ? Or are you ignorant that all we who were baptised into Jesus Christ were baptised into his death ? We were buried, therefore, with him through our baptism into his death, that, as Christ was raised from the dead by the glory of the Father, so we also might walk in newness of life." The passage can only be rightly understood from the argument which leads up to it.

[1] *Encyclopædia of Religion and Ethics*, vol. ii., p. 382.
[2] *Op. cit.*, p. 22.
[3] See an admirable paragraph by Wernle in *Zeitschr. f. Theol. u. Kirche*, 1912, 6, pp. 339, 340.

In chapter v. Paul has shown that faith, as linking the believer to Christ, has brought him into the sphere of those high privileges which he enjoys, experience of the Divine grace, hope, the love of God, the gift of the Holy Spirit. Can a faith of this kind be accused of being a solvent of right conduct? Nay, everything belonging to justification involves a break with sin. Hence he states in verse 2 the basal principle of the Christian life, "we who died to sin". And then he proceeds to show that entrance into the Christian society accentuates and embodies the same principle. Baptism, the deliberate, decisive step which a man takes when he has surrendered his life to Christ, is not something vague or nebulous. It realises the meaning of Christ for the soul. The Christ into whose name the believer is baptised, that is, whose possession he becomes, is the Christ who was crucified, and who, in dying, made an end of sin both for His own person and for all who are united to Him by faith. And the very symbolism of the rite is an impressive picture of the believer's experiences. His disappearance beneath the water is a vivid illustration of his separation from the old life of sin. It is a burial of the old existence, just as Christ's burial was a palpable proof that He had left all earthly conditions behind Him. Emergence from the baptismal water typifies entrance into a new environment, the life of the Christian society which is the life of the living Lord Himself, mediated to His followers by their fellowship with Him.

The real significance of this new life in Christ is made clear by the remarkable words of Colossians ii. 13 (which belong to a baptismal context): "You who were dead by reason of your transgressions and the uncircumcision of your flesh he (*i.e.*, God) made alive with him (*i.e.*, Christ), having forgiven us all our transgressions". Forgiveness is the presupposition of newness of life. But the Romans-passage is evidence that there is something more than symbolism in the baptismal celebration. There is indeed no suggestion that the pronunciation of the "name" of the Lord Jesus Christ, " if properly used, could enable the user to enjoy the benefits of the attributes attached to the owner of the name ".[1] Nor is there any indication whatever of "the sacramental effect of water". But a comparison with baptism on the mission field to-day helps us to

[1] So Lake, *Encyclopædia of Religion and Ethics*, ii., p. 382.

realise a situation with which Paul the missionary was quite familiar. Whether in the early Church, as Lambert holds, "there was no such thing . . . as a prolonged probation of the convert . . . but faith and baptism were connected with each other immediately,"[1] or whether, as we believe must frequently have happened, there intervened a period of instruction,[2] baptism must have meant a decision of momentous importance for the convert. Now, for the first time, he deliberately affirmed his allegiance to Christ before the world, and solemnly identified himself with the Christian brotherhood. This was the actual spiritual crisis in which he turned his back upon his old associations, faced all manner of costly sacrifices, and committed himself, in utter dependence on the Divine grace and power, to a new mode of live. Rendtorff is fully justified in saying that an act which thus liberated the most powerful ethical motives "became a religious experience of the first rank".[3] In

[1] *The Sacraments in the N.T.*, p. 172.

[2] So also Harnack, *Mission and Expansion of Christianity* (Eng. Tr.), i., p. 391.

[3] *Die Taufe im Urchristentum*, p. 32.

baptism (of course, adult) something happened. Faith had been there before, receptiveness toward the good news of Christ. The Divine Spirit had been already present, taking of the things of Christ and showing them to the believer. But now, once for all, the convert makes his own the movings of the Divine love in his heart. And thus there would come to him in his baptism a wonderful spiritual quickening, a new enhancing of the power and grasp of faith, a fresh realisation of communion with the once crucified and now risen Lord. Hence there is good ground for the statement of Von Dobschütz that "according to the early Christian view we may speak of real effects of baptism in the sense that here the person does not give himself something by his activity, but God gives him what he has only to receive".[1]

What is true of the Romans-passage holds good also for the rest. "Ye are all sons of God," he declares in Galatians iii. 26, "through faith in Christ Jesus. For all of you who were baptized into Christ put on Christ." Does this mean that their faith is due to baptism? Obviously not,

[1] See his most valuable article, "Sacrament und Symbol im Urchristentum," in *Studien u. Kritiken*, 1905, i., p. 20.

for this Epistle is as emphatic as Romans in regarding faith as the first stage in the relation of the soul to Christ. The Apostle's words can only signify that in the solemn act of baptism this faith is re-charged with spiritual energy and indeed reaches its crowning expression. In such a crisis, therefore, it may be expected to achieve great things. And chief among its results will be an intensified consciousness of intimate fellowship with Christ, a fellowship which is here compared to the putting-on of a garment. Paul's special object on this occasion is to set forth the spiritual unity which springs from faith. And baptism is the sacrament in which that unity becomes visible.[1]

A similar view appears in the difficult passage, Colossians ii. 11, 12 : " In whom [Christ] you also were circumcised with a circumcision not made with hands in the stripping off of the body of flesh, in the circumcision of Christ, having been buried with him in baptism, in which (or in whom) you were also raised up through faith in the working of God, who raised him from the dead ". Here, as we have already noted, it seems

[1] See a suggestive paragraph in Lambert, *op. cit.*, p. 153, and *cf*. the close parallel in Ephesians iv. 4-6.

impossible to identify the "circumcision not made with hands" with the rite of baptism. This is an inward experience, that profound fellowship with Christ crucified (Gal. ii. 20 ; Rom. vi. 6), that conformity to His death (Phil. iii. 10), which means the doing away of "the body of sin". The new life which it involves he associates directly, in verse 13, with the forgiveness of sins. But when he speaks of those who have undergone this change as "buried with Christ in baptism," he doubtless has in view, as in Romans vi. 1 ff., on the one hand the symbolism of the solemn rite as showing forth the completion of the process, and on the other the real recognition and assurance of the new life, which are quickened in the soul by the baptismal experience. It is highly significant that he immediately postulates the presence of faith as the psychological medium of the life of Christ in which they participate.[1]

In Ephesians v. 26 Paul speaks of Christ as "having purified the church by the bath of water with the word". The language used has an obvious reference to the lustration of the bride

[1] See Lueken's admirable notes *ad loc.* (in *Die Schriften d. N.T.*, ed. J. Weiss).

before marriage.[1] The notion of a baptism of the ἐκκλησία is plainly metaphorical. The most notable feature in the passage is the phrase ἐν ῥήματι, which no doubt must be interpreted, as in Romans x. 8, 17, of the proclamation of the Gospel. This accords with the place given to faith in the other passages on baptism which we have examined.

There remain for consideration two references in 1 Corinthians. In chapter vi. Paul has been upbraiding his converts for going to law with their brethren before courts presided over by unrighteous men, who can have no share in the Kingdom of God. After enumerating glaring forms of unrighteousness he bursts forth (ver. 11): "and such were some of you: but you had yourselves cleansed, you were sanctified, you were justified in the name of the Lord Jesus Christ and by the Spirit of our God". Not much can be based on so incidental an allusion. But probably Lambert is right in holding that the use of the middle here (ἀπελούσασθε) is intended "to remind them of the way in which at baptism they had consciously and deliberately separated themselves from the sinful

---

[1] Note the technical expression παραστήσῃ (ver. 27), and see Von Soden *ad loc.* (in Holtzmann's *Hand-Commentar*).

world in which they previously lived, and joined themselves to that fellowship of the holy which was theirs by right, inasmuch as their baptism, precisely because they were believers, was the baptism of men . . . already sanctified in principle and justified in fact ".[1]

Heitmüller and others have made much of 1 Corinthians xv. 29 as evidence for a crass form of sacramentalism approved by Paul. "Otherwise (*i.e.*, if there be no resurrection) what shall they do who are baptised on behalf of the dead ?" This curious reference occurs in a most varied series of arguments for the resurrection. The practice must undoubtedly have existed in certain communities. No clear analogies have been detected in the Mystery-cults, though it is quite probable that it had its origin in these.[2] But it is wholly illegitimate to suppose that because Paul pronounces no condemnation on a custom to which he refers, he must have given it his approval. This is surely a misapprehension of the very nature of an *argumentum ad hominem*. And there is force in Von Dobschütz's suggestion that

[1] *Op. cit.*, p. 157.

[2] The parallels given by Rendtorff, *op. cit.*, p. 33, note 1, are far from convincing.

the superstition belonged to the circle of the "sceptical" at Corinth, as "lack of faith and superstition come of the same lineage".[1]

We may conclude with a brief summary. Our material for estimating the significance of baptismal rites in the Mystery-Religions is far too meagre to admit of dogmatic conclusions. But it is highly probable that they were conceived as working *ex opere operato*. An examination of Paul's references to baptism does not suggest that in it we have a second principle of salvation, and that "the conception of justification and the forgiveness of sins are connected with baptism only in a quite cursory fashion".[2] On the contrary, the faith which welcomes the Divine message of forgiveness and new life in Christ crucified and risen is invariably presupposed as the background of the solemn ritual. It is in virtue of their faith that converts proceed to baptism. But the ordinance is far more than a symbol of spiritual processes. It is a sacrament, that is, as Prof. Bartlet admirably defines it, " a symbol conditioning a present deeper and decisive experience of the Divine grace, already

[1] *Loc. cit.*, p. 37.
[2] So Heitmüller, *op. cit.*, p. 14.

embraced by faith. But all is psychologically conditioned, being thereby raised above the level of the magical or quasi-physical conception of sacramental grace."[1]

[1] *Encyclopædia of Religion and Ethics*, vol. ii., p. 377.

CHAPTER VII

SACRAMENTAL MEALS

The evidence regarding Sacramental Meals in the Mystery-Religions is both meagre and difficult to interpret. Conclusions have been drawn from one or two mystic formulæ which go beyond the data. Thus, *e.g.*, the Eleusinian fragment preserved by Clement of Alexandria:[1] "I fasted, I drank the κυκεών," has been explained of a sacrament in which the initiated drank of the same cup as the goddess Demeter in her sorrow. This is indeed an attractive hypothesis, but it can be nothing more. A similar explanation has been given of the formula handed down by Firmicus Maternus[2] and (with variations) by Clement:[3] "I have eaten out of the τύμπανον, I have drunk out of the κύμβαλον, I have become an initiate of Attis". It is quite possible that

---

[1] Ed. Stählin, i., p. 16, 18.
[2] Ed. Ziegler, p. 43, 17.   [3] i., p. 13, 10.

SACRAMENTAL MEALS

these ritual actions may have been the symbols of the bestowal of new life, but there is no hint of how they became sacramental. Attempts have been made to find a sacramental significance in the Dionysiac-Orphic cults, but even Dieterich admits that our knowledge of the facts is altogether inadequate [1] for constructing any hypothesis, although he himself attempts a construction on the basis of a fragment from the Κρῆτες of Euripides: "lengthening out a life of purity from the day that I became an initiate of Idaean Zeus and a herdsman of night-roaming Zagreus, a celebrant of the meal of raw flesh".[2] This obviously refers to the ancient Dionysiac orgies in which the frenzied votaries of the god flung themselves on the sacrificial victim and devoured it raw. There are occasional hints of the idea that the victim was identified with the god himself. But the usage belongs to a different epoch from that with which we are concerned. Nevertheless, in the search of parallels to Christian usage, various scholars, notably Dieterich and Heitmüller, have collected evidence from the most primitive phases of religion

[1] *Eine Mithrasliturgie,*[2] p. 105.
[2] *Ibid., loc. cit.*

to illustrate the idea of communion with the god through feeding upon him. This ranges from the Aztecs of Mexico to the ancient Egyptians whose rites are preserved in the texts of the Pyramids.[1] But to establish the validity of their position it would be necessary to show, first, that this idea survived in the Hellenistic environment of early Christianity, and second, that it forms an element in Paul's conception of the Lord's Supper. Now it seems to us impossible to demonstrate its presence in the Mystery-ritual itself.[2] But the case may be different when we turn to the sacrificial meals of Paganism, meals which had their counterpart in the practice of mystery-brotherhoods. Perhaps the chief aim of these was, as Cumont suggests,[3] the maintenance of communion between the "brethren". This would of course rest on the basis of their common fellowship with their deity.

Yet the question still remains: How was that

---

[1] See *Eine Mithrasliturgie*,[2] p. 100 f.; Heitmüller, *Taufe u. Abendmahl bei Paulus*, p. 40 ff.

[2] See also Schweitzer, *Geschichte d. Paulin. Forschung*, p. 154.

[3] *Les Religions Orientales*,[2] p. 64.

fellowship supposed to be established? And it is not easy to answer with certainty. It is possible, but by no means proved, that in a primitive stage of society the partakers of the sacrificial animal believed they were thereby partaking of the very life of their deity, either as embodied in the victim or somehow associated with it. But at least as probable an explanation is the notion that the god himself is present and shares with his worshippers in the sacrificial meal. Striking exemplifications of the latter conception are given by Lietzmann in an *excursus* on 1 Corinthians x. 21, *e.g.*, *Pap. Oxyr.*, i., 110: "Chairemon invites you to dinner at the table of the Lord Serapis in the Serapæum, to-morrow, *i.e.*, the 15th," etc. The "table of the god" (τράπεζα τοῦ θεοῦ) is a phrase which occurs in inscriptions and presupposes the presence of the deity as host at the sacrificial meal. The Roman religious *epulum* is an example of the same idea. It is impossible, therefore, to bring forward any convincing evidence from Hellenistic religion contemporary with Paul in support of the conception of eating the god. Heitmüller, indeed, declares that in the earliest days of Christianity "this belief and usage had a revival and a new

260   SACRAMENTAL MEALS

lease of life,"[1] but does not produce a shred of relevant proof to establish his statement. Prof. Percy Gardner, who frankly recognises the foregoing facts,[2] finds the closest parallel to the Christian celebration in Pagan "feasts of communion with departed heroes and ancestors".[3] Whether this analogy be valid or not, it at least avoids the absurdity of attributing to Paul the notion of "eating" a Divine Being.

While emphasising the sparseness of the evidence, we have admitted the possibility that, in the Mystery-Religions, certain ritual acts of eating and drinking were believed to impart new life or immortality. And we have taken for granted that in sacrificial meals some kind of communion with the deity was supposed to be established, although the method of its establishment eludes investigation. There can be little doubt, moreover, that in the commemora-

[1] *Die Religion in Geschichte u. Gegenwart* (ed. Schiele), Bd. i., sp. 45. In *Taufe u. Abendmahl bei Paulus*, pp. 48, 49, he actually postulates for the Christian view of the Lord's Supper a notion so crude as to have been transcended, by his own admission, in contemporary heathen and Jewish thought.

[2] *The Religious Experience of St. Paul*, p. 121.

[3] *Ibid.*, p. 113.

tion feasts referred to above a ritual fellowship with the departed ancestor or hero was a main element in the celebration. We must now attempt to examine the relationship which is alleged to exist between ideas such as these and Paul's conception of the Lord's Supper.

Let us note, first of all, some characteristic statements of the Apostle's position made by investigators obsessed by the phenomena of Comparative Religion, statements so often dogmatically reiterated that writers who receive them at second-hand repeat them as beyond challenge. Dieterich asserts as unquestionable that, according to Paul's view, " Christ is eaten and drunk by the faithful and is thereby in them". The process is actual (*faktisch*).[1] Heitmüller holds that, for Paul, " simple participation in the Lord's Supper produces communion with and in the body and blood of Christ ".[2] According to Schweitzer, Paul has "the most prosaic conception imaginable of the *opus operatum*" in the sacrament.[3] Weinel declares it to be obvious from 1 Corinthians x. 1·4 that "in the sacra-

[1] *Eine Mithrasliturgie*,[2] p. 106.
[2] *Taufe u. Abendmahl bei Paulus*, p. 34.
[3] *Op. cit.*, p. 166.

ment the important thing is not the *believing* participation, but the *participation* in the supernatural".[1] In Prof. Lake's judgment, the passage just mentioned implies that "in the Eucharist Christians received the 'Spirit' in the form of food and drink".[2] Reitzenstein interprets the Pauline conception of the Lord's Supper from a magical text in which the blood of Osiris is represented as a love-potion, laying a spell on the soul of him who drinks it.[3] How far are such opinions borne out by the data of the Epistles?

Our inquiry is a limited one. It is beyond our scope to enter into the controversy which has arisen regarding the institution and original significance of the Lord's Supper. It may be necessary at one or two points to refer to phases of the discussion. But in the main we must confine ourselves to the question: What did the Lord's Supper mean for Paul? Most scholars admit that Paul found the celebration already existing in the Church.[4] Scientific exegesis

[1] *Biblische Theol. d. N.T.*, p. 327.
[2] *Earlier Epistles of St. Paul*, p. 213.
[3] *H.M.R.*, p. 51.
[4] See, *e.g.*, Holtzmann, *N.T. Theologie*,[2] ii., p. 208.

rightly rejects the interpretation of παρέλαβον ἀπὸ τοῦ κυρίου ὃ καὶ παρέδωκα ὑμῖν ("I received from the Lord that which also I handed on to you," 1 Cor. xi. 23) as a special revelation.[1] And great caution must be exercised in attributing this feature or that in the institution to the creative activity of Paul. Many modern investigators claim a totally unwarranted knowledge of the mind of Jesus when they assume that the sacramental in any shape or form contradicts His entire standpoint. We grant that if the sacramental is synonymous with the magical it must have been foreign to His thought. But, as we pointed out in the last chapter, there is a sacramentalism which is ethical to the core, having its foundations laid in a genuine religious faith. It is no excrescence of primitive superstition, but corresponds to a permanent demand of the human consciousness, the demand that the visible and tangible should be a seal to faith of that which is unseen and eternal.

The Pauline material on the Lord's Supper is contained in three sections of 1 Corinthians : (1) x. 1-5 ; (2) x. 14-22 ; (3) xi. 17-34. Section (1) is far less important than the others, as

[1] See the excellent note of J. Weiss, *ad loc.*

being no more than an illustration used in passing by the Apostle. Sections (2) and (3) supply real evidence of his position. It is wholly illegitimate to assign a superior authority, as Heitmüller does, to section (2) for the determination of Paul's actual conception. As a matter of fact, an unprejudiced interpretation of the two passages reveals, as we shall see, no discrepancy between them. Heitmüller, however, asserts that in chapter xi. we find "a more individual, theological explanation of the Lord's Supper," while in chapter x. there is presented "the unchanging fundamental idea of the celebration and its effect".[1] But this distinction is a mere assertion which there is not a syllable in the Epistle to justify. If we are obliged to choose between the two passages for an authoritative statement, Paul's own language is decisive in favour of chapter xi. For, on his definite testimony, the Apostle simply repeats in xi. 23 ff. the instructions which he had given his Corinthian converts regarding the Lord's Supper when they entered the Christian Church (ὃ καὶ παρέδωκα ὑμῖν). He nowhere suggests that this is a new communication or a discussion of "doubtful

[1] *Op. cit.*, p. 30. So also Lake, *op. cit.*, p. 213.

points," as Lake represents it.[1] He deliberately recalls to their minds the familiar ordinance, that they may realise how flagrantly they have abused it.

It is unnecessary to spend much time on chapter x. 1-5. It forms part of Paul's admonition to those who claim the possession of γνῶσις, against wounding the consciences of their "weak" brethren in the matter of eating sacrificial meat. For the latter this meat still carries with it "the consciousness of the idol" (ch. viii. 7), and so involves them in perilous associations. But the "strong" have gone further, and even partaken of meals in heathen temples (viii. 10).[2] Paul deals fully with this practice in x. 14-22, which we shall discuss immediately. Meanwhile he prepares them for his later warning by a more general caution based on the experiences of the Israelites as narrated in the Old Testament. He reminds them that the chosen people, in spite of the extraordinary tokens of God's favour manifested in their miraculous

---

[1] *Loc. cit.*

[2] Lietzmann holds that this is the situation presupposed throughout the discussion. That is possible, but not necessary.

deliverance from the power of Pharaoh, and their no less miraculous preservation in the wilderness, fell into idolatry, impurity, and rebellion against God. And God, in His displeasure with the greater number, cast them off. Christians also must lay aside the self-confidence with which they view situations that are a stumbling-block to their brethren. They themselves are exposed to the seductive environment of heathen practice. Let them beware of idolatry, for the man who thinks he stands may suddenly fall (ver. 12). It is very natural that in connection with the sacrificial meals of Paganism the Apostle's mind should move forward to the cognate celebration in the Christian Church, more especially as he is going on to demonstrate the incompatibility of partaking in both. And so he hints at the Lord's Supper and Baptism as experiences typical of God's gracious dealings under the new dispensation, in order to warn his readers that the enjoyment of high privileges, as in the case of Israel, does not necessarily ensure acceptance with God. There is no infallible safeguard in these means of grace. "Our fathers," he says, "were all baptised into Moses in the cloud and in the sea, and all ate the same spiritual ($\pi\nu\epsilon\upsilon\mu\alpha\tau\iota\kappa\grave{o}\nu$) food, and all drank the same spiritual drink: for they drank of the spiritual rock that accompanied them: now that rock was Christ." What light do these words shed on Paul's conception of the Lord's Supper?

The nature of the reference to Baptism clearly shows that here we have to do with a somewhat daring analogy, and warns us against reading into the language more than it contains. On the surface Paul follows the exegetical method common to the Rabbis and Philo. And it is possible that he actually derived the idea of the never-failing spring of water from Jewish Haggada.[1] But this description of the Divinely-provided manna and the miraculous supply of water as "spiritual" has no suggestion in it that he regarded either as supernatural in quality, or as the medium of a spiritual "substance". Nor is there a hint that he associated with them any extraordinary effect. If he did, the whole force of his argument would be vitiated, for its very purpose is to show that this wonderful Divine provision afforded no guarantee against a subsequent fatal lapse. Perhaps the best comment

[1] See Lietzmann, *ad loc.*

on the epithet πνευματικός is to be found in Deuteronomy viii. 3: "He humbled thee and suffered thee to hunger, and fed thee with manna, which thou knewest not, neither did thy fathers know, that he might make thee know that man doth not live by bread alone, but by everything that proceedeth out of the mouth of the Lord" [*i.e.*, the creative word of God by which He can call into being new means of preserving life]. Thus the manna and the water from the rock were "spiritual," not as possessing any magical properties, but as a direct pledge of the loving-kindness of God. They were intended to convince the Covenant-people of God's special relation to them. They were evidences of the redeeming purpose of God in history. It is from the same standpoint that he can identify the rock with Christ. For he regards the Divine working in the old and the new dispensation as an indissoluble unity. Hence he feels justified in making a comparison between the tokens of God's gracious favour to Israel and those Christian ordinances which are the seal of the new Covenant.

In the second crucial passage, x. 14-21, the Apostle passes beyond vague hints and deliber-

SACRAMENTAL MEALS

ately charges with idolatry those "strong" Christians who do not shrink from participating in sacrificial meals. "The cup of blessing which we bless, is it not a communion with the blood of Christ? The bread (loaf) which we break, is it not a communion with the body of Christ? For as there is one bread, so we the many are one body, for we all partake of the one bread. Look at Israel according to the flesh: do not those who eat the sacrifices enter into communion with the altar? What then do I say? That sacrificial meat is anything or that an idol is anything? No, but I say that the things which the Gentiles sacrifice 'they sacrifice to demons and not to God'.[1] Now I would not have you in communion with demons. You cannot drink the cup of the Lord and the cup of demons: you cannot share in 'the table of the Lord'[2] and in that of demons."

"Sharing in the table of the Lord" is shown in the opening sentences of the paragraph to mean partaking of the cup and the bread. And this participation is described as a communion with the body and blood of Christ. Now this last

[1] Deuteronomy xxxii. 17 (LXX).
[2] Malachi i. 12 (LXX).

conception cannot be explained in the isolation of its present context. But its meaning becomes clear from the expressive interpretation of it which Paul has given in chapter xi. There he deliberately states its significance: "As often as you eat this bread and drink this cup, you represent (καταγγέλλετε) the Lord's death till he come" (xi. 26). That is to say, the bread and wine represent not the flesh and blood of Christ as such, but His human person as slain on the Cross. Therefore communion with the body and blood of Christ means communion with the Lord as crucified and all that this involves. Hence we never find the Apostle speaking of "eating the flesh" or "drinking the blood" of Christ. He is careful to associate the solemn actions only with the bread and the cup. It is thus apparent that the Lord's Supper sets forth visibly for Paul and his fellow-Christians the supreme spiritual experience which he has described in Galatians ii. 20 : "I have been crucified with Christ". And as the Apostle can never dissociate the Crucifixion from the Resurrection, the appropriation of the benefits of the death of Christ which is quickened by the sacred celebration will carry with it a like appropria-

SACRAMENTAL MEALS

tion of the resources of the risen Lord : "No longer do I live, but Christ liveth in me : and that which I now live in the flesh I live by faith, faith in the Son of God who loved me and gave himself for me". Language of this kind reminds us that Paul's thought must not be interpreted atomistically, but in the light of his entire Christian experience.

There is nothing in the paragraph under review to conflict with the explanation which we have seen to be necessitated by the Apostle's instruction on the Lord's Supper in chapter xi. 23 ff. Indeed, the comparisons which he employs are sufficient in themselves to put us on our guard against supposing that Paul's notion here is, to quote Weinel, that " the communion with the Lord into which one enters at the table of the Lord is of a sensible-hypersensible real kind," that " the idea is not of a mere spiritual reception of Christ, but somehow of His glorified corporeality ".[1] It is impossible to associate with the eating of the sacrifices in Israel (x. 18) the notion of partaking of the Deity. Such an idea is foreign to Jewish thought. Nor is it otherwise in the case of the

[1] *Biblische Theologie d. N.T.*, p. 325.

demons whom Paul regards as the real forces existing behind Pagan idols. His language is not obscure. The communion with the demons against which he warns is described as "drinking the cup of demons," "partaking of the table of demons". These phrases, when viewed in the light of the examples cited from papyri at the beginning of this chapter, suggest that Paul regards the demons as hosts at the sacrificial meals, and communion with them is pictured by the relation of the guests to their hosts.[1] It is quite irrelevant to quote as decisive for Paul's meaning [2] the well-known passage from Porphyrius (*De philos. ex orac. haur.*, preserved by Eusebius, *Præpar. Evang.*, iv., 23, 3), in which he relates of demons that "while we are at food they approach and settle on our bodies . . . and delight especially in blood," etc., as if this made probable for Paul the notion that they were conveyed into the bodies of the worshippers by means of the sacrificial meat. The Apostle takes for granted that the presence of any one at a sacrificial meal is necessarily a more or less distinct recognition of the superhuman Person in whose honour, or

[1] See also J. Tambornino, *De antiquorum dæmonismo*, p. 95.
[2] So Lietzmann, J. Weiss, and others.

under whose ægis, the festival is held. And these superhuman powers he calls δαιμόνια, using the term to describe the objects of Pagan worship, after the model of Deuteronomy xxxii. 17 (ἔθυσαν δαιμονίοις καὶ οὐ θεῷ), which is evidently before his mind. But Porphyrius has the diametrically opposite conception of δαιμόνια as beings who interfere with the worship of the gods, and who have to be driven away in order that the god may grant his presence. Very instructive for the view we have suggested of communion with the demons is a passage in the Pseudo-Clementine *Recognitiones* (ii., 71), which says that every one who worships "those whom the Pagans call gods, or tastes meat sacrificed to them," becomes " a guest of demons," and " has fellowship with that demon whose aspect he has fashioned in his mind, whether from fear or love ".[1] We are

[1] *Cf.* J. Réville (*Revue de l'histoire des religions*, tome 56, p. 159) : "The Apostle here appeals to the religious idea which inspired the sacred meals of the Greeks, communion with the gods by the absorption of a common food, belonging to the gods by the fact of consecration. The κοινωνία τῶν δαιμονίων . . . does not mean the absorption of the flesh of demons any more than the κοινωνία τοῦ θυσιαστηρίου means the absorption of the altar. . . . In the one and the other alternative there is involved the solidarity attested by the

justified, therefore, on the basis of an examination of the facts, in asserting that 1 Corinthians x. 14 ff. affords no evidence for the notion that Paul believes in the magical communication of the glorified body of Christ to the worshipper through the medium of the bread and wine.

The most ample material for estimating Paul's conception of the Lord's Supper is presented by 1 Corinthians xi. 23 ff. We have already seen that it is an authoritative pronouncement on the subject. And it was necessary at an earlier point to call attention to the Apostle's statement of the fundamental significance of the celebration in verse 26. Paul derives this significance from the words and actions of Jesus, as these have come down to him through the tradition of the Church. Now, apart from the injunction to repeat the celebration as a memorial, there is no essential difference between Paul and the Synoptics. Indeed, so radical a scholar as Eichhorn goes the length of admitting that no one who compares the four reports of the Lord's Supper can doubt that all four writers speak of

religious meal, on the one hand with the demons, on the other with the blood and body of Christ."

the self-same thing in the very same sense.[1] With reference to the cup, Mark, Matthew, and Luke (except the so-called " Western " text) report Jesus as saying : " This is my blood of the covenant [Luke : the new covenant in my blood] shed for many [Luke : for you] ". It is therefore wholly arbitrary to challenge the allusion to the covenant as an addition due to Paul. And the saying obviously represents the approaching death of Jesus as the sacrifice which inaugurates the new covenant. The words that accompany the giving of the cup make perfectly clear the meaning of those spoken at the distribution of the bread, even in the brief form found in Matthew and Mark : " this is my body ". The extended version in Paul and the non-Western texts of Luke is true to Jesus' thought : " This is my body which is for you [Luke : which is given for you] ".[2] The ritual action, therefore, symbolises the death of Jesus as a medium of blessing for His followers. And that part of it which consists in eating the broken

[1] *Das Abendmahl im N.T.*, p. 8 (quoted by Lambert, *The Sacraments in the N.T.*, p. 267).

[2] See an excellent paragraph by Jülicher in *Abhandlungen C. von Weizsäcker gewidmet*, pp. 242, 243.

bread and drinking the wine emphasises the necessity of appropriating the promised salvation. But there is no evidence of anything realistic or magical about the benefit received. Heitmüller, indeed, finds traces of such a conception in xi. 27 : "Whosoever shall eat the bread or drink the cup of the Lord unworthily shall be guilty of the body and blood of the Lord," taking these words in close connection with verse 30 : "On this account many among you are frail and sick, and a number have fallen asleep". He compares a belief of the Syrians that the eating of sardines,[1] which were sacred to the goddess Atargatis, produced ulcers and wasting disease.[1] But the parallel is not really valid. The unworthy partaking of the bread and wine is regarded by Paul as sacrilege committed against Christ. His idea is precisely equivalent to that of Hebrews vi. 6 : "Crucifying for themselves afresh the Son of God and putting him to open shame". The effect which he discerns in the sickness and death of members of the Christian community he does not trace to the partaking of the bread and wine, but distinctly names it a κρίμα, a judgment sent

---

[1] *Op. cit.*, pp. 50, 51.

by God for the ultimate discipline of those who have been guilty.

It is interesting to note that in this important passage Paul is exclusively concerned with the participation of believers in the benefits of the sacrifice of Christ. The same thing applies to chapter x. 14 ff. But as we indicated in discussing that section, it is impossible for him to think of Christ crucified apart from Christ risen (*cf.* Rom. iv. 25). And perhaps the significant words, "till he come," are directly intended to remind them that He whose death of love they commemorate, is with them "always until the end of the age". But for the Apostle, communion with Christ does not depend upon any sacred rite. Its essential condition is a wholehearted faith. This he makes as plain as words can make it in such passages as Galatians ii. 20 and Philippians iii. 9. And so we are brought back to the position which we sought to establish in the last chapter, where we endeavoured to show that faith is for Paul the indispensable postulate of all that has spiritual value in the experience of Baptism. It is not otherwise with the Lord's Supper. This was no feast of initiation. Those who partook of it had already professed to surrender themselves to Christ as their Saviour and Lord. They had received and welcomed the good news of salvation through His self-sacrificing death. The bread and the wine were to them symbols of all that this death involved. And when they received them with discernment, they were making acknowledgment of the dying love of the Redeemer. But, as in baptism, there was something more for Paul and his converts in this sacred meal than an impressive symbolism. The "acted parable" was amazingly fitted to rouse and invigorate their faith. Thus they were by faith carried past the symbols into what Holtzmann has fitly called "the sphere of the reconciling grace which rests upon the death of Christ".[1] There they were able to realise with new vividness the actual operation of the Divine love at work on their behalf. The symbols became a sacrament, a convincing pledge of the mercy of God in Christ the crucified.

We have dwelt only on those aspects of the Lord's Supper which have been alleged to show a kinship with the sacred meals of Paganism. We have not discussed the hypothesis that the

[1] *N.T. Theologie*,[2] ii., p. 201.

Christian feast was modelled on those Pagan celebrations which commemorated a dead hero or ancestor, because in these there was nothing to correspond to Paul's central idea of communion with Christ as crucified. But we believe enough has been said to justify the statement of Von Dobschütz that "the unique sacramental conception of the Early Church, which has no analogy in the history of religion because it belongs essentially to the Christian religion, has its origin solely in Christian faith and Christian experience".[1]

[1] *Studien u. Kritiken*, 1905, i., p. 39.

CHAPTER VIII

CONCLUSIONS

IN the preceding chapters we have sought to test at various points the assumption that Christianity was for St. Paul a Mystery-Religion, and that many of his religious conceptions were closely allied to the Mystery-cults of Paganism. It may be well in this closing section of our inquiry to gather up and emphasise the more important conclusions at which we have arrived, supplementing them at one or two points.

The relation of the Mystery-Religions to Paul's environment requires no discussion. Ample evidence has been adduced to show that throughout the sphere of his missionary operations he would be in touch with many who had been initiated into Pagan Mysteries, and had finally entered the Christian Church. We cannot picture him engrossed in the cure of souls without recognising that he must have gained a deep insight into the earlier spiritual aspirations of

CONCLUSIONS 281

his converts, and the manner in which they had sought to satisfy them. Even apart from eager inquirers, a missionary so zealous and daring would often find himself confronted by men and women who still clung to their mystic ritual and all the hopes it had kindled. It was inevitable, therefore, that he should become familiar, at least from the outside, with religious ideas current in these influential cults. Sometimes, as *e.g.* in the case of γνῶσις and δόξα, these ideas found remarkably close parallels in the thought of the Old Testament. Thus he would be impressed by their capacity for holding a genuinely spiritual content, and would use them in circumstances in which their earlier history would tend to make them all the more effective. Certain important terms like τέλειος, πνευματικός, σωτηρία, and others, were in the air. They meant one thing, no doubt, for a Christian, and quite another for a Pagan. Yet their fundamental significance for both had elements of affinity, sufficient to link together the respective usages. The essentially religious meaning, for example, of πνεῦμα and νοῦς in documents of Hellenistic Mystery-Religion provided a common standing-ground for Paul and many of his readers. What holds of separate terms may occasionally be affirmed regarding groups of ideas. Thus the combination of συμμορφιζόμενος with γνῶναι in Philippians iii. 10 seems to indicate a background for the Apostle's conception akin to the Mystery-doctrine of transformation by the vision of God. But it has also become clear that we dare not make far-reaching inferences from terminology as to the assimilation by Paul of Mystery-ideas. For we were able to show that the central conceptions of the Mystery-Religions belong to a different atmosphere from that in which the Apostle habitually moves. There is no principle determining their relations, which in any sense corresponds to the Cross of Christ in the realm of Paul's thought and experience.

It is, moreover, vain to endeavour to find points of contact between Paul and the Mystery-cults on the side of ritual. Unquestionably he was too sensitive to the practical demands of the human soul to disparage the simple rites which he found existing in the nascent Church. Indeed, he was aware that the celebration of the Lord's Supper had its origin in the Master's farewell meal with His disciples. He was ready to recognise the high spiritual impulses which were quickened in the solemn surroundings of the Christian sacraments. He knew that these actions, with lowly, believing hearts responsive to them, became real channels for the Divine grace. But the essential characteristic of his religious attitude was detachment from ceremonial. It is no wonder that interpreters like Heitmüller and Weinel, who attribute a magical view of the sacraments to Paul, are concerned to point out that his sacramentalism is a sort of erratic boulder in his system as a whole. It would be foolish to demand for Paul a rigid logic in the concatenation of his thought. But his thinking is in no sense atomistic. And the vital centre of the organism lies in his conception of faith. Independent as are the gracious movements of a God, almighty and all-loving, they demand for their effectiveness the receptivity of the human soul. That is one aspect of faith for Paul. And the other is the personal appeal to God of the surrendered life. A heart to welcome, and a will to claim the supreme Divine gifts, and behind both, as their explanation, the emotion of a love created by the unspeakable love of Christ. Every living idea in Paul is irradiated by his faith, whether its form be juristic or theosophical or sacramental. To assign a position of any importance in the complex of his ideas to an element for which faith does not count, is to ignore the indissoluble connection between his thought and his religious experience. The centrality of faith, therefore, comes to be a criterion of every attempt at reconstructing Paul's spiritual platform. And here also we discover that there is no corresponding feature in the framework of the Mystery-Religions.

Nevertheless, we have every right to speak of the Mysticism of Paul. How is the term, in his case, to be interpreted? To many natures everything that savours of mystical experience is not only alien but offensive. They regard it as a purely pathological condition, the result of auto-suggestion. Or they view it as an unethical dissociation of personality from the salutary claims of normal life, with the aim of absorption in an impersonal Absolute. It is unquestionable that mystics have often laid stress on a more or less morbid self-mortification as the pathway to their goal, and that the *via negativa*, so dear to many of them, has resulted in a conception of God which really obliterates all that we mean by character. But it is equally certain that in numerous instances those who have yearned for and professed to attain real contact with the Divine have exercised a moral power yielding astonishing results in the sphere of practical life. Mysticism, in effect, is a term which covers a manifold area of experience. It is extremely difficult in the history of Christianity to distinguish it from those conditions of overpowering faith, involving profound emotion, which belong to the soul that has "counted all things as loss" for Christ. Indeed, Pfleiderer can scarcely be said to exaggerate when he asserts that "the mystical element in Paulinism depends immediately and exclusively on Paul's notion of faith".[1] Let us briefly analyse this mystical element.

[1] *Paulinism* (E. tr.), vol. i., p. 199; *cf.* Lehmann's statement: "The culminating point in the experience of the believing Jew is the *passion of faith*" (*Mysticism*, E. tr., p. 101). The chief defect in Miss Underhill's treatment of Paulinism in her recent attractive study of Christian origins, *The Mystic Way*, published while this book was in the press, is its failure to emphasise faith as the clue to Paul's profoundest religious experience, and the attempt to force that experience into a frame-work of technical categories derived from mediæval Mysticism. See a most masterly statement of the view adopted in the text by Wernle, *Zeitschr. f. Theol. u. Kirche*, 1913, 1, pp. 69-72.

The phenomena associated with Mysticism, and appearing in every age and in all manner of environments, usually seem to presuppose a special type of temperament. In the second chapter we referred to the case of the prophet Ezekiel as a nature peculiarly sensitive to ecstatic or trance conditions, in which he received the Divine message. Yet it is plain that his "peculiar psycho-physical constitution" in no way detracted from the vigour of his ethical teaching. We have hints that the temperament of Paul was of a similar kind in the allusions he makes again and again to revelations ($\dot{a}\pi o\kappa a\lambda\acute{v}\psi\epsilon\iota s$) and visions ($\dot{o}\pi\tau a\sigma\acute{\iota}a\iota$) which came to him, and especially in the remarkable description of an ecstatic experience given in 2 Corinthians xii. 1 ff. But no reader of the Epistles could ever form the impression that these occurrences, associated with special psycho-physical conditions, constitute for the Apostle a predominant feature of his religious life. We have ample evidence as to the attitude he assumes towards abnormal workings of the Divine Spirit. In his famous discussion of spiritual $\chi a\rho\acute{\iota}\sigma\mu a\tau a$ in 1 Corinthians xii.-xiv., he makes no secret of his desire to curb all manifestations of intense spiritual emotion which are not calculated to edify the Christian community. And while he admits that such phenomena may spring from a real contact with Divine influence, he gives them no place in his impressive enumeration of the fruits of the Spirit. The distinguishing characteristic of these is their ethical quality. This is in full accord with one of Paul's most splendid achievements in the life of the Early Church, the transformation of the conception of the Spirit as a fitful energy, accompanied by extraordinary manifestations, into that of an abiding, inspiring power which controls conduct in the interest of love. His own ecstatic experiences must have been regulated by the same cautions. For this would certainly be possible. The testimony of the great Christian mystics warns us against confounding ecstasy with hysteria. They recognise, indeed, that there is often a justification for such comparison, and declare that ecstasies must be tested. The test consists "not in its outward sign, but in its inward grace, its after-value".[1] This after-value is due to the high conviction that the soul has been carried into the world of Eternal Reality. All the evidence suggests that

[1] E. Underhill, *Mysticism*, p. 431.

for Paul these experiences were not depressing but life-enhancing.

But in touching these more or less abnormal conditions, we are dealing only with the circumference of Paul's religious history. Its centre lies elsewhere. Weinel aptly remarks that the simultaneous origin of what he calls Paul's "Spirit- and Christ-mysticism" can only be explained from his experience on the Damascus road.[1] This was for the Apostle a real contact with the risen Lord, the Lord as life-giving Spirit. There and then he came to be "in Christ" (2 Cor. v. 17). There and then Christ came to be "in him" (Gal. i. 16). We pointed out in a former chapter that this language transcends all spatial categories. But while the ultimate fact which it endeavours to express eludes analysis, Paul himself supplies the material for estimating, up to a certain point, the process by which the ineffable relationship is realised. It is not established in any magical way. It is the Divine answer to faith. And the nature of the faith is not left obscure. In the most classical passage on union with Christ to be found in his Epistles, Paul illuminates the matter

[1] *Biblische Theologie d. N.T.*, p. 287.

by a single flash. For he describes the faith which is the nexus in this fellowship as "faith in the Son of God who loved me and gave himself for me" (Gal. ii. 20). Here, obviously, the intellectual element in faith is not emphasised; not even that which is involved in Paul's attitude towards the resurrection. This is a faith which has behind it the force of an all-subduing love. The emotion is the response to the redeeming love of the Cross, the most tremendous moral power with which Paul has ever come in contact.

Thus we can discern that the "Mysticism" of the Apostle has an inherently ethical quality. This might have been deduced from his conception of the Spirit, as we have briefly exhibited it. And that conception, of course, can never be dissociated from his experience of intimate communion with Christ, as appears from such crucial passages as Romans viii. 9, 10 ("Ye are not in the flesh but in the Spirit, if so be that the Spirit of God dwelleth in you. But if any man have not the Spirit of Christ, he is none of his. And if Christ is in you, the body is dead because of sin, but the Spirit is life because of righteousness"). But we have preferred to keep to the main track of his thought, a track which leads through the hard realities of an earthly life. For Paul relates his supreme experience of fellowship, that which is far more precious to him than abnormal raptures (although he valued these), to the common existence which is his daily lot : "that which I now live in the flesh" (Gal. ii. 20). It is possible to go further in our analysis on the basis of the material presented in the Epistles. We have already emphasised the nature of the content of that supreme experience which lies at the heart of Paul's mysticism.[1] He himself calls it, "being crucified with Christ". It occupies the central place in his exposition of the meaning of the Lord's Supper. There he describes it as "communion with the body and blood of the Lord" (1 Cor. x. 16). And we saw in the last chapter that, in the light of the explicit statement in 1 Corinthians xi. 26, the phrase could only mean communion with the Lord as crucified. The central implication of the idea is identification with the attitude towards sin of the crucified Redeemer and all that that involves, with its correlative of sharing

---

[1] See chapter v., p. 220 ff.

in the victorious life of Christ as risen. Here is a type of mysticism which stands by itself. Its meaning, as we have seen, is fellowship with Christ. That fellowship involves the will. It could never be the product of mere feeling or brooding contemplation. It has little in common with the notion of absorption in the Deity which links together mystical aspirations in every age and every clime. If there is any possession which Paul holds dear, it is that of his individuality. His eager speculations on the "spiritual organism" are sufficient proof. Like Plato, he escapes what may be technically called "Mysticism" by "his unwavering belief in the indissoluble personality of the human *ego*".[1] And as regards the Divine factor in the mystic fellowship, he has too keen a sense of the historical personality of the Lord to lose himself in the sea of absolute Being. These are never the categories with which he works. Indeed, to realise with vividness the limits which he imposes upon his mystical thought and feeling, we have only to reflect on his attitude towards deification.

We have pointed out the prevalence of this doctrine as the goal of mystical aspiration in

[1] See Lehmann, *Mysticism* (E. tr.), p. 89.

Hellenistic religion. Dean Inge shows clearly[1] that, in Eastern Christendom during the early centuries, owing to the fluid nature of the concept θεός, the notion of deification (θεοποίησις) was widely current in a somewhat vague sense, often scarcely distinguishable from immortality.[2] But rash inferences were sure to be drawn, such as that of Methodius that "every believer must, through participation in Christ, be born as a Christ".[3] Developed on these lines the conception of personality was bound to become nebulous, as, *e.g.*, in Eckhart's saying: "If I am to know God directly, I must become completely He, and He I: so that this He and this I become and are one I".[4] Paul is careful to avoid language or thought of this type. When he approaches it, as, *e.g.*, in Galatians ii. 20, he expressly guards against possible misunderstanding. Perhaps the reverence born of his unwavering monotheism was a determining factor of his

---

[1] *Christian Mysticism*, p. 356 ff. See also an ingenious suggestion in G. Murray's *Four Stages of Greek Religion*, p. 39 f.

[2] *Cf.* Rohde, *Psyche*,³ ii., p. 2: "He who among the Greeks says 'immortal,' says 'God'".

[3] Quoted by Inge, *op. cit.*, p. 359.

[4] See E. Underhill, *Mysticism*, p. 502.

CONCLUSIONS 293

position. In any case, he never permits his aspirations to carry him further than the Divine εἰκών into which believers are being transformed (*e.g.*, 2 Cor. iii. 18). And it is easy to exaggerate the significance of the language he employs on that subject.

We observed in chapter iv. how difficult it was to grasp the precise nature of Paul's conception of the "transformation" (μεταμορφοῦσθαι). The only assertion which could be made with confidence was that we must guard against identifying it with the magical transmutation of essence central for the Mystery-Religions, as Paul's idea of the πνεῦμα, the chief factor in the transformation, is essentially moral. As a matter of fact, the highest relationship to God recognised by the Apostle is that of "children" (τέκνα) or "sons" (υἱοί) of God. "You did not receive the spirit of bondage again, resulting in fear: but you received the spirit of adoption (υἱοθεσίας) whereby we cry, Abba, Father. The Spirit itself bears witness with our spirit that we are children of God" (Rom. viii. 15, 16). Such a relationship is, as Lehmann has aptly described it,[1] "personal, intimate; it breathes freedom; it is conscious

[1] *Mysticism* (E. tr.), p. 105.

discrimination, and therefore not mysticism," in the strict sense of the term.

A quite arbitrary emphasis has been laid by Schweitzer on the eschatological implicates of Paul's conception of union with Christ. He rightly contrasts that conception with the notion of the Mystery-Religions, that the living man, by means of gnosis and the vision of God, receives the Divine essence into his being. But he goes to the other extreme in holding that Paul attributes the experience of transformation to what he calls "a world-process". "As soon as the individual by means of faith and baptism enters into this new cosmic event (*Geschehen*), he is immediately renewed and receives Spirit, ecstasy, gnosis, and all that accompanies them."[1] We get some light upon the meaning of this extraordinary state in connection with Paul's language as to "dying with Christ". Schweitzer criticises Reitzenstein for holding, as every unbiassed exegete of Paulinism must hold, that the Apostle is here thinking of a deliberate identification of himself with the death of Christ, which involves the breaking off of relations with sin and the crucifying of the natural man. Instead, we

[1] *Geschichte d. Paulin. Forschung*, p. 175.

CONCLUSIONS

are told that Paul is not concerned with an action performed by the believer. His conception rather is that "at the moment when the individual receives baptism, the process of the dying and rising again of Christ, without the believer's co-operation, without any exercise of will on his part, without any reflection of his, starts working in him like machinery which is set in motion by pressing a spring".[1]

This grotesque misconception of Paul's religious standpoint is an arresting instance of the results of "consistent eschatology," and warns us against approaching the Epistles with a ready-made framework into which their thought has to be forced. Let us admit without hesitation that Paul has his eyes fixed on the glorious consummation of the future. But let us no less carefully recognise that for that future he has no clear-cut scheme of things. Such utterances as Philippians i. 23: "having the desire to depart and to be with Christ," remind us that his eschatological forecasts were as flexible as our own. For here the idea of the Parousia falls completely into the background, and he regards death simply as a passing into the presence of

[1] *Op. cit.*, p. 176.

the living Lord. It is only by ignoring many of the cardinal elements in his outlook that we can find the clue to his mysticism in those magical and mechanical processes which Schweitzer associates with the transference from the present to the coming Æon. How far the Apostle is removed from the notion of a salvation which works automatically, appears from such statements as Philippians iii. 11 : "if by any means I may attain unto the resurrection from the dead. Not that I have already obtained, or am already perfect : but I press on if so be that I may lay hold on that for which also I was laid hold on by Christ Jesus "; and 1 Corinthians ix. 27 : " I beat my body black and blue, and bring it into bondage, lest by any means, after having preached to others, I myself should be rejected ". It will take a bold interpreter to assert in the light of these and many similar passages that in Paul's view there was no co-operation of the believer, no exercise of will on his part in the matter of participating in the benefits of Christ's death and resurrection, but only an external, supernatural machinery, set a-going by the rite of baptism.

The central ideas of Pauline eschatology are

CONCLUSIONS 297

essentially religious. Take, for instance, those which are most intimately linked to his experience of mystical union with Christ, namely, life and salvation. In Romans vi. 4-6 Paul deliberately interprets the "newness of life," which has been reached by communion with Christ, realised with peculiar impressiveness in the solemnity of baptism, as the norm for daily living (ἵνα . . . ἐν καινότητι ζωῆς περιπατήσωμεν), and explains it as "no longer serving sin". Again, in Romans viii. 6, he describes "the mind of the flesh" (*i.e.*, the earthly nature as insensible to God) as death, while "the mind of the Spirit is life and peace". Beyond all question the terms "death" and "life" have direct eschatological bearings. But their content is in no sense exclusively eschatological. Paul invariably regards "life" as a present possession of the believer. But he would not have asserted that originally he possessed a natural life, while on surrendering himself to Christ he received a spiritual life. The new life is a renewal of the old from its very foundations. It embraces the physical (to use our distinctions) as well as the ethical and religious. Its only contrast lies in death. Death for the Apostle means the ruin of the whole personality. Life in Christ is something larger than existence and means the triumphant continuance of personality beyond the barriers of earth and time, in conformity with the nature of the glorified Lord, who is the image of the invisible God.

The same considerations apply to Paul's conception of salvation, which is really "life" regarded from a special point of view. It is needless to cite passages which reveal the eschatological colour of σωτηρία. The fact that it occurs most frequently in the phrase εἰς σωτηρίαν, where it is a goal to be reached, is proof positive. But Paul has too keen an interest in the demands of daily life to defer the reality of salvation to a future crisis. Undoubtedly like eager Christians of every time he delights to think of that consummation in which the hampering conditions of material existence shall be surmounted. It is absurd to consider as a pessimistic aberration his passionate cry: "Who shall deliver me from the body of this death?" Has any yearning been more perpetually echoed throughout the ages? But no one was ever more conscious of the reality of salvation as an existing fact of experience.

"God was pleased," he declares, "through the foolishness of the thing preached to save them that believe" (1 Cor. i. 21); "There is therefore now no condemnation to them that are in Christ Jesus" (Rom. viii. 1).

Our investigation has reached its limit. If it has accomplished anything, it has simply demonstrated afresh that in St. Paul we are confronted, not with one of those natures which is content to be the medium of the spiritual forces of its environment, but with a personality which has been shaped once for all in the throes of a tremendous crisis, and thenceforward transforms every influence to which it is sensitive with the freedom born of a triumphant faith.

INDEX

I. SUBJECTS

AKIBA, warning of, against mysteries, 45; his estimate of allegory, 51.

Apocalyptic thought, relation of, to Rabbinic, 44.

Archons, 24 f.

Ascent of soul, origin of idea of, 42; in Apocalypses, 42 f.; relation of, to 2 Cor. XII. 1 ff., 174.

Attis. See Cybele.

ἀγνωσία, 165-167.

ἀπαθανατισμός, 110, 203.

ἀποκάλυψις, in Paul, 172 f., 286.

BAPTISM, as a mystery, 2, 233; rites of, in ancient religions, 229; alleged association of, with death in Egyptian papyrus, 231; Paul's view of, held to be magical, 233; secondary place of, in Paul, 235-238; relation of, in Paul, to dying to sin, 244-247; real significance of, for Paul, 247-253; for the dead, 253 f.; summary of Paul's view of, 254 f.; in 1 Cor. x. 1 ff., 267.

CABALA, relation of, to Apocalypses, 43.

Commemoration, feasts of, 261.

Communion with God, through actual mysticism, 7, 9; through γνῶσις, 25; in O.T. prophets, 36; in relation to Divine "Name," 55; idea of, found in all Mystery-religions, 69 f.; by partaking of deity, 200 f., 271; by possession or ecstasy, 201 f.; by revelation, 203; by means of the "elements," 204 f.; as sacred marriage, 205; through voluntary death and new birth, 206-211; in sacrificial meals, 259. See Jesus Christ, Regeneration.

Cross, central significance of, for Paul, 215, 218, 220, 221, 227, 246, 270, 278, 279.

Cybele (Great Mother), as association-deity, 75; cult of, at Rome, 88; relation of, to Dionysus (— Sabazius), 89; Attis-ritual in cult of, 90; Attis-mysteries, 90-93, 209, 210; age of ritual, 93; Attis as vegetation-deity, 93, 94, 213; influence of Mithraism on Cybele-Attis cult, 94; *taurobolium*, 94 f., 211.

DEIFICATION, not found in Judaism, 50; as result of γνῶσις, 110, 163, 178; by regeneration, 200; in Liturgy of Mithra, 203; in Hermetic literature, 216; Paul's attitude towards, 291 f.; in Eastern Christianity, 292. See Regeneration, Transformation.

Demons, communion with, 269, 272, 273; idea of, in Paul, 272 f.; in Porphyrius, 273; guests of, 273.

(301)

INDEX

Dionysus, frenzy in cult of, 13 f., 89; prominence of, in religious associations, 74; affinities of, with Phrygian deities, 74, 89; affinity of, with Osiris, 75, 87, 98; at Eleusis, 85; cult of, at Rome, 89 *n.*; sacramental elements in cult of, 257.

Doresche Reschumoth, as allegorical exegetes, 52; mystical tendencies of, 53.

δόξα, O.T. basis of, 191; Paul's use of, 192-194, 281; alleged connection of, with Egyptian mysticism, 194 ff.; origin of Paul's idea of, traced to Persia, 194 *n.*

δύναμις, as central in γνῶσις, 25; of God, in human soul, 108, 203.

ECKHART, 292.

Ecstasy, in Paul, 32, 173 f., 176, 286, 290; in Philo, 66; in Suso, 174 ff.; affinity of, to ἐνθουσιασμός, 202; test of, 287. See Mysticism.

Elemental spirits, in Gnosticism, 24; in Paul, 24 f.; redemption from, 25; in Judaism, 60; Babylonian origin of idea, 60-62. See στοιχεῖα.

Eleusinian Mysteries, effect of, 71; national character of, 81; Foucart's theory of, 82; description of, 83; significance of ritual in, 83 f.; Rohde's hypothesis of, 84; ὅσιος in, 85 *n.*; deeper sense of, 85, 86 f.; connection of, with Dionysus, 86; Thracian influence on, 87.

Eschatology, relation of, to Paul's mysticism, 295, 296; central ideas of Pauline, 297.

Esoteric doctrines, in Jochanan, b. Zakkai, 49; basis of, in Gen. I. and Ezek. I., 49: not in Paul, 128, 129.

Ezekiel, as sensitive to ecstatic conditions, 37 f., 286.

εἰκών (of God), relation of, to σῶμα πνευματικόν, 189; connection of, with δόξα, 189; as goal for Paul, 293.

εἱμαρμένη, in Babylonian theology, 19; in Gnosticism, 24. See Fate.

ἐνθουσιασμός, 14, 201.

ἔρως, as Orphic term, 10.

FAITH. See Mysticism, Paul.

Fate, tyranny of, in Hellenistic religion, 19, 23, 198, 216.

GNOSTICISM, flexibility of term, 24, 26; essential character of, 25; relation of, to Hellenistic syncretism, 27, 29; "vulgar" type of, 28; Persian dualism in, 29; censured by Paul, 29; as channel for Christian influence on Paganism, 64.

God, formula of relationship to, 9; "hand" of, in prophets, 34 f.; "knowledge" of, 36; mystical "name" of, 54-56; connection of "name" with Hellenistic religion, 56. See Communion.

HERMES, as revealer, 106; dialogue between, and Tat, 107; character of dialogue, 109; in Arcadia, 112.

Hermetic literature, Egyptian elements in, 19; "vulgar" γνῶσις in, 28; connection of, with Valentinian Gnosticism, 64; problems of, 103; complex strata in, 104, 109, 111; Reitzenstein's account of origin of, 105, 106, 111; as a revelation, 106; spiritualising of cult in, 111; theories of Cumont, Otto, Zielinski, as to, 111, 112; estimate of theories, 113; alleged acquaintance of Paul with, 118; possible influence of semi-Christian Gnosticism on, 167.

Hippolytus, on connection between Orphics and Gnosticism, 27.

INITIATION, repetitions of, 22; Lord's Supper not a feast of, 277.

I. SUBJECTS

Isis (Osiris-Serapis) cult, date of Apuleius' account of, 69; wide diffusion of, 75, 98; relation of Ptolemies to, 75, 76, 96 f.; in Rome, 77, 98; origin of Serapis, 97; Osiris-festivals, 97 ff.; assimilation of initiates to Osiris, 99; fascination of, 99; fundamental ideas of, 99, 100; description of, by Apuleius, 100-102; religious significance of, 102, 103.

JESUS CHRIST, comparison of, with Mystery-deities, 211; communion with, in Paul, alien to Mystery-conceptions, 213-215, 220, 221; nature of communion with, for Paul, 221-223, 269-271, 290, 291; relation of communion with, to Spirit, 224; ethical character of communion with, 225, 277; death and resurrection with, in Paul, 225; difference of content in this idea from Mystery-conceptions, 227; baptism and communion with, in Paul, 241; communion with body and blood of, 269 ff., 290. See Communion.

JUDAISM, influence of Paganism on, 57 f., 61; contact of, with Oriental mysticism, 59; pressure of Babylonian and Persian thought on, 60-62.

καταγγέλλειν, meaning of, in Paul's account of Lord's Supper, 270.
κύριος Σαβαώθ, relation of, to κύριος Σαβάζιος, 58.

LITURGY of Mithra, difficulty of dating, 69; hymn in, 108 n.; prosaic elements in, 110; fundamental character of, 114 n.; regeneration in, 143, 146, 178; deification in, 203.
Lord's Supper, meaning of, for Paul, 262-279; data for Paul's view of, 263, 264; authoritative pronounce-

ment on, in 1 Cor. XI. 28 ff., 274 ff.; various aspects of, 275; no magical element in, for Paul, 276; central place of faith in, 277 ff.

MAGIC, in Egyptian religion, 63; Jewish elements in Egyptian, 63; in Liturgy of Mithra, 110; in Hermetic literature, 112, 113; alleged traces of, in Paul's idea of sacraments, 233, 283.
Manna, comparison of, with bread in Lord's Supper, 267.
Methodius, 292.
Mithraism, 114, n.
Mystery-religions, scanty evidence for, 68; difficulties as to chronology of, 69; features common to, 69 f.; influence of Greek Mysticism on, 70; wide diffusion of, 72 ff.; aim of, 79, 199 ff.; Isis-ritual typical of, 102; terminology of, in Paul, 117-120; as elements of Paul's environment, 79 f., 115, 280 f.; crude conceptions in, 200 ff.; Loisy's parallel between, and Paulinism, 211 ff.; central ideas of, different from Paul's, 213-215, 219, 221, 223, 228, 282. See Communion, Deification, Regeneration, Salvation.
Mysticism, astral, 6, 7; in earliest Hebrew prophets, 33 f.; in Psalms, 36; in relation to Jewish mind, 38, 47, 48; in Judaism, 43, 47; disparagement of, in Rabbinism, 45; connected with famous Rabbis, 50; relation of, to allegorical exegesis, 51; in Paul, 31, 33, 223 n., 284-293; common suspicion of, 284; faith central in Paul's, 285, 288, 289; universal phenomena of, 32, 286; relation of Paul's, to his conversion, 288; ethical quality of Paul's, 289; special character of Paul's, 290, 291; limits of Paul's, 291, 292; eschatological elements in Paul's, 294 f.

μύσται, associations of, 73 f.; ideal of, 78 f. See Religious associations.

μυστήριον, in LXX and Synoptics, 123, 124; in Paul, 124-130; used with verbs of revealing, 128; reference of, to Divine purpose for Gentiles, 126, 128; eschatological strain in, 128 f.; Gardner's view of, 129; relation of, in Paul, to τέλειος, 130; as current terms, 281.

NEPHESH, relation of, in Paul, to ψυχή, 157.

νοῦς, in Hermetic literature, 106 n., 108, 112; in Paul, 138; relation of, to πνεῦμα, 139; affinity of Paul's use of, with Hermetic usage, 149, 150, 281; Paul's use of, determined by O.T., 158, 159.

ORIENTAL cults, reverence for, in West, 20; as *personal* religion, 21, 87; adherents of, 21, 88; fundamental elements of, 22; as Mystery-religions, 88.

Orphism, origins of, 10; theology of, 11 f.; relation of, to Pythagoreanism, 12, 13; ecstasy in, 15; cathartic ritual of, 15 f.; degradations of, 16, 71 f.; hymns of, 17; relation of, to Dionysus-cult, 11, 13-15, 71; Oriental elements in, 16 f.; religious aspirations of, 18.

Osiris. See Isis.

ὀργεῶνες, 72, 75.

PAUL, Christianity of, as Mystery-religion, 2; his knowledge of Mystery-religions, 70, 79, 115 f.; attitude of, to Mystery-religions, 116 f.; Reitzenstein's theory of two-fold personality in, 145 f.; comparison of, with initiates, 146, 147; his conception of Christ compared with Mystery-deities, 213; detachment of, from ritual, 234-238, 277, 282, 283 f.; the Spirit and baptism in, 238-240; the Spirit and faith in, 240 f.; faith central for, 242-245, 277, 278, 283, 284; alleged realistic view of Lord's Supper in, 261 f. See Baptism, Ecstasy, Lord's Supper, Jesus Christ, Mystery-religions, Mysticism.

Philo, relation of, to Posidonius, 8; mysticism of, 65-67.

Plato, references of, to Orphism, 10, 13; mysticism of, 291.

Pneumatic phenomena, in apocalypses, 39-41; current in all ages, 41; in Rabbinic piety, 46; in Mystery-religions, 161.

Posidonius, influence of, 6-9.

Pseudo-Aristotle, περὶ κόσμου, 8.

πνεῦμα, ethicised by Paul, 39, 159, 287; fundamental uses of, in Paul, 136, 137; contrasted with σάρξ, 137, 154; as equivalent to ψυχή, 138; Paul's use of, as Hellenistic, 140; in Hellenistic Mystery-documents, 141, 142, 281; relation of, to νοῦς and ψυχή, in Mystery-religions, 151; theory of Oriental influence on, 152; Paul's conception of, alleged to be animistic, 152 f.; basis of Paul's idea of, in O.T., 155; relation of, to ψυχή, based on O.T., 156; possession by Divine, fundamental for Paul, 238. See Baptism.

πνευματικός, relation of, in Paul, to τέλειος, 135; basal meaning of, in Paul, 135, 136; contrasted with ψυχικός, 138; Paul's use of, alleged to be Hellenistic, 140; in Mystery-literature, 142-144; comparison of, in Paul, with Mystery-usage, 147, 281; criticism of Reitzenstein's view of, in Paul, 148 f.; Paul's view of, due to O.T., 156; in Hellenistic religion, 160; meaning of, in 1 Cor. x. 3 f., 268.

προφῆται, used of Egyptian priests, 35.

I. SUBJECTS

φωτίζειν (φωτισμός), in LXX, 197; in Paul, 198.
ψυχικός, meaning of, in Paul, 138; Paul's use of, as Hellenistic, 140; in Mystery-literature, 142-144; comparison of, in Paul, to Mystery-usage, 147 f.; use of, in Paul, due to O.T., 156.

REGENERATION, idea of, in all Mystery-religions, 69 f.; in Hermetic literature, 107, 108, 110; in Isis-mysteries, 209; in Cybele-Attis cult, 210 f.; comparison of, in Paul and Mystery-religions, 216, 220; through baptismal rites, 229. See Transformation.
Religious associations, evidence for, in inscriptions, 72; rise of, 72; predominance of foreigners in, 73, 77; chiefly in commercial centres, 77 f.; spirit and influence of, 78, 81, 82; as part of Paul's environment, 79; relation of, to early Christianity, 80, 119.
Revelation, esoteric, 23; in Hermetic literature, 106, 108, 109.
Ruach of Jahweh (Elohim), and prophecy, 34; lack of emphasis on, in pre-exilic prophets, 35; in Ezekiel, 38 f.; ethicised in post-exilic period, 39; in relation to wisdom, 46 f.; relation of, in Paul, to πνεῦμα, 155, 157.
Ruysbroeck, 205.

SACRAMENTAL meals, meagre evidence for, in Mystery-religions, 256.
Sacraments, in early Church, 254, 255, 278, 279.
Sacrificial meals, aim of, 258; danger of, for Christians, 265, 266; Paul's estimate of, 269.
Samothracian Mystery-deities, 76.
Salvation (σωτηρία), in Cybele-Attis cult, 95; as aim of Mystery-religions, 199, 216; character of,

in Mystery-religions, 216 f.; in Paul, 217-219; mediation of, in Paul, 219 f.; not exclusively eschatological in Paul, 298.
Shechinah, as parallel to Holy Spirit, 48; immanence of, 52.
Serapis. See Isis.
Sethians, alleged Orphic affinities of, 27.
Spiritual "organism" (σῶμα), in Paul, 184 f.; relation of, to Mystery-ideas, 186 f.; relation of, to "heavenly garments," 188 f.
Stoicism, as popular religion, 4; mystical strain in, 5.
Suso, 175.
Syncretism, Hellenistic, 18 ff.; in Egypt, 19; alleged, in Paul, 30.
σάρξ, disparaging sense of, in Greek writers, 137 n.; basis of Paul's conception of, in O.T., 155.
σταυρός, in Valentinian Gnosticism, 23 n.
στοιχεῖα, in Paul, 24 f., 61. See Elemental Spirits.
συνείδησις, in Paul, 158.

TAT, in Hermetic literature, 106, 107; prayer of, 108.
Taurobolium, 94 ff., 208, 211.
Terms of Mystery-religions, in Paul, 117-120, 281; as involving mystery-ideas, 119 f.; groups of, in Epistles, 121, 282; general significance of, for Paul, 122; inaccurate use of, 212 f.
Therapeutae, syncretism of, 59.
Tongues, speaking with, 160.
Transformation, in Mystery cults, 178 f.; in Paul, 180-183, 293; Schweitzer's view of, 294 f. See Regeneration.
τέλειος, relation of, in Paul, to σοφία, 130 f.; use of, in Plato, 131; in Hermetic writings, 132; in Philo, 131, 133; contrasted by Paul with νήπιος, 132 f.; in Stoicism, 133; probable meaning of, in

Paul, 133 f.; in LXX, 134; as current term, 281.

θεὸς ὕψιστος, in semi-Pagan associations, 58 n.; relation of, to Sabazius, 75.

θίασοι, 73.

WHEEL of births, 12.

ZAGREUS, in Orphism, 11, 257.

II. AUTHORS.

ABELSON, 48, 52.
Achelis, H., 148.
Anrich, 20, 216.
Anz, 23.

BACHER, 45, 46, 49, 51, 54.
Barth, C., 23.
Bartlet, V., 254.
Bauer, W., 131.
Bertholet, 45.
Blass, 48, 50.
Böhlig, 114, 159, 194.
Bonhöffer, 158.
Bousset, 4, 29, 42, 43, 50, 60, 62, 64, 66, 170, 188.
Bréhier, 66, 117.
Brückner, M., 206, 212, 216.
Burnet, J., 10, 19.

CAPELLE, W., 8, 137, 154.
Charles, 188.
Cheyne, 192.
Clemen, 190.
Conybeare, F. C., 59.
Cornford, F. M., 12, 204, 207, 208.
Cumont, 6, 20, 22, 58, 62, 88, 94, 95, 96, 111, 112, 118, 145, 188, 211, 212, 230, 258.

DEISSMANN, 195, 196, 222.
Denney, 128, 221.
Dieterich, 17, 24, 25, 42, 55, 63, 92, 93, 187, 195, 201, 204, 205, 208, 210, 211, 212, 222, 257, 261.
Dill, 21, 77, 94, 100.
Dillmann, 192.
Dobschütz, Von, 249, 253, 279.

Drexler, 98, 100.
Duhm, 36, 192.

EICHHORN, 274.
Eisele, 17, 89, 92, 94.
Eisler, 16, 17, 82, 87.
Erman, 63, 99.

FARNELL, 85.
Feine, 184.
Foucart, 73, 74, 78, 82.
Frazer, J. G., 93, 98.

GALL, Von, 192.
Gardner, P., 129, 216, 260.
Graillot, 145.
Gray, G. B., 191.
Gruppe, 58.
Gunkel, 30, 40, 41, 44.

HARNACK, 26, 248.
Harrison, J. E., 10, 14, 16.
Hatch, 127.
Heinrici, 80, 119, 177.
Heitmüller, 152, 153, 222, 230, 238, 242, 243, 245, 253, 254, 257, 259, 264, 276, 283.
Hepding, 68, 90, 92, 95, 208, 211, 230.
Holtzmann, H. J., 237, 239, 262, 278.
Hubert, 63.

INGE, 38, 145, 175, 205, 292.

JACOB, 62.
Jacoby, A., 79, 88, 108.

INDEX

Jong, De, 34, 87.
Jülicher, 275.

KAERST, J., 72, 76.
Klein, 53, 54, 55.
Kohler, K, 36, 59.
Kornemann, 77.
Krebs, 64, 107, 167, 195.
Kroll, W., 19, 28, 64, 67, 105, 113, 132.

LAKE, K., 2, 212, 232, 233, 234, 235, 236, 238, 244, 247, 262, 265.
Lambert, 237, 248, 250, 252.
Lauterbach, 52, 53.
Lehmann, 285, 291, 293.
Lietzmann, H., 172, 230, 259, 265.
Lightfoot, 135.
Loisy, 2, 211, 215.
Lueken, 251.

MILLIGAN, 232.
Monceaux, 71.
Murray, G., 12, 90, 93, 107, 212, 292.

NORDEN, 9, 27, 159, 167, 170.

OTTO, W., 19, 70, 111.

PFLEIDERER, 223, 285.
Pohlenz, 170.
Poland, F., 73, 76, 78.
Pringle-Pattison, 223.

RAMSAY, Sir W. M., 57, 58, 86.
Reitzenstein, 19, 21, 33, 61, 63, 65, 102, 104, 105, 106, 109, 110, *et passim*.

Rendtorff, 248, 253.
Réville, J., 273.
Robinson, H. W., 155, 156, 157, 158.
Robinson, J. A., 172.
Rohde, 11, 34, 84, 85, 88, 89, 201, 202, 292.

SCHECHTER, 47, 70.
Schlatter, 45.
Schmidt, C., 56.
Schürer, 58.
Schweitzer, 1, 90, 183, 213, 240, 261, 294, 296.
Soden, Von, 252.
Sokolowski, 194.
Stade, 192.

TAMBORNINO, 272.
Taylor, A. E., 10, 13, 71.

UNDERHILL, E., 120, 174, 175, 206, 285, 287.

VOLZ, 34, 35, 38, 39, 42, 47, 152, 156.

WACHSMUTH, 115.
Weinel, 220, 237, 261, 271, 283, 288.
Weiss, J., 129, 133, 134, 139, 160, 172, 185, 186, 263.
Wendland, P., 3, 26, 57, 120, 121, 122, 174, 179, 187.
Wernle, 245, 285.
Wilcken, 97.
Wobbermin, 85.
Wünsch, 69.

ZIELINSKI, 28, 112, 150.

III. BIBLICAL REFERENCES

I. OLD TESTAMENT

Genesis—		Isaiah—	
I.	45	VIII. 11	35
I. 27 (LXX)	190	XI. 2	171
Deuteronomy—		XV. 17	35
VIII. 3	268	XXVI. 9	157
XXX. 14	36	XXXI. 3	155
XXXII. 17 (LXX)	269, 273	XL. 6	155
Judges—		XL. 13	139
VI. 34	189	LXI. 1 f.	156
1 Samuel—		Jeremiah—	
X. 5, 6, 10	33	XV. 19	35
XIX. 20, 24	33	XVII. 5	155
2 Kings—		Ezekiel—	
III. 15	34	I.	46
XVII. 27, 28	197	II. 2	37, 155
1 Chronicles—		II. 9 ff.	38
XXV. 8	134	VIII. 3	37
Job—		XI. 19	156
IV. 13 f.	46	XXXVI. 26	155, 156
IV. 15	155	Daniel—	
Psalms—		I. 8	44
XVIII. 8 (LXX)	197	II. 18 (LXX)	124
XXVI. 1 (LXX)	197	Hosea—	
LI. 11	36, 156	II. 20	36, 171
LVI. 4	155	Amos—	
LXXIII. 23-26	36	III. 8	35
LXXXVII. 2, 3	157	Zechariah—	
LXXXIV. 2	155	VII. 12	156
CXXXII. 9	189	Malachi—	
Proverbs—		I. 12 (LXX)	269
II. 5	171		

II. NEW TESTAMENT

Matthew—		Luke—	
XIII. 11	124	VIII. 10	124
Mark—		Acts—	
IV. 11	124	XIX. 18, 19	30

INDEX

Romans—
I. 9	137
I. 16	219
I. 18-32	166
III. 5-8	233
IV. 25	277
V. 1	242
V. 5	219
V. 8-10	218
VI. 1 ff.	233, 245
VI. 3 ff.	237, 297
VI. 4	193
VI. 6	226
VI. 10 ff.	243
VII. 4	226, 243
VII. 10	156
VII. 14	135
VII. 25	139
VIII. 1	299
VIII. 6	297
VIII. 9	238
VIII. 9, 10	136, 289
VIII. 12	218
VIII. 13	225
VIII. 15	224, 293
VIII. 16	137, 219, 293
VIII. 18	193
VIII. 23	180
VIII. 29	180, 190
VIII. 30	197
X. 17	240
XI. 25	124, 128
XI. 34	139
XII. 2	139, 182

1 Corinthians—
I. 17, 18	235
I. 21	299
I. 23	128
II. 1-10	129
II. 4, 5	241
II. 6 ff.	121, 133
II. 7	128
II. 10-16	135
II. 11	138
II. 16	139, 140
III. 1 ff.	132, 135, 144
III. 3	148
III. 4	149
IV. 1	125

1 Corinthians—*cont.*
IV. 15	241
V. 4, 5	140
VI. 11	252
VI. 15-17	171
VI. 17	137, 224
VII. 11	119
VII. 14	153
VIII. 3	172
VIII. 6	9
VIII. 10	265
IX. 19, 22	117
IX. 27	296
X. 1	54, 235
X. 1-4	261
X. 1-5	263, 265
X. 3 ff.	135
X. 14-22	263, 268, 277
X. 16	290
X. 18	271
X. 21	259
XI. 7	189
XI. 17-34	263
XI. 23 ff.	263, 274
XI. 26	270, 290
XI. 27, 30	276
XII. 1 ff.	161
XII. 2	119
XII. 10	172
XII. 11	239
XII. 14	119
XIII. 2	168
XIII. 10	133
XIII. 13	239
XIV. 1 ff.	135
XIV. 2	125, 176
XIV. 6, 29, 30	172
XIV. 13 ff.	139
XIV. 20	132
XIV. 37	136
XV. 29	253
XV. 34	165
XV. 44	135, 181
XV. 49	184, 189
XV. 50	184
XV. 51	125, 128, 185
XVI. 8	168

2 Corinthians—
III. 8	193

III. BIBLICAL REFERENCES

2 Corinthians—*cont.*
- III. 13 f. 182
- III. 17 224
- III. 18 . . 180, 181, 189, 293
- IV. 2, 3 182
- IV. 3, 4 182
- IV. 4 190
- IV. 4, 6 197
- IV. 16 182
- V. 1, 2 . . . 184, 185
- V. 3 185
- V. 4, 5 181
- V. 5 149
- V. 13 176
- V. 14, 15 219
- V. 14, 18 220
- V. 17 . . . . 220, 288
- V. 20 128
- VII. 1 138
- XII. 1 ff. . 32, 33, 44, 173, 286

Galatians—
- I. 16 288
- II. 19 226
- II. 19, 20 242
- II. 20 146, 219, 222, 270, 277, 289
- III. 2 240
- III. 26 249
- III. 27 188
- IV. 3, 9 . . . . 61, 169
- IV. 8, 9 . . . . 24, 25
- V. 22 f. 148
- VI. 1 f. 149
- VI. 14 226

Ephesians—
- I. 9 ff. 127, 128
- I. 13 240
- I. 17 172
- I. 18 197
- I. 21 56
- III. 1 ff. 126
- IV. 13, 14 132
- V. 26 251
- V. 32 127
- VI. 12 135
- VI. 19 127

Philippians—
- I. 19 217
- I. 23 295
- III. 8-10 . . 169, 222, 243
- III. 9 277
- III. 10 . . . 182, 227
- III. 12 133
- III. 15 133
- III. 21 . . 180, 184, 189
- IV. 2 130
- IV. 8 116

Colossians—
- I. 11 193
- I. 15 190
- I. 21 f. 226
- I. 25 ff. . . . 126, 128
- I. 27 193
- II. 2 . . . . 79, 126
- II. 8, 20 61
- II. 11 244
- II. 11, 12 250
- II. 13 247
- II. 14, 15 227
- II. 20 . . . . 29, 226
- III. 3 224
- III. 10 189
- IV. 3 127

1 Thessalonians—
- II. 12 193
- II. 13 241
- V. 4 ff. 165

2 Thessalonians—
- I. 9 193
- II. 6-8 127
- II. 7 129

Hebrews—
- VI. 6 276

1 Peter—
- II. 15 166

Jude 19 138

Apocalypse—
- XIV. 18 60
- XVI. 5 60